JOHN MACARTHUR

AND THE LEADERSHIP TEAM AT GRACE COMMUNITY CHURCH

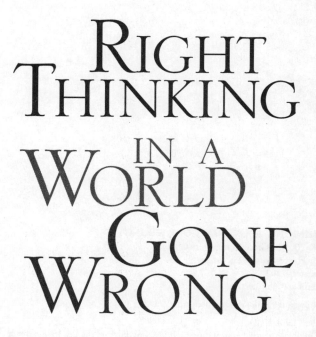

RIGHT THINKING
IN A WORLD GONE WRONG

NATHAN BUSENITZ
Associate Editor

HARVEST HOUSE PUBLISHERS
EUGENE, OREGON

Unless otherwise indicated, all Scripture quotations are taken from the New American Standard Bible®, © 1960, 1962, 1963, 1968, 1971, 1972, 1973, 1975, 1977, 1995 by The Lockman Foundation. Used by permission. (www.Lockman.org)

Verses marked NIV are taken from the HOLY BIBLE, NEW INTERNATIONAL VERSION®. NIV®. Copyright © 1973, 1978, 1984 by the International Bible Society. Used by permission of Zondervan. All rights reserved.

Cover by Abris, Veneta, Oregon

John MacArthur: Published in association with the literary agency of Wolgemuth & Associates, Inc.

RIGHT THINKING IN A WORLD GONE WRONG
Copyright © 2009 by Grace Community Church
Published by Harvest House Publishers
Eugene, Oregon 97402
www.harvesthousepublishers.com

Library of Congress Cataloging-in-Publication Data

MacArthur, John, 1939-
Right thinking in a world gone wrong / John MacArthur and the Leadership Team at Grace Community Church.
    p. cm.
ISBN 978-0-7369-2643-0 (pbk.)
1. Christianity and culture. 2. Thought and thinking—Religious aspects—Christianity. I. Grace Community Church (Sun Valley, Calif.) II. Title.
BR115.C8M2145 2009
261.0973--dc22

2008045619

Printed in the United States of America

09 10 11 12 13 14 15 16 17 / BP-SK / 10 9 8 7 6 5 4 3 2

To our beloved flock at Grace Community Church, who make the responsibility of shepherding the sweetest task on earth.

CONTENTS

Introduction

The Bible and Real Life
God's Word and Everyday Ethics

John MacArthur

I t is common in the evangelical church today for people to verbally
acknowledge that the Bible, as God's Word, is the final authority
for both what they believe and how they live. Yet in reality, a clear connection between that public confession and personal conduct is rare.

Claiming that Scripture is true and complete should preclude evangelicals from turning to other sources for establishing thought and life.
Yet many do just that. In cosmology, for example, a straightforward
reading of Genesis 1–2 is often dismissed on the basis of modern
evolutionary theories. In apologetics, philosophy and human reason
frequently take precedence over Scripture. And in church growth,
demographic surveys, marketing techniques, and a man-centered theology with a watered-down gospel override clear biblical truth.

To this list, the subject of morality and ethics must be added.
Instead of looking to the Bible, many professing Christians look to
psychology and sociology for supposed solutions to personal needs and
social ills. The rise of postmodern thought has similarly skewed the
church's understanding of right and wrong—as an unbiblical tolerance
(in the name of love) has weakened churches to the point where they
are as soft on truth as they are on sin. Popular television shows, from

Oprah to *The Tonight Show* to the average sitcom, have had a tangible effect (and not for the better) on how American Christians think through everyday issues. The political arena, too, has played a major role in shaping an evangelical understanding of morality, as words such as *Republican* and *Democrat* or *liberal* and *conservative* have come to redefine the difference between what is good and what is evil.

The fact is that far too many professing Christians live their lives, day in and day out, on the basis of something other than the Bible. As a result, their priorities reflect the world's priorities, not God's. Their patterns of behavior and their plans for the future differ only slightly from those of their unsaved friends and neighbors. Their expenditures reveal that their perspective is temporal, and that they are vainly pursuing the elusive American Dream. Their shortcomings, when they admit to them, receive the same fault-free labels that the world ascribes ("mistakes" or "diseases" or "addictions" rather than "sins"), as they search for answers in psychology, medication, or the self-help section of the bookstore. Though they adhere to an external form of traditional Christian moralism, there isn't anything particularly biblical or Christ-centered about how they live.

Yet it is in the lives of sinners who have been transformed by the gospel of grace that a distinctly Christian ethic must be fleshed out. True Christianity is not defined on the basis of external moralism, religious traditionalism, or partisan politics, but on the basis of a personal love for Jesus Christ and a desire to follow Him no matter what the cost (John 14:15). It is only because believers have been transformed on the inside (through the regeneration of the Holy Spirit) that they are able to exhibit godliness in their behavior. And the world cannot help but take notice. As Jesus told His hearers in the Sermon on the Mount, "Let your light shine before men in such a way that they may see your good works, and glorify your Father who is in heaven" (Matthew 5:16; cf. 1 Peter 2:12).

The Heart of the Christian Ethic

The heart of the Christian ethic, of course, is the gospel. Only those who have been transformed from within (Titus 3:5-8), being indwelt by the Spirit of God (Romans 8:13-14), are able to exhibit genuine holiness (Galatians 5:22-23; 1 Peter 1:16). Biblical Christianity is not primarily concerned with external behavior modification (cf. Matthew 5–7), but with a change of heart that subsequently manifests itself in a changed life (1 Corinthians 6:9-11).

A true Christian ethic, then, is not possible without the regenerating work of the Holy Spirit. Unless the inner man is washed first, external morality and religious observances are only a superficial façade. Jesus rebuked the hypocrites of His day with these words: "Woe to you, scribes and Pharisees, hypocrites! For you are like whitewashed tombs which on the outside appear beautiful, but inside they are full of dead men's bones and all uncleanness" (Matthew 23:27). Christ was not saying that behavior is unimportant. But rather that from God's perspective, the heart is what matters most (cf. 1 Samuel 16:7; Mark 12:30-31).

Of course, a heart that has been truly transformed by God will respond in love to His Son, Jesus Christ (cf. John 8:42). And those who love Jesus Christ will eagerly desire to follow and obey His commands (John 14:15), as found in His Word (cf. Colossians 3:16). A truly Christian ethic, then, eagerly affirms and applies the moral instructions found in the Bible. But it does not do so in an attempt to legalistically earn salvation (Isaiah 64:6). Rather, having received salvation as the free gift of God through faith in Christ (Ephesians 2:8-9), it readily obeys out of a heart of love (Ephesians 2:10).

If Christians are to live in keeping with who they are as children of God, they must live according to the Word of God through the power of His Spirit. No other source of wisdom or moral insight will do. By definition, they are people of the Book—and not just on Sundays, but every day of the week (cf. Isaiah 66:2).

The Total Sufficiency of Scripture

Psalm 19:7-9 is one of the clearest and most concise sections of Scripture detailing the sufficiency and authority of Scripture, especially as it applies to everyday Christian living.[1] In that passage, we learn first of all that the "law of the LORD is perfect, restoring the soul" (verse 7a). The Hebrew word translated "perfect" means complete or whole; and "soul" actually speaks of the whole inner person. Thus, God's Word is sufficient to transform people completely from within, beginning with conversion and extending to the sanctification of the whole person (2 Timothy 3:15-17). Unlike the imperfect and incomplete wisdom of men (1 Corinthians 1:18-31; 2:10-16), the Bible is so comprehensive that by pointing sinners to Jesus Christ it can change people, through the power of the Holy Spirit, into whom God desires them to be.

Psalm 19:7 goes on to assert that "the testimony of the LORD is sure, making wise the simple." God's Word is His "testimony" to us about Himself, for if He had not revealed Himself to us we would have no way to know about Him or His requirements for us. God's self-testimony in Scripture is absolutely trustworthy—His promises can be believed and His prescriptions obeyed. Those who do so will find wisdom, which in the Old Testament refers to the skill of godly living. The Bible, then, can take naive, uninstructed, and undiscerning people and make them skilled in wise decision-making and practical holiness. Scripture touches every area of life, including how we think, what we say, what we do, and why we do it. Everything we need to know to live a godly life is covered in the pages of God's Word. Nothing else is necessary.

Third, the psalmist notes that "the precepts of the LORD are right, rejoicing the heart" (19:8a), meaning that the divine principles found in Scripture lay out a sure path for us to follow. God has given us His Word so that we can successfully navigate our way through this life, and as we do so, we will experience true joy. Ironically, those who run away from the Word of God (to any other source of supposed wisdom) simultaneously run away from joy and peace. Too many Christians think they will find happiness in riches, accomplishment, or fame. But these worldly allurements are nothing more than mirages, as Solomon found out the hard way (Ecclesiastes 2:1-26). Though our world often views biblical morality as an obstacle to happiness, nothing could be further from the truth. Lasting happiness, fulfillment, and satisfaction cannot be found in the sensual pleasures of sin. They are instead found only in God.

Next, the psalmist writes, "The commandment of the LORD is pure, enlightening the eyes" (19:8b). The Word of God that we are commanded to obey is "pure," meaning clear or understandable. To be sure, some sections are more difficult to understand than others (2 Peter 3:15–16), but in general the Word of God is unmistakably plain. It is not mystifying, confusing, or puzzling. Its message of salvation is not hard to understand, and it leaves no doubt as to necessary truth. In the midst of a world characterized by darkness and confusion, the Word of God brings clarity. Through the Scriptures, we can know truth in a world that is searching for it; we can understand right and wrong in a society that cannot tell the difference; and we can be comforted in times when those around us are worried by what is happening.

The simplest Christian knows a lot of things that many scholarly unbelievers do not know (Psalm 119:99). We know how the world came to be. We know where humanity began and what our purpose is in this life. We know how sinful men and women can be made right with their Creator. We know what the ultimate future of our planet will be. And we know what will happen to us after we die. When someone loses a child or a spouse, when national or personal crises arise, when economic or natural disasters take place—where can we go for the dark things of life to be made clear? For a world clouded in confusion, God's Word offers sanity, clarity, and hope.

Psalm 19 continues in verse 9 by noting that "the fear of the LORD is clean, enduring forever." The Bible conveys the awesome grandeur of God and thereby invokes in us a reverential awe (or fear) that draws us to worship our Creator. Thus, the Scriptures give us the right way to worship the true God. There is no taint of evil or impurity in the Bible's presentation of God or His expectations. The words of the Bible are pure words that produce a holy reverence for God (cf. Psalm 12:6). And they endure forever, meaning they can always be trusted, at any time and in any age. Moreover, the worship they command will characterize the people of God not just in this life, but also for eternity.

Critics and skeptics (and sometimes even professing Christians) may claim that the Bible is not sophisticated enough for modern times. Such claims only expose their own foolishness. The Bible is absolutely pure, flawless, and error-free. There is no need to update, edit, or refine it. It is perfect. When I was in college I learned about philosophy. Almost every philosophy I studied was already long dead. I also had to learn about psychology. Almost every form of psychotherapy I read about back then is now obsolete and has been replaced by new theories or techniques. But there's one thing that never changes, and that is the eternal Word of God. It is always relevant.

Finally, and most pointedly, Psalm 19:9 says that "the judgments of the LORD are true; they are righteous altogether." In Scripture, the Judge of all the earth has revealed to us His decrees and determinations. Thus, the Bible speaks truth without compromise and without apology. Christians therefore need not play the postmodern shell games that try to redefine truth. The Word of God is truth (John 17:17). It is eternally true, because its Author is eternally true. It is "righteous altogether" because it reflects the One who wrote it. In all of its comprehensiveness, it is not only without error, but it is a sufficient source of truth. Nothing needs to be added to it, and nothing subtracted from it (Deuteronomy 4:2; Revelation 22:18-19). In its wholeness it is perfect, and it produces that completeness in those who are transformed by its power (2 Timothy 3:16-17).

I remember meeting a young man on drugs who was living in an overturned refrigerator box by a stream in the mountains of northern California. I was hiking through the area and asked if I could introduce myself. We talked a little while. It turned out he was a graduate of Boston University. He said, "I've escaped." I asked, "Have you found the answers?" "No," he said, "but at least I've gotten myself into a situation where I don't ask the questions." How hopeless! But such is the despair and dejection of those who do not have the truth.

Scripture describes some people as "always learning and never able to come to the knowledge of the truth" (2 Timothy 3:7). That is not referring to intellectual truth or the wisdom of this world; it is referring instead to the truth of life, death, God, man, sin, right, wrong, heaven, hell, hope, joy, and peace. People cannot find that kind of truth on their own. That is why God has given us His Word.

Putting It All Together

These few lines from Psalm 19 beautifully underscore the fact that God's Word must be our final rule of faith and practice. It is the basis and determiner of a truly Christian ethic. Consisting of the revealed knowledge of God, the Bible is everything we need for life and godliness (2 Peter 1:3). Why would we look elsewhere for how to live this life when we have the answers from the Creator and Judge Himself?

Every time we pick up the Bible, we pick up the truth. Jesus said, "If you continue in My word...you will know the truth, and the truth will make you free" (John 8:31-32). Man will search and struggle and grapple and grope for the truth until he finds it. Only then is he free. The Bible is the final source of truth—about God, creation, life, death, men, women, children, husbands, wives, fathers, mothers, friends, and enemies. It shows us how to live, and to do so abundantly.

Any ethic that starts outside of Scripture, or that does not have Scripture as its foundation, may not rightly be called a Christian ethic. Our response to moral questions is not determined by politics, economics, personal preference, popular opinion, or human reasoning. It is, instead, grounded in what God has told us is true about ourselves and our world.

For each of us, our own Christian ethic begins with daily obedience, which stems from a heart that loves Jesus Christ (cf. John 14:15). God's expectations for us are clearly laid out in His Word. Thus, if we are to practically apply true godliness and righteousness, we must know and submit to the Scriptures. They are perfect, sure, right, pure, clean, and true.

The Scriptures are our authority because God is our authority, and His Word stands forever. To sidestep or ignore the Bible not only ensures moral disaster, it also slights the Author of the Bible. May we honor Him by living and thinking according to His Word.

Part 1

ENTERTAINMENT AND LEISURE

1

Glorifying God in the Gray Areas
Christian Liberty and the World of Entertainment[1]

John MacArthur

As a pastor, I have the privilege of guiding people through God's Word, explaining its implications in their lives by clarifying a passage of Scripture or a point of doctrine. Among the concerns people raise, however, I can't remember anyone ever asking me if it was wrong to cheat, steal, lie, commit murder, commit adultery, or covet. I can't recall a time when someone wanted to know whether a Christian should read the Bible, pray, worship, love, or tell others about salvation in Jesus Christ. God's Word is unmistakably clear about those things.

There is, however, one class of questions that I often receive, and it is with regard to issues or activities that are not specifically addressed in Scripture, and thus fall somewhere between what is obviously right and obviously wrong. Being neither "black or white," these issues involve aspects of Christian freedom that fall into what has been dubbed "the gray areas." What entertainment is acceptable? What kind of music is okay? What about what you wear, where you go, or how you spend your free time? How does the Bible speak to those things?

Some would say, "The Bible doesn't address them. You can do what you want to do. You're free in Christ!" Though it is true that the Bible doesn't specifically mention every possible decision you might face in life, it does address all choices with general *principles* and *parameters* that govern Christian freedom. When you run your choices in the gray areas through the following grid of seven biblical principles (drawn primarily from the book of 1 Corinthians, in which the apostle Paul gave detailed instructions on liberty issues), I trust you will find both clarity and true freedom to live your life to God's glory.

Principles for Living to God's Glory

1. *The Edification Principle:*
   Will this activity produce spiritual benefit?

In 1 Corinthians 10:23, Paul explained that "all things are lawful, but not all things are profitable. All things are lawful, but not all things edify." Some people in the Corinthian congregation were exercising their Christian liberty without any regard for the spiritual good of others, or even the good of themselves. Paul corrected that thinking by reminding them that, unless something is spiritually profitable, it's not worth doing. Something that is *profitable* is useful, helpful, or advantageous; and that which *edifies* builds up spiritually. So based on this verse, believers should ask themselves, "Will doing this activity enhance my spiritual life and the spiritual lives of others? Will it cultivate godliness in me and in them? Will it build us up spiritually?" If not, then is it really a wise choice?

There are a plethora of ways, of course, in which we can build up others in the faith, and in which we ourselves can "grow in the grace and knowledge of our Lord and Savior Jesus Christ" (2 Peter 3:18). But at a foundational level, edification comes from studying the Word and listening to it taught (cf. Acts 20:32; Colossians 3:16; 2 Timothy 3:16-17); from showing true love to fellow believers as you fellowship with them (cf. 1 Corinthians 8:1; Hebrews 10:24); and from obediently serving within the context of the local church (cf. Ephesians 4:12). When it comes to the gray areas of life, we should begin by asking if the choice we are about to make is spiritually profitable, both for ourselves and for those around us.

2. The Enslavement Principle:
Will this activity lead to spiritual bondage?

Earlier in 1 Corinthians, Paul had already told his readers, "All things are lawful for me, but not all things are profitable. All things are lawful for me, but I will not be mastered by anything" (1 Corinthians 6:12). Again, the apostle underscored the fact that he wanted to do only those things that are spiritually profitable. Part of that entails avoiding those temptations or activities that might result in personal enslavement. Paul knew that his only Master was Jesus Christ; thus he would not allow himself to be mastered by anything or anyone else.

The immediate context in 1 Corinthians 6 refers to sexual sin, which is uniquely enslaving. However, the principle extends beyond sensuality to any habit or behavior that might become life-dominating or Spirit-quenching. In Ephesians 5:18, speaking of alcoholism, Paul commanded, "Do not get drunk with wine...but be filled with the Spirit." Though the context there is different, the idea is similar. Don't allow yourself to become addicted or enslaved to that which is sinful or even just potentially destructive. If what you are considering can be habit-forming, why pursue it? Don't allow yourself to be in bondage to anything or anyone. You are a slave of the Lord Jesus Christ, and Him alone.

3. The Exposure Principle:
Will this activity expose my mind or body to defilement?

Speaking specifically of sexual immorality, Paul commanded the Corinthians to avoid anything that might defile them. "Do you not know that your body is a temple of the Holy Spirit who is in you, whom you have from God, and that you are not your own? For you have been bought with a price: therefore glorify God in your body" (1 Corinthians 6:19-20). Elsewhere, he told the Ephesians to reprove and avoid the sensual deeds that characterize the wicked, "for it is disgraceful even to speak of the things which are done by them in secret" (Ephesians 5:12). Instead, believers are to dwell on those things that are true, honorable, right, pure, lovely, excellent, praiseworthy, and of good repute (Philippians 4:8).

So ask yourself if the decision you are about to make will expose you to the sinful, lewd, and debauched elements of fallen society. If it will, then stay away from it. In Romans 12:1-2 Paul wrote, "I urge you, brethren, by the mercies of God, to present your bodies a living and holy sacrifice, acceptable to God, which is your spiritual service of worship. And do not be conformed to this world, but be transformed by the renewing of your mind, so that you may prove what the will of God is, that which is good and acceptable and perfect." How you choose to use your body, along with what you choose to put into your mind, should always reflect your concern to honor Jesus Christ (cf. Romans 6:12-13). Thus anything that defiles your body or pollutes your mind ought to be avoided.

4. The Esteem Principle:
Will this activity benefit others, or cause them to stumble?

Regarding the eating of food offered to idols, a gray area in the early church, Paul wrote, "Food will not commend us to God; we are neither the worse if we do not eat, nor the better if we do eat. But take care lest this liberty of yours somehow become a stumbling block to the weak" (1 Corinthians 8:8-9). In exercising our Christian liberty, we must be sensitive to weaker believers who might have more sensitive consciences. When we esteem them as more important than ourselves, putting their spiritual interests above our own freedom, we are following the example of Christ (Philippians 2:1-5).

This is the principle of love. As Romans 13:10 says, "Love does no wrong to a neighbor; therefore love is the fulfillment of the law." If you know that your choice—what you consider "in bounds" and approved by God—will cause another Christian to stumble and sin, love that brother or sister enough to restrict your own freedom. That is not very popular in our self-absorbed society, but it is biblical. In fact, to cause a fellow Christian to violate his or her conscience is ultimately to sin against the Lord. For "by sinning against the brethren and wounding their conscience when it is weak, you sin against Christ. Therefore," Paul said, "if food causes my brother to stumble, I will never eat meat again, that I will not cause my brother to stumble" (1 Corinthians 8:12-13).

5. *The Evangelism Principle:*
Will this activity further the cause of the gospel?

As those seeking to live out the Great Commission (Matthew 28:18-20), Christians should always consider how their actions will affect their witness to a watching world. Speaking of his own evangelistic ministry, Paul wrote, "Give no offense either to Jews or to Greeks or to the church of God; just as I also please all men in all things, not seeking my own profit but the profit of the many, that they may be saved" (1 Corinthians 10:32-33). Paul was far more concerned with seeing sinners embrace Christ than he was with the exercise of his liberty. Thus he was willing to set his freedom aside for the sake of the gospel (1 Corinthians 9:19-23).

Whether or not you are aware of it, what you allow or disallow in your behavior affects your witness for Christ. It is an issue of *testimony*—what your life says about God—to the friends, relatives, coworkers, neighbors, or even strangers who might be watching you. Your testimony either tells the truth about God, or it tells a lie. The choices you make in the gray areas should reflect your concern not to bring offense to God's reputation but to bring Him praise instead.

6. *The Ethics Principle:*
Will this activity violate my conscience?

In a parallel passage to 1 Corinthians 8–10, Paul gave the Romans similar instructions regarding food offered to idols. In so doing, he made one point very clear—it is dangerous to do anything that violates your conscience and causes you to doubt your actions, even if other Christians feel free to so act. "He who doubts is condemned if he eats, because his eating is not from faith; and whatever is not from faith is sin" (Romans 14:23). We sin if we act in any way that goes contrary to the convictions of our own faith and good conscience.

First Corinthians 10:25-29 contains three references to abstaining from certain practices "for conscience' sake." Never train yourself to violate your conscience. If your conscience is troubled by what you are thinking about doing, don't do it. If you are not sure about it, don't do it. It is hard to overstate the value of a clear conscience, and it is definitely worth keeping your conscience clear so that your relationship with God will not be hindered (cf. Psalm 66:18). If you will keep yourself in prayer and the study of God's Word, you will rightly inform your conscience so you can "walk as children of Light...trying to learn what is pleasing to the Lord" (Ephesians 5:8,10).

7. The Exaltation Principle:
Will this activity bring glory to God?

The summary and goal of the aforementioned six principles is found in this one. Paul declared, "Whether, then, you eat or drink or whatever you do, do all to the glory of God" (1 Corinthians 10:31). We were created to glorify God and worship Him forever. As those who have been transformed by His grace and transferred into His kingdom, pleasing Him is both our highest aim and our greatest delight (2 Corinthians 5:9).

Our heart's cry is to glorify our Lord and Savior with our lives. So when it comes to the gray areas, think about your decision. Will God be glorified, praised, and exalted? We genuinely honor Him when we make choices that are consistent with the principles found in His Word. On the flip side, when we make foolish and sinful choices, our actions dishonor Him. If an activity will glorify God, then do it. If it won't, or if it is questionable, then do something else.

A Few More Thoughts About the World of Entertainment

The seven principles we've examined can apply to every gray area in life, including those related to entertainment, amusement, and leisure.

At the same time, however, there are some additional principles that are specifically helpful in considering how we choose to be entertained. Having pastored for four decades a church ten miles from Hollywood, I am well aware of how entertainment media saturates our culture. During my lifetime, I have noticed the cultural shift away from active and intellectual pastimes (including recreations such as sports and reading) to passive and less stimulating amusements (such as television, movies, video games, and computer media). Technological advancements have improved our society in many ways, yet they have also introduced a host of powerful new temptations. Though sin is still sin at its root (cf. 1 John 2:16), some of its forms have never before been so accessible.

The world of entertainment, electronically speaking, is big business. Today's top films gross hundreds of millions of dollars, as do some of the most popular video games. Television shows broadcast to millions of viewers; radio programs reach millions of listeners; and music retailers sell millions (or if you're iTunes, billions) of popular songs. Access to this media is also more convenient than ever before, thanks to the Internet. Since it opened to commercial interests two decades ago, the Internet has grown to roughly one-and-a-half billion users worldwide.

None of these technologies, in and of themselves, are inherently evil. In fact, each of them can be used to dispense God's truth and promote righteousness. Yet the reality is that we live in a fallen world deeply corrupted by sin and under the influence of supernaturally hostile forces. Hence we must not be so naïve as to assume that all entertainment is spiritually neutral and safe, as though we could immerse our minds in everything the world offers and remain spiritually unscathed.

So how can we live a consistent Christian life in our entertainment-saturated culture? Those who claim Jesus Christ as the Lord of their lives are called to submit to His authority in all areas of life. Every choice we make, including how we are entertained, must be submitted to His lordship. Here then are four principles to consider in addition to the seven we surveyed earlier in this chapter. These principles presuppose a genuine Christian faith on the part of the reader—a faith that loves Christ and wants to glorify Him in every area of life, including entertainment choices.

Entertainment in Light of Our Submission to Christ

The Lordship of Christ Demands Good Stewardship

God has given each of us a limited number of resources—in particular, time, money, talents, and energy; and we are commanded to be good stewards of each (cf. Ephesians 5:15; Proverbs 13:11; Ecclesiastes 11:9; Matthew 25:14-34; Mark 12:30). How we use those resources is reflective of our priorities. As Jesus said, speaking specifically of money, "Where your treasure is, there your heart will be also" (Matthew 6:21). Christians must consider how they can use their resources not for their own leisure and entertainment, but for the work of the gospel.

Recent studies show that the average American watches more than four hours of television per day, which, spread over a 70-year lifespan, amounts to nearly 12 years of viewing time. Some of that may be instructive and diversionary, but such statistics make one wonder what Christ will say to those believers who have spent a sixth of their lives staring at the tube (Romans 14:10-12). (Amazingly, watching television is only *one* of many ways in which people can waste time being entertained. The trend today is to spend nearly as much time on the Internet.)

So ask yourself how much real benefit you receive by watching television and movies or playing video games, and how that compares to the time you spend in spiritual pursuits. How much money do you spend on temporal amusements, and how does that relate to your eternal investments? How hard do you labor not to advance your own agenda but to further the work of Christ's kingdom? These are heart questions every believer needs to ask. As stewards of the King (Matthew 25:14-30), we have been called to so much more than our own entertainment.

The Lordship of Christ Denounces Impurity and Worldliness

Ephesians 5:3-4 has excellent words in this regard: "Immorality or any impurity or greed must not even be named among you, as is proper among saints; and there must be no filthiness and silly talk, or coarse jesting, which are not fitting, but rather giving of thanks." Those two verses alone rule out much of what passes as entertainment in our world today—sexual immorality and impurity, dirty jokes and silly talk, and anything that promotes greed or undermines the giving of thanks. That list is a pretty good summary of what is wrong with much of contemporary American media.

Movies, for example, are usually rated according to language, violence, sexual content, and thematic elements. Many of them are not just *non*-Christian, they are *anti*-Christian. I don't mean that they openly attack the Christian faith. But at least in some cases they might as well. They employ filthy language and lewd humor (Colossians 3:8; Titus 2:6-8); they glorify violence rather than peace (Titus 1:7; 1 John 4:7-8); they glamorize lust and immorality rather than holiness (1 Thessalonians 4:3-5; 1 Peter 1:16); they instill feelings of discontentment and desire rather than thankfulness (Ephesians 5:20; 1 Timothy 6:6); and they promote worldviews that are antithetical to biblical Christianity (2 Corinthians 10:5). Does that mean a Christian should never watch movies? Not necessarily. But we must be discriminating about the things we allow into our minds. We are called to renew our minds (Romans 12:2; Ephesians 4:23; Colossians 3:16). When we continually fill our minds with the filth of this world, we do ourselves a great spiritual disservice.

The Lordship of Christ Determines Right Priorities

Our media-driven culture has redefined the pursuit of happiness. The American Dream—which used to consist of a loving family, a nice house, and a white picket fence—now includes instant fame, endless riches, easy romance, and the blank-check promise that anyone can achieve his or her dreams. Reality television and the rise of the Internet are perhaps somewhat to blame for this phenomenon. But ultimately the problem lies in the human heart.

We were created to long for satisfaction, fulfillment, and joy, and those desires are good in and of themselves. But our fallen world tries to meet those desires with money, romance, fame, and other earthly pleasures. Yet temporal things can never bring lasting satisfaction to a heart that was created to find its ultimate joy in God. King Solomon learned this lesson the hard way. After experimenting with everything the world could offer, Solomon finally concluded it was all vanity, and that without God, no one can have true enjoyment (Ecclesiastes 2:25-26; 11:9; 12:13-14).

Christians should not allow entertainment to define their understanding of happiness, romance, modesty, masculinity, success, fulfillment, justice, or anything else. The Word and the Spirit should shape our worldview, not Hollywood. Sadly, however, many Christians today are more affected by the movies they watch than the sermons they hear. They show more enthusiasm for video games or television sporting events than they do for pursuing Christlikeness. They fill their minds with the sounds of talk radio or perhaps the latest hit albums rather than letting the Word of Christ richly dwell within them. Deep down, they enjoy exploring the pleasures of the world—even if only vicariously—as they watch actors play out scenes in which sinful pursuits are seemingly rewarded with happiness. The irony, of course, is that in real life those same actors are just as miserable as everyone else, a sobering reality that keeps supermarket tabloids in business.

Our priorities, passions, plans, and pursuits must be grounded in our love for Jesus Christ. Only in Him can we find true satisfaction (cf. Matthew 11:28; John 7:37). In serving Him we can lay up eternal treasure (Matthew 6:20). In pleasing and glorifying Him we fulfill life's greatest purpose (cf. 2 Corinthians 5:9). He is to be the object of our affections, ambitions, and hopes (cf. Romans 14:7-8; Galatians 2:20; Philippians 1:20-21). As the author of Hebrews exhorted his readers, "Let us also lay aside every encumbrance and the sin which so easily entangles us, and let us run with endurance the race that is set before us, fixing our eyes on Jesus, the author and perfecter of faith, who for the joy set before Him endured the cross, despising the shame, and has sat down at the right hand of the throne of God" (Hebrews 12:1-2).

The Lordship of Christ Defines a Proper Perspective

Right priorities and godly passions stem out of a proper perspective—a heavenly mind-set that understands eternal realities and interprets this life accordingly. If this world were all there was, we would be wise to amass treasure and search for happiness in the here and now. But that is not reality. This world is *not* all there is.

Reality, as revealed by the truth of Scripture, encompasses much more than the temporal pleasures, priorities, and pursuits of this world. God is real; His Word is real; heaven and hell are real; the gospel is real; Jesus is real; His death, resurrection, and ascension are all real, as is the fact that He will soon be coming back. The brevity of this life is real; the certainty of death is real; the promise of future reward is real; and the threat of eternal destruction is also real. In contrast, the world of entertainment is not real. In fact, most entertainment is about escaping from reality, not portraying it accurately.

As Christians, our worldview must be grounded in reality, not in the imaginary worlds of Hollywood. People can deny reality, and they can distract themselves with fantasy, but they cannot change the fact that one day they will stand before God (Hebrews 9:27). At that moment, the riches, pleasures, and accomplishments of this world will be of no use to them.

The parable of the rich fool is a striking example of this type of foolhardy shortsightedness. Jesus tells the story in Luke 12:16-21:

> The land of a rich man was very productive. And he began reasoning to himself, saying, "What shall I do, since I have no place to store my crops?" Then he said, "This is what I will do: I will tear down my barns and build larger ones, and there I will store all my grain and my goods. And I will say to my soul, 'Soul, you have many goods laid up for many years to come; take your ease, eat, drink and be merry.'"

But God said to him, "You fool! This very night your soul is required of you; and now who will own what you have prepared?"

So is the man who stores up treasure for himself, and is not rich toward God.

Jesus' words ring out as a wake-up call for those who profess to know God and yet live as though God were no more real than whatever movie they watched last. For those who keep hitting the spiritual snooze button, it is time to wake up and focus on what really matters (cf. Romans 13:11). As Christians, our perspective must be eternal in scope. And entertainment, though enjoyable in the moment, is not eternal.

Are You Defined by Christ, or Society?

Movies, television, radio, video games, MP3s, and the Internet—these and other forms of mass media pervade our world. In and of themselves, these technologies are not inherently sinful. Most other forms of leisure and recreation are not inherently sinful either. In fact, fun, happiness, and joy are gifts from God.

But before we wholeheartedly embrace the media-driven entertainment of our culture, we must not forget that we are *Christians*. Our identity is defined by Jesus Christ, not by the society around us. That distinction should be reflected in everything we think, say, and do. We live in a world carried along by ungodly lusts and entertained by sin. Yet we are called to walk in thankful holiness. Though we are in this world, we are not *of* this world (John 17:14-16). That means we can't watch every movie, laugh at every joke on television, download every new music album, click on every online video, or visit every Internet page. Taking a stand for righteousness in your own life and family is not being legalistic. It's being Christian.

2

A Match Made in e-Heaven

Internet Dating and God-Honoring Romance

Rick Holland

I will be forever thankful that there were no Internet dating services when I met my wife. The truth is that no computer logarithms or binary calculations would have ever put the two of us together. Compatibility? Are you kidding?! She loves mushrooms; I hate them. She enjoys old movies; I like watching college football. Her idea of a relaxing weekend is at a nice hotel with room service and a pool. Mine is to be ten miles back in the woods on a deer hunt. I could go on and on, but the point is simple—we had very few points of compatibility except for our common love for Jesus Christ and ministering in His church. As incompatible as we were (and are), we deeply love each other and adore our marriage.

Since neither eHarmony nor any of its cousins would have put my wife and me together, I must admit my hesitations about Internet dating. At the same time, I am not completely opposed to the concept either. I know at least two married couples in our church who met through Internet dating services, and they are both very happy.

As a pastor to about a thousand collegians, the topics of dating, romance, and marriage are never far from my thinking. I am not claiming to be an expert on relationships; I'm just experienced in watching them develop in a variety of ways. The latest trend is e-dating. With conservative estimates stating that there are some 50 million people who use online dating sites, this is obviously more than just a passing fad.

You've Got Mail

Finding romance via the Internet is not new. But the concept attained pop culture status in the 1998 movie *You've Got Mail,* starring Tom Hanks and Meg Ryan. Though not about Internet dating services per se, the film romanticized cyberspace as the new and hip place for falling in love. With a keyboard, a mouse, and a high-speed connection, you could find romance without leaving home. But Internet romance can have its share of sticky possibilities, as the movie pointed out. With a few strokes of the keyboard you can create an identity far different from that which you have in the real world. One of the film's subplots involved that very issue. Are we more real in person or behind a computer screen? *You've Got Mail* suggested the computer persona as the authentic self. Whatever our assessment of the film's overall message, *You've Got Mail* raised some important questions about online romance and its compatibility (pun intended) with a biblical worldview.

A Question of Compatibility

In the course of putting together this chapter, I saw a television commercial for eHarmony, currently the most popular Internet dating service. Smiling at the camera, a clean-cut young man in his twenties enthusiastically announced, "eHarmony is going to find me a very compatible person." A subsequent visit to their Web site confirmed what I suspected: Compatibility is the holy grail of Internet dating services. Here is what they say about themselves:

> At eHarmony, our patented Compatibility Matching System® narrows the field from millions of candidates to a highly select group of singles that are compatible with you.

> Unlike other sites where you can post a picture and para-
> graph and then browse the profiles of other users, eHarmony
> does the matching for you based on 29 Dimensions™ of
> personality that are scientifically-based predictors of long-term
> relationship success.[1]

Elsewhere, the Web site claims that "eHarmony carefully pre-
screens each match to ensure compatibility based on 29 Dimensions™
that are crucial for relationship success."[2] Don't miss the key words:
"scientifically-based predictors of long-term relationship success." Internet dating services are fiercely competing for willing subscribers who
may become successful matches. They use these success stories and
statistics as advertisements and enticements for new customers. And
they all use "compatibility" as their relational magnet.

But this raises a critical question: Is compatibility a legitimate biblical foundation for relationships? The Bible has a lot to say about
relationships and marriage. Yet it says nothing of compatibility as
either the initial or sustaining criteria for Christian marriage. At the
same time, it doesn't say it is wrong to pursue someone who shares
"dimensions of compatibility." Scripture's silence on the subject makes
it a matter of wisdom (cf. Romans 14).

But God's Word *does* talk a lot about Christian couples *complement-*
ing each other (Genesis 2:18). For a couple to complement one another
there must be differences to reconcile, incompletion to complete, and
incompatibilities to overcome. In Ephesians 5:22-33, the apostle Paul
described marriage as having a reciprocal relationship with the gospel.
Christ's relationship with His bride, the church, is to be the pattern for
Christian marriage. And Christian marriages are to serve as compasses
pointing to Christ's relationship with the church. The beautiful mystery
of Jesus' relationship with sinners is the massive incompatibility that
the cross overcame.

The many differences that exist between my wife and I have been
fertile ground for learning selflessness and becoming more like Christ.
Our "incompatibilities" have allowed us to serve and complete the

other by deferring to these differing desires, preferences, and needs. We have both changed for the better because we were so different.

It is not an oversimplification to say that the fact that God made man male and female was His creative slant on marital compatibility. This compatibility was demonstrated in his anatomical design (Genesis 2:24), constitutional make up (1 Peter 3:1-7), and the pleasure that comes from heterosexual union (Proverbs 18:22; 31:10; Ecclesiastes 9:9; Song of Solomon 1:2). Biblical compatibility has little to do with similar interests, but rather, differing roles (Ephesians 5:22-33; Titus 2:2-8).

Still, couples who develop a relationship in which they share common interests have advantages. Their overlapping interests certainly minimize the sources of conflict and provide common points of joy. But even with these points of compatibility, they still have sin to deal with in themselves and each other. Compatibility does not diminish the need for completing the other with sanctifying interaction.

Moreover, Christian couples must understand that their true compatibility is found in Christ—not in shared interests, similar likes and dislikes, or common personality traits. It is the gospel and their identity in Christ that ultimately makes them compatible. Two people can share a lot of similar tastes, but if they do not share faith in Jesus Christ, they are not truly compatible. On the flip side, two people who love Christ can also love each other, no matter what their differences.

Even two Christians who come from vastly different theological backgrounds should consider the fact that compatibility at the theological level is more important than at the personality level. Believers with strongly different views on issues like the doctrines of grace, charismatic gifts, gender roles, or even baptism may not be as compatible as their online quotient suggests.

A Question of Reality

This should go without saying, but the real world of everyday life and the virtual world of the Internet don't always match up. This is perhaps illustrated most clearly in the e-mail hoaxes that pepper our in-boxes. Pyramid schemes, fraudulent scams, and false alarms are commonplace in the electronic world, where things (in reality) are not always what they seem (on screen). If an e-mail is a forward of a forward of a forward, or if the "free offer" requires personal information, or if the reward is a sum of several million dollars, chances are you're being scammed. Of course, not every e-mail is malicious. But discernment (along with a good spam filter) is necessary to avoid unwanted hassles and heartaches.

The same is true in the world of Internet dating. Recent reports suggest that up to 90 percent of online daters lie about themselves in an effort to make themselves look better to potential matches.[3] Robert Epstein writes, "For men, the major areas of deception are educational level, income, height, age and marital status; at least 13 percent of online male suitors are thought to be married. For women, the major areas of deception are weight, physical appearance and age."[4] In other words, what you see online may not be what (or who) you'll get in real life.

Granted, not everyone who posts their profile on an Internet dating Web site is doing so with intentions to deceive. But even so, it is human nature to emphasize our best character traits while minimizing our weaknesses. Without even thinking about it, people naturally put their best foot forward in an effort to make themselves appear as attractive as possible. This is especially easy to do online, where people know that how they answer certain questions will affect their "match-ability" with others. They fabricate what psychologists call an "ideal self" that projects the best image. One study even found that these people actually regret when they do tell the truth since they are most concerned with the impression they make on others. People drop their inhibitions because their anonymity encourages their tendency to create fantasies and half-truths. Even when the motivation is not to be dishonest, the resulting profile can still be a generally improved depiction (or distortion?) of the real person.

All of this to say, Christians who use online dating services should do so with a great deal of discernment. They should be aware that some "profiles" may actually be predators, and that even genuine prospects tend to exaggerate their positive qualities. Again, this is not to say that online dating services are inherently wrong or that believers can't use them. But they do pose some unique challenges, especially when it comes to differentiating what is real from what is a façade.

An important side note, also under the category of reality, should be mentioned here. There is a danger in every dating relationship—which is perhaps heightened in Internet dating—with regard to unrealistic expectations. Hollywood has taught us to view romance in terms of "happily ever after" as the flawless knight in shining armor and the fair maiden of impeccable beauty ride off together into the sunset. But romance in real life involves two sinners, each with their own weaknesses and foibles. Though the delights of a Christ-centered marriage are both profound and plentiful, they are not enjoyed without significant self-sacrifice and hard work.

Dating, both online and off, is generally self-oriented. Singles ask themselves, *What do I want in my future spouse?* By contrast, a godly marriage is others-oriented. Christians should ask, *How can I serve and show love to my spouse?* Reflecting this kind of selfless humility when thinking about dating will prepare single believers for fruitful service in marriage. Anticipating what the reality of married life entails, as outlined in Ephesians 5:22-33 and elsewhere, will give them much-needed perspective as they consider their romantic pursuits.

A Question of Accountability

A final question about online dating centers on the question of accountability. When romance blossoms in the context of the church, or even work or school, it comes with a built-in level of accountability. Pastors, parents, and peers quickly become aware of the "special interest" that is forming between two people. The time they spend together includes group activities, social outings, and ministry events—circumstances in which other Christians can observe the couple and offer counsel or feedback. The couple understands that they are being watched, and that people who care about their souls also care about their growing friendship. As a result, rash decisions that might lead to either heartbreak (when a relationship is broken off) or heartache (when purity is not preserved) are weighed against the consequences that a sense of corporate accountability provides.

But online dating is essentially accountability-free. Time on a computer is almost always spent in isolation, making it impossible for pastors, parents, or peers to watch the relationship develop. A sense of anonymity gives the heart a greater sense of freedom in expressing that which might not be said in real life. Moreover, the person on the other end is a complete stranger—not only to the would-be suitor, but also to his or her friends and family. There is no one to vouch for that person as a suitable potential mate, or to affirm that the relationship is going well, or to give informed counsel should issues arise down the road. This puts Christian singles in a much more difficult place as they attempt to pursue romance in a way that is righteous.

It should also be noted that real-world romance often begins in friendship, as two people get to know each other to some degree before expressing romantic interest. But this is not the case in online dating relationships. From the outset, the mind-set is geared toward romance, meaning no opportunity is provided for establishing a simple friendship first. If at any point the romance no longer seems viable, the friendship immediately dies with it. Breaking up is relatively painless (unless you are on the receiving end of the bad news), since there are often no real-world implications to ending the relationship. Online daters may also be tempted to continually look for "someone better" or to entertain multiple prospects at one time. But such practices, and the perspective that fuels them, can develop dangerous habits if left unchecked.

The accountability that comes with real-world relationships guards against these kinds of temptations. Hopefully, no single Christian guy would attempt to date multiple young ladies in his church at the same time. Nor would he arbitrarily end a romantic relationship without considering the consequences or first seeking the counsel of friends and mentors.

On balance, the Christian single who is renewing his or her mind through the Scriptures and seeking to live in a way that honors Christ through the power of the Spirit can certainly navigate the electronic waters of online dating with purity and integrity. The conscience informed by the Scriptures provides believers with a stronger level of accountability than anything external. Remembering the omnipresence of God also goes a long way to countering the thought of sin (Proverbs 15:3). At the same time, wisdom suggests that isolation and temptation often go hand-in-glove (Proverbs 18:1). Whether they enter the world of online dating or not, those who desire to live righteously will seek out accountability from other believers.

To Date or Not to Date

I meant what I said at the beginning: There is nothing inherently sinful about online dating. I am sincerely happy for my married friends who met that way. But there are some unique challenges that come with Internet dating services. For instance, the foundation for online relationships is found in compatibility, while the biblical basis for romance centers on completing one another in Christ. Also, being realistic about oneself and one's expectations tends to be much easier in real-world settings than on the Internet. And finding accountability for how the relationship is being conducted can be much more difficult when, at least at the beginning, it is isolated to a computer.

I fear that too many Christians today are fishing for online love. Given the choice of shopping online or in the local church for a spouse, I am convinced that the local church is the best place for marriages to germinate. After weighing the options, I would probably counsel most of the collegians I serve not to jump online and create a profile.

Ten Important Principles

Below is a brief overview of ten principles for righteous romance.[5] These principles were developed over the years, primarily in working with collegians. No matter what method of dating or courting is used, I believe these ten principles can serve singles seeking to glorify God through their relationships.

1. **Character principle:** The character principle focuses in *being* the right person more than on *finding* the right person. God prioritizes the condition of the heart over externals (1 Samuel 16:7), and so should we. Evaluation of a potential spouse should first be based upon character. At the same time, we need to remember that we ourselves must be maturing in righteousness through the Word, prayer, and spiritual discipleship (Titus 2:1-8). One of the best ways to prepare for marriage is to learn from an older, wiser, and godlier mentor of the same gender.

2. **Confirmation principle:** The confirmation principle is a willingness to submit oneself to the spiritual oversight and accountability God has placed in one's life. Parental affirmation (Ephesians 6:1-2), pastoral affirmation (Ephesians 4:11-16), and peer affirmation (Proverbs 15:22) are three types of confirmation one should seek in determining the wisdom of continuing a romantic relationship.

3. **Contentment principle:** The contentment principle recognizes that the starting point for developing a righteous relationship with another person is the ultimate relationship— your relationship with God. If you are not first satisfied in God alone, you will never find lasting happiness with anyone else (Psalm 63; 84:11; Philippians 4:10-13).

4. **Common ground principle:** A believer should develop a romantic relationship only with another Christian (2 Corinthians 6:14-18). If marrying an unbeliever is outside of God's will, then dating one must also be off limits. You cannot date someone who is spiritually dead and simultaneously please Christ.

5. **Cultivation principle:** Relationships need to be cultivated if they are to grow. Believers can develop relationships in a group setting with other believers. Believers should see each

other as spiritual siblings first and as romantic options second. There is value in couples spending time alone, but it should be done in a public setting to minimize temptation.

6. **Complementarian principle:** Men and women have different God-given roles for the purpose of complementing each other (Genesis 1–3, Ephesians 5:21-33). "At the heart of mature masculinity is a sense of benevolent responsibility to lead, provide for, and protect women in ways appropriate to a man's differing relationships...At the heart of true femininity is a freeing disposition to affirm, receive, and nurture strength and leadership from worthy men in ways appropriate to a woman's differing relationships."[6] With this in mind, men should be the initiators in a relationship. Internet dating potentially puts a woman in the place of being an initiator with men.

7. **Companionship principle:** God instituted marriage so that mankind could glorify the Creator through purposeful companionship. Marriage was created so that a husband and wife together, as a two-in-one team, would serve, reflect, and honor God. Make sure you get to know the other person before you decide that he or she is "the one." Try to observe him or her in as many different settings as possible.

8. **Commitment principle:** This principle stresses that true love, biblically defined, involves self-sacrifice and commitment. Christian love imitates God's love for us, which is an unconditional commitment to imperfect people. In romantic pursuits, great care must be made to distinguish butterflies and feelings from genuine love and commitment. Love is a commitment that culminates in marriage. We too often confuse emotions for love.

9. **Communication principle:** Successful relationships require biblical modes of communication. Biblical communication

includes communicating verbally, honestly, regularly, and purposefully (Ephesians 4:25-29). The key to successful communication is humility. Those who desire to be better communicators and listeners must place the focus of their communication and attention on the other person.

10. **Chastity principle:** A question frequently asked in Christian relationships is, How far can we go physically? This question is really asking, How close can we get to the line without crossing over into sin? By contrast, the chastity principle asks, How pure and holy can I be? Sex is God's wedding gift, and He does not want it opened early! Avoid behavior you would one day regret if your relationship were to be broken off. The safest approach is to treat the person you are dating as if he or she might become someone else's spouse (cf. 1 Thessalonians 4:3-7).

3

WHERE VIRTUAL REALITY
MEETS REAL LIFE

Video Games and a Biblical Worldview

AUSTIN DUNCAN

T his chapter is rated E for Everyone.

After all, it seems everyone is playing video games these days. What used to be the digital domain of a few teenagers cooped up in their parents' basement is now a global phenomenon. A national survey conducted by the Pew Internet & American Life Project exposes just how pervasive video games have become among young people. In the 2008 survey *97 percent* of young respondents said they played video games. That's 99 percent of boys and 94 percent of girls, with no significant differences between various ethnicities and income levels. In fact, 7 percent of those surveyed said they didn't even have a computer at home, but did have a game console (such as a PlayStation, Xbox, or Wii).[1]

Video Games Have Grown Up

Video games are still ingrained in youth culture, but that is no longer their exclusive domain. As each generation of gamers grows up, video games are becoming more and more an adult leisure activity and no longer the hallmark of adolescence. According to a 2008 report by global market research company NPD Group, 63 percent of the U.S. population now plays video games. The average game player is 35 years old and has been playing for 13 years. This statistic grows as gamers get older, as video games become a more regular activity at senior centers, and as games are marketed with an adult audience in mind.[2]

They Play a Lot

When Pew conducted its survey, half the respondents said they had played a video game the previous day. According to Forbes.com, "One British study polled 7,000 'gamers' and found that 12 percent of them met World Health Organization criteria for addictive behaviors."[3] According to Nielsen, which recently started monitoring video game usage in homes in the same manner they have monitored television ratings for years, the most-played game in 2007 was the Massive Multiplayer Online Role Playing Game (MMORPG), *World of Warcraft*. It was played by the average gamer for 1023 minutes per week.[4] That is over 17 hours a week, or the equivalent of a part-time job.

Mario Collected Coins, So Does the Industry

Gaming has moved from a minority childhood pastime to a mainstream avenue of entertainment and media. The industry itself has developed into a massive and formidable economic giant. PricewaterhouseCoopers expects the video game market to be worth about $55.6 billion dollars in 2008—up from $22.3 billion in 2003. The economic reach of game developers is reflected in the amazing advancements of games so visually stimulating and technologically impressive that their realism nearly rivals films. Prerelease sales of *Halo 3* (the number one Christmas 2007 pick by teenage boys according to the retail chain Game Crazy) were in excess of one million copies. The day the game went on sale, the company that produced it made $170 million.

The Word of God and the World of Gaming

This chapter is not a wholesale condemnation of electronic entertainment. Video games are not automatically disqualified as legitimate pastimes just because they're amusing. Having fun is not inherently sinful. And the blame given to video games for our world's ills—from childhood obesity to poor eyesight to dismal social skills—has at least in some cases been overstated.

Nonetheless, the incredible popularity of video games warrants a biblical evaluation of the role they have in the lives of those who play them. Every Christian should seek to think biblically about each aspect of his or her life, desiring to honor Christ in all forms of work and play (including video games). Parents in particular need to shepherd their children in this area, as habits formed during the childhood and teenage years can be hard to break later in life.

A Biblical Worldview on Gaming

A biblical worldview will require an application of wisdom to the topic of video games in the areas of maturity, reality, eternity, and purity.

Maturity

That guy in line at GameStop is 37!

"We don't stop playing because we grow old, we grow old because we stop playing." George Bernard Shaw's often-quoted line is a favorite of time wasters and game players, and it would make sense if growing old was a bad thing. In our culture, youthfulness is prized and folly is praised. But not so from a biblical perspective, where old age, maturity, and wisdom are revered (1 Corinthians 14:20; Ephesians 4:13; Hebrews 5:14). Adults who spend all their time playing games don't stay young, they stay immature.

Many authors, both Christian and secular, have commented on the modern phenomenon of extended adolescence. Dr. Leonard Sax, in his book *Boys Adrift,* states,

> The proportion of young men (age eighteen to thirty-five) living at home with parents or relatives has surged over the [last] thirty years. That proportion has roughly doubled, while the proportion of young women in the same age group living

with parents or relatives has remained constant. Young women and young men are now following different life scripts. Young women are getting jobs, establishing themselves in the workplace, then (in many cases) thinking about having children. But a growing number of young men are just not on the same page.[5]

In part due to video games (one of the factors Dr. Sax considers in his book), young men particularly are clinging to adolescence far beyond the teenage years.

As a result, many young men shun adult responsibilities, delaying marriage (but not necessarily sexual intimacy) and maintaining a high-school maturity level well into their twenties. Like real-life Peter Pans, they just don't want to grow up. Their carefree mentality carries with it more than a disdain for gray hairs; it is marked by a foolhardy rejection of wisdom, a stunted understanding of beauty, and a juvenile infatuation with fun and selfish pursuits. At some point the responsibilities of adulthood should make regular devotion to video games impossible. Young men need to consider the end of their gaming days as they embrace those responsibilities—launching careers, getting married, and starting a family (cf. 1 Corinthians 16:13).

Biblical maturity involves growing in Christlikeness, wisdom, conviction, service, self-control, faithfulness, and the embracing of responsibility. Young men today know a lot about games like *Halo 3* and *World of Warcraft,* but little about integrity, theology, hard work, and how to acquire a wife in a way that honors God. They've role-played virtual heroes, yet they themselves have no knowledge of true sacrifice, honor, or courage. They've traveled to digital worlds in imaginary spacecraft, yet many still haven't moved away from home (cf. Genesis 2:24). They're disciplined enough to play for as long as it takes to reach the next level; yet they lack discipline in every other area of life. Somehow, playing games for eight hours straight does not transition well to working eight-hour days.

Self-control and self-discipline are defining aspects of spiritual maturity (cf. 1 Timothy 3:2). While occasional gaming can be a perfectly legitimate leisure activity, addiction to video games is generally reflective of sinful patterns of behavior (laziness, selfishness, a lack of discipline, etc.). As Peter warned his readers, "For by what a man is overcome, by this he is enslaved" (2 Peter 2:19). And as Paul explained to the Corinthians, "All things are lawful for me, but not all things are profitable. All things are lawful for me, but I will not be mastered by anything" (1 Corinthians 6:12). An immature Christian needs to learn self-control, a character trait that comes from being Spirit-led as the mind is filled with the Word of Christ (Galatians 5:23; Ephesians 5:18; Colossians 3:16). On the other hand, a lack of discipline in one area of life, left unchecked, will inevitably spread to infect other areas.

Reality

Why face reality when you can instantly have everything you've ever wanted—including adventure, money, romance, power, property, popularity, charm, and intrigue—in the virtual fantasy world of your own choosing?

Well, for starters, it's not real. Hardcore gamers may be disappointed to hear this, but there is no galactic alliance; there are no ring-shaped planets harboring enemy aliens; and there are no dwarves, trolls, or goblins wandering in the woods. Your video game character is not really you. *You* are not a futuristic soldier, an international super spy, an immigrant car thief, a local crime boss, a guitar-strumming rock star, or even a sports hero. No, *you* are a Christian, called by God to make your life about something other than a digital fantasy world. And if video games are getting in the way of your ability to take care of life's priorities and responsibilities, you need to make some drastic changes.

A recent article for Yahoo! Games tells the sad story of a marriage breaking apart because of the husband's addiction to *World of Warcraft*. "He would get home from work at 6:00, start playing at 6:30, and he'd play until three A.M. Weekends were worse—it was from morning straight through until the middle of the night," his wife said in an interview. "It took away all of our time that we spent together. I ceased to exist in his life."[6] According to the article, the husband had been neglecting his normal responsibilities, such as paying bills and doing his share of housework. On one occasion, he could not even take a 30-minute break to spend time with his wife. Feeling abandoned, the wife is pursuing a divorce. Video game addiction is the reason. "I'm real," she says, directing her words to her husband, "and you're giving me up for a fantasy land. You're destroying your life, your six-year marriage, and you're giving it up for something that isn't even real."[7]

Neglecting one's family for a fantasy world is senseless, self-indulgent, and sinful. But apparently that hasn't stopped too many people. *World of Warcraft,* for example, boasts over ten million players online.

In simulating real life, many games provide players with control over an avatar (an online character/personality that represents the human player in a virtual world). The avatar is under the gamer's total control and may or may not accurately reflect the gamer's true physique, age, gender, race, ideology, hairstyle, and more. Games like *The Sims* and *Second Life* have become increasingly personal as players have spent hours vicariously pursuing fantasy lives through their avatars—controlling the virtual movements, decisions, relationships, finances, and futures of their computerized creations.

But how does such overt self-indulgence and personal preoccupation mesh with a biblical worldview? Not very well. The heart of Christianity is about loving God (Mark 12:30) and loving others (Mark 12:31), while denying oneself and one's selfish pursuits (Mark 8:34). When we spend long periods of time serving ourselves and indulging our own fanciful desires, we not only cultivate a spirit of hedonism and selfishness within ourselves (creating an even greater appetite for our own entertainment), we simultaneously neglect opportunities to actively pursue Christ and serve others (cf. Philippians 2:1-4).

Moreover, we endanger an accurate understanding of our own self-identity which must be grounded in reality. Christine Rosen, author of *Playgrounds of the Self,* makes this insightful observation: "We have created video games, the new playgrounds of the self. And while we worry, with good reason, about having our identities stolen by others, we ignore the great irony of our own mass identity theft—our own high-tech ways of inventing and reinventing the protean self, wherein the line between reality and virtual reality ultimately erodes and disappears."[8] For Christians, the situation becomes even worse when the lines between fantasy and fact begin to blur. This life is not a game, nor is the life to come. The reality of God's future judgment is not the stuff of science fiction or electronic role-playing. Nonetheless, those who continually fill their minds with things of the virtual world may, at points in their thinking, find it difficult to distinguish between the virtual realm and reality. Insofar as a video game can dull our spiritual senses or divert our focus away from Christ (Hebrews 12:1-3), it is better left unplayed.

Christ is real and so is His gospel. Ministry opportunities are abundant. Yet too many Christians are wasting precious hours engrossed in what amounts to a cheap substitute for reality. They may be able to outsmart electronic dragons and save digital damsels, but all the while their unsaved friends and neighbors remain trapped in the clutches of the evil one. As new creations (2 Corinthians 5:17), believers are to live in the overwhelming reality of the death and resurrection of Jesus Christ. We have been raised in Christ (Colossians 3:1), and He lives in us (Colossians 1:27). He is therefore the basis of our self-identity (Galatians 2:20).

Eternity

From the most complex games to solitaire on your cell phone, games take time. Much of what can be said about video games in this regard could also be applied to other aspects of electronic entertainment—such as blogging, watching television, and surfing the Internet. When large amounts of time each day are devoted to such entertainment, it means that in fact large portions of life are being wasted. Regarding television in particular, John Piper says this: "No one will ever want to say to the Lord of the universe five minutes after death, I spent every night playing games and watching clean TV with my family because I loved them so much…. Television is one of the greatest life-wasters of the modern age."[9] The same could easily be said about video games.

Due to their computerized complexity, today's video games often require days to master and weeks to beat. A game that costs only $40 or $50 to purchase may actually cost hundreds of hours in wasted time. In many games, the player's character develops as he advances through the virtual storyline and becomes more skilled and better equipped. Yet from a real-world standpoint, players themselves may gain little more than carpal tunnel syndrome and an otherwise useless knowledge of fictional weaponry.

Time invested in such pursuits is forever lost and cannot be reused for things that matter. Hours that could be spent working, praying, reading, serving, fellowshipping, evangelizing, or just thinking are instead spent on activities that have no lasting value. God's Word teaches us that time is precious (Psalm 90:12; cf. 39:4-5). Using it wisely is an issue of good stewardship. We must not forget that our lives are not our own; we belong to Christ (1 Corinthians 6:20). When we waste time consistently, a few hours each day, we waste the very lives we have dedicated to Christ.

One of the central themes of the book of Ephesians is the "walk" of the believer. The apostle Paul uses "walk" as a metaphor to represent living. Believers are to walk in good works (Ephesians 2:10), in love (5:1-5), in holiness (5:6-13), and in a way consistent with their calling (4:1-16). They are also to walk in a way that is purposeful and wise. Paul wrote, "Look carefully then how you walk, not as unwise but as wise, making the best use of the time, because the days are evil. Therefore do not be foolish, but understand what the will of the Lord is" (Ephesians 5:15-17). Paul's point here is not strictly about time management (in terms of better scheduling), but life management (in terms of making the most of every opportunity to honor, serve, and worship God). The one who walks wisely will view his or her limited time in this life in light of eternity, taking advantage of every opportunity to bring glory to God.

Purity

Many of the most popular video games are rated M for Mature. A few are even AO (or Adults Only). Yet, in spite of the warnings, one recent survey found that half of teenage boys listed a game with an M rating as one of their favorites.[10]

Video games, not unlike movies, receive these ratings because they contain elements that are considered objectionable and inappropriate for children. Often such games are also inappropriate for Christians. It should be obvious, but games (no matter how popular) that glorify violence, denigrate the value of human life, promote greed, reward deceit, contain profanity, or flirt with sexual immorality should be avoided by believers (Proverbs 6:17; Ephesians 5:3; 1 Timothy 4:12). Our entertainment must honor the Lord and reflect His character. Our amusements should not reinforce values that are diametrically opposed to how we ought to think (Philippians 4:8) and what we are to do (Mark 12:30-31; 1 Corinthians 10:31).

By way of illustration, consider the recently released *Grand Theft Auto IV*. From a business perspective, the game was a major success. It broke sales records by selling over three-and-a-half million units on the day it became available, and banking more than $500 million in its first week on the market. According to studies, the Grand Theft Auto series is the most popular video game for boys ages 12 to 14.

The game itself is rated M for Mature, meaning it is supposed to be sold only to customers over 17 years old. Its label warns buyers of "blood," "intense violence," "strong language," "use of drugs and alcohol," "strong sexual content," and "partial nudity." The story behind the game isn't much better. Players gain points as they murder, steal, deceive, covet, and solicit sexual favors, all while trying not to get caught. To make matters worse, the highly detailed graphics make the entire experience all the more lifelike. According to MTV News correspondent Stephen Totilo,

> [The creators have] tried to make *Grand Theft Auto IV* feel like less of a video game. Shooting a policeman, a criminal or a civilian will cause them to tumble with convincing physics. Shot people look hurt. Cars handle more realistically and more distinctly, depending on the type, making driving feel more true to life. The improved physics and animation make the game feel more real, the player's actions more fraught with consequence…. Is it still "just" a game? That depends on your perspective and what your hopes are for how something like this might impact those who play it.[11]

Even one of the game's creators, Lazlo Jones, told the *Washington Post,* "If you let your child play this game, you're a bad parent."[12]

Contrast this description of the game's contents to Paul's words in Ephesians 5, where believers are told to avoid the sinful amusements of the world:

> Immorality or any impurity or greed must not even be named among you, as is proper among saints; and there must be no filthiness and silly talk, or coarse jesting, which are not fitting, but rather giving of thanks. For this you know with certainty, that no immoral or impure person or covetous man, who is an idolater, has an inheritance in the kingdom of Christ and God. Let no one deceive you with empty words, for because of these things the wrath of God comes upon the sons of disobedience. Therefore do not be partakers with them; for you were formerly darkness, but now you are Light in the Lord; walk as children of Light (5:3-8).

It is difficult to see how any Christian could enjoy playing a game like *Grand Theft Auto,* and not simultaneously violate the very heart of these (and a host of other) verses. If we are to make no provision for lusts of the flesh (Romans 13:14), we must be careful about what temptations we expose ourselves to in the name of entertainment.

Purity must be a priority in every aspect of a Christian's life, including video games. If playing a game violates either biblical principles or the believer's conscience, it is sinful. There's just no other way to say it. As Paul told the Philippians:

> Finally, brethren, whatever is true, whatever is honorable, whatever is right, whatever is pure, whatever is lovely, whatever is of good repute, if there is any excellence and if anything worthy of praise, dwell on these things (4:8).

Press "Escape" to Quit

Will playing video games turn your brain into oatmeal and unleash untold violence on the public, as some people claim? Probably not. Do they require a tremendous amount of discernment from pastors, parents, and players? Absolutely.

By all accounts, video game fixation has taken American culture by storm. On the one hand, there are many video games that are perfectly appropriate for Christians to enjoy—being both fun and nonobjectionable. When played in moderation, they pose no major spiritual threat to anyone. On the other hand, growing numbers of games *do* represent a considerable risk to believers. Their portrayal of sin has become more explicit as graphic quality has improved, and their proclivity to addict and enslave has also increased as game play has been enhanced and plots thickened. The Christian's thinking on this issue must be submitted to the counsel of Scripture. Biblical principles must govern the believer's entertainment.

Those principles include a call to spiritual maturity, a responsiveness to reality, an awareness of eternity, and a commitment to personal purity. Pastors and parents, children and teenagers, gamers and nongamers must let biblical priorities govern their entertainment choices. Doing so may mean turning off the game console. Yet doing so will mean more time for finding true life and joy in something (or more rightly, Someone) far greater than anything video games can ever offer—namely, God Himself.

4

Parental Guidance Required
Making Wise Media Choices for You and Your Family

Kurt Gebhards

No one would argue that our culture is media-saturated. And few would disagree that, as Christians, our consumption of media needs to be moderated. But how can believers make wise media choices for both themselves and their families? It's a question most of us face every day.

Western culture is awash in an ocean of electronic media. Movie theaters, televisions, video games, laptops, cell phones, text messages, music downloads, e-mails, podcasts, and blogs bombard us with a constant flow of audiovisual stimuli. Every day, our lives are inundated with more media than we can possibly process; and much of it, from the dramas on cable to the banner ads online, is decidedly ungodly—depicting sin as pleasurable and without consequence.

When one stops to think about it, the rapid growth and unrelenting pervasiveness of media is quite alarming. We no longer have to leave our homes in order to be exposed to sins and temptations of every kind. Just turning on the television or logging onto the Internet can be a spiritually dangerous undertaking. Yet most Christians do not seem appropriately concerned.

They should be.

As those who are called to walk in holiness and purity, believers need to take care to protect the purity of their minds. Dads and moms, especially, have a responsibility to safeguard their children. In a culture where parents excel at sanitizing little hands, bandaging little cuts, and vaccinating little immune systems, we must not neglect the spiritual well-being of little eyes, ears, and hearts.

So what are God's safety instructions to countermand the crush of entertainment? How can we, by God's help, protect our kids from the evil influences of the world? We need to go to the Scriptures to help us make wise decisions for both ourselves and our families. The challenge of this chapter is twofold: (1) to identify the scriptural principles that should shape our media choices, and (2) to assist parents in shepherding their families in a media-crazed society.

Biblical Principles that Address Media Choices

Media is a powerful influence in our world and lives. But it is not more powerful than the Spirit of God, who indwells believers. By filling our minds with the Word of God (which is the sword of the Spirit), and resting in His strength, we can make godly choices that will neutralize the threat media poses to us and our families. Though the Bible does not mention electronic media specifically, it does provide us with the principles we need to make godly decisions. Let's consider three major scriptural points.

1. Carefully avoid temptations that feed your areas of weakness

Sometimes we need to be reminded that we are weak, frail creatures. Even as Christians our hearts are still prone to wander away from the Lord (Isaiah 53:6), and we can be tempted in many ways (James 1:13-16). If one of the champions of our faith, the great apostle Paul, struggled with indwelling sin, we are certainly vulnerable as well (Romans 7:15,24). Scripture makes it plain that we are easily tempted and spiritually vulnerable (1 Peter 2:11).

God warns us repeatedly in His Word regarding immorality. James 1:27 states that pure religion includes "keep[ing] oneself unstained by the world." We are also called to distance ourselves from the influence of the world (1 John 2:15-17). To disregard God's warnings is to foolishly place ourselves in danger.

With these realities in the forefront of our thinking, we must accordingly be careful to watch over our hearts "with all diligence" (Proverbs 4:23). We are our own worst enemy, and it is the enemy within (the sinful lusts of our flesh) that must be conquered (Jeremiah 17:9). Though Satan can tempt us, using the worldly pleasures around us as bait, it is ultimately our own sinful lusts that cause us to sin (James 1:14). Since a battle rages in the heart we must make no provision for the flesh (Romans 14:13), but rather "sow seeds" to the Spirit (Galatians 6:8). If we sow seeds of holiness, we will reap righteousness as a consequence. And vice versa.

Temptations are cunning and often so subtle that it can be difficult to discern morality from immorality. We must not adopt Hollywood's view of sin as our own. There is a stark contrast between the Bible's depiction of sin and the media's. Consider the sins of adultery, witchcraft, homosexuality, lying, stealing, cheating, and slandering. In Scripture, the consequences of engaging in these are grief, regret, remorse, pain, difficulty, and discipline. Non-Christians will ultimately suffer eternal death in hell (1 Corinthians 6:9-11).

In the media, however, these same sins are usually glorified and upheld as fun, satisfying, and fulfilling. The negative consequences of sin are rarely depicted. Popular films, shows, sites, and songs feed us the tempting lie that sin leads to happiness and carries few if any repercussions. However, this is the polar opposite of biblical truth. When we buy into the world's lies, we bring danger to our souls.

Repeated indulgence in media has a way of dulling the senses. If we are not vigilant, our thinking can become jaded, and lines of morality blurred. But, as one of my fellow pastors has stated, "We should not be entertained by the sins for which Christ died." Lusting after electronic images, laughing at immorality, becoming discontent with our life circumstances, and filling our minds with anti-Christian messages are sins we must avoid.

But *avoidance* is only part of the biblical approach to media. The Christian life is not only concerned with avoiding immorality; it is also consumed with pursuing Christ. In putting off "the deeds of darkness," we must also "put on the armor of light" (Romans 13:12). With that in mind, let's consider two additional major principles believers need to apply.

2. Make the most of the time God has given you

Ephesians 5:16 challenges believers to be "making the most of your time, because the days are evil." James reminds us that our life is fleeting (4:14). Redeeming the time means that we are zealous for good works (Titus 2:14) and that we are "careful to engage in good deeds" (Titus 3:8). God saved each of us from our sins for the purpose of performing good works (Ephesians 2:10).

Movies, TV shows, the Internet, and other forms of media present a daily temptation to pull us away from God's purposes for our lives. How many times have we sat down for "a quick show" and three hours later wondered where the evening went? Or logged on to check our e-mail and two hours later found ourselves still surfing the Web? Even relatively small amounts of wasted time on a daily basis can add up to large amounts of life spent mindlessly gazing at a screen. Wasted time means wasted opportunity; wasted opportunity means poor stewardship; and we will give an account to God for how we spend our lives (Romans 14:10,12; 2 Corinthians 5:10).

Thoughtless media consumption runs counter to the purposefulness of the Christian sojourn. Along with the psalmist, ask God to teach you to number your days (Psalm 90:12). How are you using God's precious gift of time?

3. Worship God above all else, even in your media choices

As Christians, God is to be our all-encompassing passion. Jesus Christ is the pearl of great price (Matthew 13:45-46). There is nothing greater than knowing and pursuing Him (Philippians 3:8). Christ is our supreme value (1 Peter 2:7). He offers us unending joy and satisfaction (Psalm 16:11). The treasures of His fellowship are found deep within the mines of prayer, Scripture-reading, and worship (Psalm 63:1-5). In our relationship with Christ, we invest whatever is necessary to gain infinite returns.

How shocking that we can know these truths, and yet still be pulled into the mundane and immoral things of life! If we know that His "lovingkindness is better than life" (Psalm 63:3), why are we so easily lured into so many lesser things? We must fight to worship Him above all else (1 Timothy 6:12). In what ways might your exposure to media dim your desire for God and quench your passion for Jesus Christ? Why would you not give those things up and pursue the Lord with that time instead? It will not be wasted time!

Along with the three points above, consider these additional biblical principles that can inform our media choices:

- Ensure that Jesus Christ is exalted in all that you do (Colossians 1:18)

- Understand that all things are lawful but not all things are profitable (Romans 6:14)

- Do not fall under the dominating influence of anything except God (1 Corinthians 6:12)

- Beware especially of sexual lust because of the severity of sexual sins (1 Corinthians 6:15-20)

- Fear the destructiveness of worldliness (Matthew 13:22)

- Realize that exposure to sinful examples is corrupting (1 Corinthians 15:33)

- Recognize that even small amounts of foolishness are significant (Ecclesiastes 10:1)

- Do not give serious consideration to the world's philosophies (Psalm 1:1)

- Avoid friendship with the world (James 4:4)

- Be inexperienced and a novice in regards to wickedness (1 Corinthians 14:20)

- Avoid exposure to evil (Proverbs 22:3)

- Flee lust and all inducements to sin (2 Timothy 2:22)

- Fight materialism and covetousness, which are idolatry (Colossians 3:5)

- Protect your eyes from sinful and worthless images (Psalm 101:3)

- Pursue purity in both thought and deed (Hebrews 12:14)

- Make no provision for the flesh and its sinful desires (Romans 13:14)

- Thank God that He has given us all things to freely enjoy (1 Timothy 6:17)

- Use your freedom not for selfishness but for service (Galatians 5:13)

- Train your senses to discern between good and evil (Hebrews 5:14)

- Take every thought captive to Christ (2 Corinthians 10:5)

- Distance yourself from the entangling corruption of the world's lusts (2 Peter 2:20)

- Look to Christ for rest, joy, peace, and fulfillment (Matthew 11:28-30)

- Rejoice in the fact that heavenly rewards await those who are faithful (Hebrews 11:6)

- Fill your life with thoughts that honor Christ (Philippians 4:8)

- Remember that the eyes of the Lord are in every place, watching the evil and the good (Proverbs 15:3)

- Cultivate your contentment through godliness (1 Timothy 6:6)

- Set your mind on the things of Christ (Colossians 3:1-2)

- Expend yourself in spiritual ministry toward others (2 Corinthians 12:15)

- Live to the end that God is glorified in all that you do (1 Corinthians 10:31)

Shepherding Your Children Through Media Choices

In addition to the principles listed above, Christian parents must take special care to make wise decisions for their families. Whether we like it or not, our children are targeted as prime consumers in the media market. Without parental guidance, they are especially vulnerable, not only because they generally lack discernment but also because they are being exposed to media more than any previous generation. Parents need to be aware of the threats media can pose, and alertly stand guard. Dads and moms should set the tone in the home and uphold a godly standard for their kids. The effort parents make in this regard will not go unrewarded (cf. Proverbs 22:6).

Be a good example of self-control with media. Parents must set an example that is worthy to be followed. Wise choices must be made, and self-control must be employed. The sobering fact is that our children will emulate what they see in us. They learn as much by how we live as they do by what we tell them. If we are always watching television, even if it is relatively good television, what message does that send to our kids? If we skip church to watch the game, if we justify dirty movies by "fast-forwarding the bad parts," if we laugh at the sensual or irreverent sitcom jokes, what lessons do we teach our children? No matter what we say, we will not convince them that Jesus Christ is our highest love if the way we spend our free time suggests otherwise.

Stand guard against sinful influences. Parents must watch over their family with vigilance. They need to know (and be in control of) the influences to which their children are being exposed. Ignorance is no excuse. If a child is wearing headphones, the parents should know what is on the MP3 player. If there is an Internet connection in a child's room, the parents should know what Web sites are being visited and ensure that sinful content is blocked. If there is a television in the bedroom closet, the parents should know what shows are being watched. (For that matter, parents should seriously think through the potential temptations and risks involved *before* allowing their children to have private access to any media device, especially televisions, cell phones, or Internet-capable computers.)

Media must be muted in our homes so that the noise doesn't drown out the voice of God. If we are not careful to shield ourselves, we will be overtaken by the deluge, and more significantly, so will our children. As their spiritual (and legal) guardians, we must be proactive in the struggle against the assault of entertainment. Parents are called by God to be the prime influencers of their children. They must not surrender that role to a corded box that sits in the living room.

Stimulate spirituality with your family. Your evenings at home are *prime time* not for watching television but for investing in your family. If you spend that time watching television instead of with your kids, you are neglecting your God-given responsibilities as a parent. Consider two things—among many others—that you trade for a few fleeting moments of relaxation and entertainment: a deep relationship with your children, and gospel opportunities to lead them to Christ.

If you spend time with your kids, investing in them, learning about them, showering love upon them, and playing with them, *they* will want to turn off the television. When your children are all grown and gone from the house and you think back on the years you spent with them as a parent, what things will you regret? I've never met anyone who wishes they had watched more television and spent less time investing in relationships.

Parents (especially fathers) need to take an active role in the spiritual development of their children. Youth pastors and other spiritual influences can be helpful supplements. But the primary spiritual responsibility for raising up godly children rests in the home. As God commanded Israelite parents 3,500 years ago, "You shall teach [God's statutes] to your sons and shall talk of them when you sit in your house and when you walk by the way and when you lie down and when you rise up" (Deuteronomy 6:7). If we are to fully counter the effects of media, we must diligently teach our children the truth about God, sin, and salvation.

As an aside, here are five practical questions parents should consider as they create a strategy for their families when it comes to media:

1. Honestly assess your media consumption. List the TV shows you watch regularly. From the biblical standards you've learned in this chapter, do you need to make some changes? Are you exposing yourself to corrupting influences?

2. Understand your responsibility to redeem the time and use it wisely for God's glory. Are you spending too much time watching television, surfing the Web, or participating in other media-driven activities (such as video games)?

3. Consider what you want to make of your life in light of Christ's call for faithfulness to Him (Matthew 25:23). Are you abusing your freedom in Christ for your own leisure and pleasure (Galatians 5:13)? Or are you exerting yourself in service to the Lord?

4. Compare your media intake with your intake of God's Word. Are you more devoted to your own entertainment and amusement than you are to God's precious Word? What plan of action will you take to address this?

5. Honestly assess the example you offer to your kids. Do you need to make any changes or improvements? Will you sit down with your family, admit your failure in this area, and set up a new plan of action? Remember that your responsibility as a parent is to provide spiritual leadership and guidance for your children in the home.

Setting a Higher Standard

Our culture yearns for recreation and rest. The entertainment industry feeds us the notion that we all deserve a little relaxation, and then happily presents us with many options. You work hard all day, so you *deserve* a little time in front of the television to unwind. Yet God's Word sets a more exacting standard for those who follow Jesus Christ. We are called to live our lives exerting all of our energy for Christ, to spend and be spent, to fight the good fight of faith, to clamor after something far more worthy and infinitely more fulfilling than anything this world has to offer. We are to live for the glory of Christ!

If we do, not only will our homes be bastions of godliness in a wicked world, the sacrifices we make for His sake will be abundantly rewarded in heaven. We would do well to join with the great theologian and writer Jonathan Edwards in being "resolved, that I will live so, as I shall wish I had done when I come to die." Why would we spend our lives being amused by the dim hue of the television when we could be breathlessly enraptured in the blazing brilliance of Christ's glory? Let us keep our eyes on Christ, the Author and Perfecter of the faith. In so doing, we will have little appetite for the fading illusions of this passing world.

5

AMERICAN IDOLS

Entertainment, Escapism, and the Cult of Celebrity

TOM PATTON

We live in a culture obsessed with the promise of fame and renown. Our nation has become a civilization unashamedly committed to the proposition that all people are created "celebrities." We are told that the inalienable rights endowed to us by the Creator include life, liberty, and the pursuit of the American Dream. From gossip columnists who disguise themselves as evening news reporters to nationwide talent scouts who offer fame and fortune like a carousel's golden ring, our society has been infected with the virus of human entertainment…and almost no one is standing in line for the vaccine.

American Idolatry and Popular Culture

It is no coincidence that, at the time of this writing, the most popular television show in America is *American Idol*. Each season a group of no-name hopefuls compete for the chance to be the next object of media adoration. A host of similar shows, such as *Nashville Star, America's Got Talent,* and the re-launch of *Star Search* have followed in its wake—demonstrating our culture's widespread intoxication with stardom. The question is no longer just "Who wants to be a millionaire?" It's "Who wants to be a star?"

The prophets of this American idolatry, armed with the lie that happiness is "making it big," market the mirage with passion and pizzazz. Entertainment, it seems, has now been crowned as the sole standard upon which our culture evaluates everything. Accordingly, the status of celebrity has apparently become the most transcendent state that can ever be bestowed upon someone.

Celebrity worshippers are everywhere, proselytizing their man-centered religion in all avenues of the public domain. Magazines unapologetically named *People* or *Vanity Fair* market stardom with fervor and great skill. Talk radio broadcasters boast of the resumes of rising politicians with the passionate rhetoric usually reserved for demigods. Olympic athletes are adorned with gold and silver and then sold to the highest bidder to advertise everything from breakfast cereal to basketball shoes. From actors that star in blockbuster movies to television evangelists who brag of Rolls Royce lifestyles, everyone in America wants to be famous; and now thanks to the explosive advances of widespread media, it appears as if everyone can be.

The mass appeal of *reality television* allows the most ignoble and bizarre lifestyles of the rude and reckless to become the new standard for success. Colossal Internet campaigns are launched to persuade a myriad of customers to "broadcast" themselves. The underlying philosophy is that everyone has "a story" to tell. Whether or not there is a moral or redeeming quality to the tale doesn't matter. What matters is whether it can be used to create an opportunity to gain notoriety and thus partake in the greatly coveted American Dream.

American Idolatry and the American Dream

In modern times, the American Dream has become an unspoken promise propagated by this culture through billboards, media, film, and every other possible imaginable venue that promotes the celebrity lifestyle. It implies that because of our immense freedoms and the unprecedented opportunities granted to us in this country, we can achieve our dreams. If we work hard enough or believe in ourselves long enough then regardless of our background or education or any other possible restraint, we can become not only financially secure but also wealthy, revered, famous, and happy.

Some have seen this as a primary theme of the United States from the very beginning. Founding father Alexander Hamilton noted the motivation behind the origin of our country as the "love of fame which is the ruling passion of the noblest minds." However, where *fame* was once the *recognition of exceptional accomplishment,* it has now been replaced by *celebrity,* the less dignified notion of *recognition for simply being recognizable.* What now inspires the culture is the prospect of viewing their lives through the American Story as they seek to escape from their unfulfilling lives by vicariously placing themselves in every movie or television show they watch. Craving to be stars in their own right, they look to media to gain for themselves meaning, purpose, and their own 15 minutes of glory. Whereas entertainment once provided escape from reality, it seems now that entertainment has become the reality from which no one desires to escape.

American Idolatry and the Cult of Celebrity

It is impossible to overexaggerate the widespread influence on our culture of what might be termed the *cult of celebrity,* where the aspirations of an entire society converge on the desire to be known. The cult of celebrity is a virtual religion whose congregants inadvertently worship themselves by giving envious praise to the rich and famous whom they long to emulate. With faith in their dreams, they embrace the promise that one day they too might find their own sacred status. Long gone are the days in which exceptional ability and excellent character combined together to create a public prototype worthy of emulation. Today, under the influence of Hollywood, we see a new sect of devotees who have abandoned any objective criteria for their idol worship and given themselves fully to the pursuit of personality.

The central issue being addressed is the bottomless appetite our culture possesses for entertainment and how this ferocious hunger has subtly morphed itself into a full-fledged brand of American idolatry. It has taken the positive influence that once came from model heroes of bravery and morality and replaced them with negative examples of self-aggrandizement and arrogance. What was once an innocent platform for the budding abilities of talented children has been twisted into an exploitive license for self-promotion. As a result, the obsession for recognition in this culture is not only more desirable than real ability, but also vastly more necessary for career success.

To whatever degree this new entrepreneurial strand of idolatry may seem shocking to the innocently naïve, the truth remains that the *worship of people* throughout world history has always been a central human fascination and struggle. For example, it was customary for a victorious first-century Roman military general to return from a successful campaign and be granted what was termed a "triumph." A triumph was the apex of public recognition for the homecoming commander, who along with his troops would parade the streets with both the spoils and prisoners of war. In response, they would receive the thunderous accolades of the people.

Accompanying the general in his chariot was a slave of his own choosing who was commissioned to stand at his shoulder to perform a very specific task. As the roar of the crowd echoed in the air and the glory of the state was magnified about them, the chosen slave would whisper into the ear of the victorious general a phrase reserved for those tempted to think themselves a god in any generation: "Remember, you are only human!"

Whether this corruption manifests in the scandalous *deification of humanity* (as seen in the first-century Roman cult that worshipped both dead and living emperors) or in the sacrilegious *humanization of deity* (as witnessed in the twentieth-century production of the rock opera *Jesus Christ Superstar*), mankind has constantly attempted to redefine himself as something more than a creature so as to worship his own image.

American Idolatry and the Sin of Self-Worship

The sin of idolatry is a sin of the heart (cf. Ezekiel 14:3-7). It occurs when men and women love something else more than they love God

(Mark 12:30-31; cf. Revelation 2:4-5); when they serve something other than Him (cf. 1 Thessalonians 1:9); when He is not the object of their praise and adoration (cf. Deuteronomy 6:14). Though the term can conjure up images of robed worshippers bowing before golden statues in ornate buildings, idolatry is often evidenced in more subtle forms, such as the self-worship that pervades the American culture of self-exaltation and self-gratification. When people want to be like God, they inevitably fall into sin (cf. Genesis 3:5).

One of the most dramatic illustrations of idolatrous worship is found in the Old Testament account of the giving of the Ten Commandments. When the Lord thundered forth His holy law at Mt. Sinai He began by denouncing the sin of idolatry: "You shall have no other gods before Me" (Exodus 20:3) and "You shall not make for yourself an idol, or any likeness of what is in heaven above or on the earth beneath or in the water under the earth" (Exodus 20:4). Yet only a short time later, Aaron led the people of Israel in an idolatrous delusion as they worshipped a calf-shaped statue made of pure gold (Exodus 32:1-4). From this point forward, throughout the entirety of Israel's history, the deception of idolatry remained a constant threat. All too often, the sad irony of Israel's legacy was that God's chosen people had chosen other gods.

In the New Testament, the apostle Paul explained the rationale behind idolatry in the first chapter of Romans. God created human beings to worship Him, and when they reject Him on account of their sin, they naturally worship something else. Man cannot push away the truth of God that has been implanted deep within the human heart without simultaneously redirecting its wonder into expressions of a much lesser kind. Paul said it this way: "They exchanged the truth of God for a lie, and worshiped and served the creature rather than the Creator, who is blessed forever, Amen" (Romans 1:25). By refusing to worship God, sinful men exchange the true object of worship for a counterfeit. Instead of rightly acknowledging the Creator, they ironically give their praise to something He has made.

So men and women worship "mother earth" or false religion or themselves and their own happiness. Whatever the object, if it is not the true God, it is idolatry. In all of this, men are without excuse. As Paul explained, speaking of God, "His invisible attributes, His eternal power and divine nature, have been clearly seen, being understood through what has been made, so that they are without excuse" (Romans 1:20). Such idolaters "suppress the truth [about God] in unrighteousness" (verse 18), ignoring the witness of both the creation around them and the conscience inside them (2:15). Having been blatantly confronted with the undeniable reality of God's existence, they willfully rebuff the tug of truth on their hard hearts and seek their deepest satisfaction in gratifying themselves.

The Emptiness of American Idolatry

Until sinners submit to the truth about God, they will never acquire what it is they truly seek. They are like the Samaritan woman who met Jesus at Jacob's well, confusing the true remedy for spiritual thirst with the temporary satisfaction of an earthly spring (John 4:14). Sadly, the unbeliever attempts the whole of his life to quench the unquenchable with something other than God. So he pursues fame, money, power, wealth, fitness, work, wisdom, education, love, or any other created thing that can perhaps quiet the desperate cry of his empty soul. But none of the things he finds—whether politics or popularity or creativity or anything else this world offers—can ever answer the call of his heart. He can pursue happiness, but he will never find it. As soon as he acquires one desire it turns into dust—as does the next, and the next after that, until life finally ends in disappointment.

This is the cotton-candy fate of the American Dream that befalls all who embrace the cult of celebrity. From a distance it looks so appealing—a big and beautiful ball of glistening spun sugar. But those who finally get it and taste it find that it isn't very filling. Sure, it is sweet for a moment. But it doesn't bring lasting happiness. After a quick melt in the mouth it is gone forever. Then what?

King Solomon understood this perhaps better than anyone else ever has. He was the richest, most famous, and most powerful man of his day. He was also the smartest, because God had given him supernatural wisdom. Solomon used all the resources at his disposal in the pursuit of his own happiness. He experimented with pleasure (Ecclesiastes 2:1-3), hard work (2:4-6), material possessions (2:7-8), popularity and prestige (2:9-10), and even his own wisdom (2:12-14), all in an effort to find lasting joy. Yet he found it all to be empty, finally concluding that true joy and fulfillment cannot be found in the things of this world, but only in God (2:24-26; 12:13-14).

As Solomon learned after a lifetime of trial and error, if you want happiness in this life you must look to God. You must deny everything you once thought could give you happiness for the sake of following the risen Lord. His salvation is the satisfaction you seek. It cannot be found in fame and fortune any more than it can be found at the end of a rainbow. It is only found in embracing the true source of all satisfaction, God Himself.

A Right Response to American Idolatry

The cult of celebrity promises something only God can provide. Those who love it and follow after it, like all who worship idols, will ultimately be disappointed and find it empty. But what is a right response to the bottomless appetite our culture possesses for entertainment?

The answer begins with finding true life in Jesus Christ. If you want happiness and joy in this life you must deny everything you once thought could give you happiness for the sake of following a risen Lord. When you realize that all your life you have pushed away from the God of your creation, when you understand that your sin is such a great offense against God that He sent His Son to die for sinners, and when you come to see that what you seek is ultimately a saving knowledge of the Savior and not the acclaim of man, then your heart will joyfully break in two, for ultimately His salvation is the satisfaction you seek. The Spirit comes and turns your heart away from the lust of being known by men to the joy of being known by God.

Next, we must continue to guard our hearts against the powerful seduction of the cult of celebrity. Though we have repented of our idolatry and consequently been granted salvation by grace through faith in Jesus Christ, we must also recognize that our vulnerability to such temptation still exists. At times we too have redirected the glory that belongs only to God into a man-made vehicle for our own self-congratulation. At times we too are like those whom the Lord rebuked through Jeremiah: "Are you seeking great things for yourself? Do not seek them" (Jeremiah 45:5).

Even those who have found their sole satisfaction in Jesus Christ can at times place their attention back on their preconversion desires for self-adoration. Initially we view American idolatry with disdain and disappointment, but over time the pull of its allurement and the magnitude of its influence can erode even our best-planned defenses and perspectives. It is not wrong to encourage the talents of our children and strive to develop whatever giftedness we may have received from God. But before we can be a light to our star-studded world we must first remember to dim the flame for our own glory.

Finally, we must use the cult of celebrity in our evangelism. It is a reality that transcends all cultures, that no one is satisfied with what they have until they have the one true God! A rich young ruler sought out Christ even though he had wealth, health, and prosperity because he sensed that *eternity* was what he really needed (Luke 18:18). He knew that what he was pursuing and all that he owned could not and did not make him happy. Yet when Jesus instructed him to throw it all away he refused to do so, believing instead that maybe a little more worldly wealth would do the trick...and that finally he would be satisfied. All that people *want*—a bigger office, a higher salary, a better career, a different spouse, a healthier body, an earlier retirement, a happier life, or an exalted celebrity status—is not in fact what they *need,* and it never was! The Bible's answer to sinful man is this: You will never be satisfied until you realize that your every desire for more in this life is, in reality, a desire for more of God. That must be our answer as well.

Part 2

MORALITY AND ETHICS

WHAT GOD HATH JOINED TOGETHER

Issues Related to Divorce and Remarriage

PASTORAL PERSPECTIVE

*Several years ago, the elders of Grace Community Church pub-
lished a booklet entitled* The Biblical Position on Divorce and
Remarriage: The Elders' Perspective. *The material in this chapter has been adapted from that document.*[1]

God hates divorce, because it always involves unfaithfulness to
the solemn covenant of marriage that two partners have entered
into before God, and because it brings harmful consequences to those
partners and their children (Malachi 2:14-16). Divorce, in Scripture,
is permitted only because of mankind's sin. Since divorce is a concession to man's sin and is not part of God's original plan for marriage,
all believers should hate divorce as God does and pursue it only when
there is no other recourse. With God's help, a marriage can survive
the worst sins.

In Matthew 19:3-9, Christ taught clearly that divorce is an accom-
modation to man's sin that violates God's original purpose for the
intimate unity and permanence of the marriage bond (Genesis 2:24).
He taught that God's law allowed divorce only because of "hardness of
heart" (Matthew 19:8). Legal divorce was a concession for the faithful

partner due to sexual sin or abandonment on the part of his or her spouse, such that the faithful partner was no longer bound to the marriage (Matthew 5:32; 19:9; 1 Corinthians 7:12-15). Although Jesus did say that divorce is permitted in some situations, we must remember that His primary point in this discourse is to correct the then-popular notion that people could divorce one another "for any reason at all" (Matthew 19:3) and to show the gravity of pursuing a sinful divorce. Therefore believers should never consider divorce except in specific circumstances (see below), and even in those circumstances it should be pursued reluctantly because there is no other recourse.

Biblical Grounds for Divorce

The only New Testament grounds for divorce are sexual sin or desertion by an unbeliever.

The first is found in Jesus' use of the Greek word *porneia* (Matthew 5:32; 19:9). This is a general term that encompasses sexual sin, such as adultery, homosexuality, bestiality, and incest. In the Old Testament, God Himself divorced the northern kingdom of Israel because of her idolatry, which He likened to sexual sin (Jeremiah 3:6-9).[2] When one partner violates the unity and intimacy of a marriage by committing sexual sin—thereby forsaking his or her covenant obligation—the faithful partner is placed in an extremely difficult and painful situation. After every attempt has been made to bring the sinning partner to repentance (so that forgiveness and reconciliation can take place), the Bible permits release for the faithful partner through divorce (Matthew 5:32; 1 Corinthians 7:15).

The second reason for permitting a divorce is in cases where an unbelieving spouse does not desire to live with his or her believing partner (1 Corinthians 7:12-15). Because "God has called us to peace" (verse 15), divorce is allowed and may be advisable in such situations. When an unbeliever desires to leave, trying to keep him or her in the marriage may create greater tension and conflict. Hence Paul stated, "If the unbelieving one leaves, let him [or her] leave" (verse 15). Also, if the unbeliever leaves the marriage relationship permanently but is not willing to file for divorce—perhaps because of a chosen lifestyle, irresponsibility, or to avoid monetary obligations—then the believer is put in the impossible situation of having legal and moral obligations that he or she cannot fulfill. Because "the brother or the sister is not under bondage in such cases" (1 Corinthians 7:15), meaning that the believing spouse is no longer bound to the marriage, divorce is acceptable without fearing the displeasure of God. (The unbeliever would be considered the covenant-breaker, thus releasing the innocent party.)

Biblical Grounds for Remarriage

Remarriage is permitted for the faithful partner only when a divorce is based on biblical grounds (Romans 7:1-3; 1 Corinthians 7:39).

Those who divorce on any other grounds have sinned against God and their spouse, and for them to marry another is an act of "adultery" (Mark 10:11-12). This is why Paul says a believing woman who sinfully divorces should "remain unmarried, or else be reconciled to her husband" (1 Corinthians 7:10-11). If she repents from her sin of unbiblical divorce, the true fruits of that repentance would include seeking reconciliation with her former spouse (Matthew 5:23-24). The same is true for a believing man who divorces unbiblically but later repents (1 Corinthians 7:11). Such a person could remarry someone else only if the former spouse had remarried or died, in which case reconciliation would be impossible.

The Bible also gives a word of caution to anyone who is considering marriage to a divorcee. If the divorce was not on biblical grounds and there is still a responsibility to reconcile, the person who marries the divorcee is considered an adulterer (Mark 10:12).

Divorce and Church Discipline

Believers who pursue divorce on unbiblical grounds are subject to church discipline because they openly reject God's instructions in the Bible. The person who obtains an unbiblical divorce and remarries is guilty of adultery because God did not permit the original divorce (Matthew 5:32; Mark 10:11-12). That person is subject to the steps of church discipline as outlined in Matthew 18:15-17.

If a professing Christian violates the marriage covenant by abandoning his or her spouse, and subsequently refuses to repent during the process of church discipline, Scripture instructs that he or she should be put out of the church and treated as an unbeliever (verse 17). At that point, the faithful partner is then free to divorce according to the provision in 1 Corinthians 7:15 regarding unbelievers who have departed. Before such a divorce, however, reasonable time should be allowed for the possibility that the unfaithful spouse might return as a result of the discipline.

The leaders in a local church should help single believers who have been divorced to understand their situation biblically, especially in cases where the appropriate application of biblical teaching does not seem clear. In some instances, the church leadership may need to help divorcees determine whether one or both of the former partners were genuine believers at the time of their past divorce, because this will affect the application of biblical principles to their current situation (1 Corinthians 7:17-24). Also, because not all churches practice church discipline, pastors and elders must recognize that in some cases estranged or former spouses might be rightly regarded as unbelievers (on the basis of unrepentant and ongoing sin) even if they are currently attending church somewhere else. In such instances this would affect the application of biblical principles to their believing partners (1 Corinthians 7:15; 2 Corinthians 6:14).

Any believer who is in a divorce situation that seems unclear should humbly seek the help and direction of church leaders, because God has placed those men in the church for such purposes (Matthew 18:18; Ephesians 4:11-16; Hebrews 13:17).

Divorce Prior to Conversion

Salvation indicates that a person has begun a new life. That new life is defined by a pattern of obedience to what God has revealed about every area of life—including marriage and divorce. According to 2 Corinthians 5:17, the believer has become a "new creature" when he believes in Jesus Christ. This does not mean that painful memories, bad habits, or the underlying causes for past marital problems will no longer exist, but it does mean that Christ begins a process of transformation through the Holy Spirit and the Word. A sign of saving faith will be a receptivity and a willingness to obey what God has revealed in His Word about marriage and divorce.

According to 1 Corinthians 7:20-27, there is nothing in salvation that demands a particular social or marital status. The apostle Paul, therefore, instructs believers to recognize that God providentially allows the circumstances they find themselves in when they come to Christ. If they are called to Christ while married, they should seek to remain in their marriage unless the unbelieving spouse subsequently desires to leave (1 Corinthians 7:15; 1 Peter 3:1). If they are converted after being divorced and cannot be reconciled to their former spouse (because that spouse is an unbeliever, is remarried, or has died), then they are free to either remain single or be remarried to another believer (1 Corinthians 7:39; 2 Corinthians 6:14).

Unbiblical Divorce and Divine Forgiveness

In cases where a divorce took place on unbiblical grounds and the guilty partner later repents, the grace of God is operative at the point of repentance. A sign of true repentance will be a desire to implement 1 Corinthians 7:10-11, which would involve an eagerness to pursue reconciliation with his or her former spouse, if that is possible. If reconciliation is no longer possible (per the reasons listed in the section "Biblical Grounds for Remarriage"), then the forgiven believer could pursue another relationship under the careful guidance and counsel of church leadership.

In cases where a believer obtained a divorce on unbiblical grounds and remarried, he or she is guilty of the sin of adultery until that sin is confessed (Mark 10:11-12). God does forgive that sin immediately when repentance takes place, and there is nothing in Scripture to indicate anything other than the fact that from that point on, the believer should continue in his or her current marriage.

Divorce and Pastoral Qualification

Obviously, the church has a responsibility to uphold the biblical ideal of marriage, especially as exemplified by its leadership. First Timothy 3:2 says that leaders must be "the husband of one wife" (literally, "a one-woman man"). That phrase, repeated in verse 12, does not mean that an elder or deacon cannot have been remarried,[3] but that he be solely and consistently faithful to his wife in an exemplary manner. It says nothing about the past before his salvation, because none of the other qualifications listed refer to specific acts in the past (prior or subsequent to salvation). Rather, they all refer to qualities that characterize a man's Christian life.

A pastor's marriage should be a model demonstration of Ephesians 5:22-29, which describes the relationship of Christ to His church. In cases where a potential pastor, elder, or even deacon has been divorced, the church must be confident that he has given evidence of ruling his family well and proven his ability to lead those close to him to salvation and sanctification. His family is to be a model of faithful and righteous living (1 Timothy 3:4-5; Titus 1:6). It would be necessary to carefully examine the circumstances surrounding his divorce (whether it was before or after salvation, on what grounds, etc.) and any consequences still remaining that may affect his reputation—because God desires the pastors of His church to be the best possible models of godliness before others. If a leader truly desires to be "above reproach" (1 Timothy 3:2), he will be willing to undergo such scrutiny.

When Life Is Reduced to a Choice
Opposing Abortion While Reaching Out to Hurting Women

Bill Shannon

I'll never forget meeting my third granddaughter for the first time. She was beautiful. As my wife and I stood in that ordinary hospital room, we stared with joyful fascination at the extraordinary miracle of life. We marveled out loud at how God had fashioned her little arms, legs, fingers, and toes. We wondered about which side of the family she might grow up to look like; and we rejoiced in the fact that she was healthy and strong. We could hardly take our eyes off her. She was undoubtedly part of our family, and we were so thankful that God had brought her into our lives.

Now we just had to wait until she was born.

But it would be seven more months before her birthday would come. In fact, our granddaughter was still in her first trimester of life when we met her for the first time. Her mom had been hospitalized for pregnancy-related sickness; and our first glimpses of her were via a three-dimensional ultrasound machine. But there she was as a seven-week-old fetus—affectionately known as *Peanut*—with recognizable ears, eyes, elbows, fingers, toes, and a nose. I was shocked at how distinct her features were. "How could anyone think this is not a human being?" I asked my wife. The images we saw were not of an indistinct blob. No, we clearly saw our granddaughter, her tiny heart beating inside her tiny body. There she was, complete in all the beauty of personhood.

Abortion in American Culture

My granddaughter was not even two months along when I first met her. As impossible as it is for me to imagine, that is the same stage of development at which millions of other unborn babies are killed each year. According to recent statistics, 22 percent of all pregnancies in the United States (excluding miscarriages) end in abortion. Since *Roe v. Wade,* over 45 million abortions have taken place in the United States. Some 61 percent of these take place before the fetus is 9 weeks old, with another 28 percent occurring between 9 to 12 weeks. By far, the most common reasons for having an abortion are social in nature, meaning that the pregnancy is inconvenient or the child is unwanted by the mother for one reason or another. And of those women who have abortions, at least 65 percent would consider themselves Christians (with 43 percent identifying themselves as Protestant, and 27 percent as Catholic).[1]

The American legal system, ever since the landmark *Roe v. Wade* Supreme Court decision in 1973, has held that women in the United States have a constitutional right to obtain an abortion in the early stages of pregnancy—that is, before the fetus is considered "viable" (or able to live on his or her own outside of the mother's womb). Beyond the fact that "viability" is an inherently subjective standard, a point admitted even by abortion advocates, the irony is that a newborn baby is immediately granted full legal rights as a human being; yet only a few months (or even hours) earlier, that same child is not even considered a person.

Abortion and the Bible

Ever since the Supreme Court decided against the unborn, abortion as a medical practice has been widely accepted in American society. But does the legalization of abortion in the eyes of the government make it right in the sight of God? To answer this question, one must begin by determining God's view of the human fetus. Does He consider the fetus a person or merely protoplasm? If the Bible fails to grant personhood to the unborn fetus, then perhaps the premature extermination of such life is morally inconsequential. But, if God's Word demonstrates that the unborn fetus is indeed a person, then abortion is nothing less than murder (Genesis 9:6; Exodus 20:13).

A number of Bible passages make it clear that God regards conception as the moment at which personhood begins. Job 10:8-12 and 31:13-15, for example, attribute divine value and human qualities to the unborn fetus. Psalm 139:13-16 similarly exalts God for His creative work in the fashioning of the unborn baby. Isaiah 49:1-5, Jeremiah 1:4-5, and Galatians 1:15-16 all note that God can work in the lives of His chosen servants even before they are born. Furthermore, Luke 1:41-45 documents the emotional joy of the unborn John the Baptist when Mary visited Elizabeth. And Psalm 51:5 points to conception as the beginning of a person's sinful nature. None of these things would be possible if personhood did not come until after birth.

In some passages, the Bible speaks of an unborn child in the same way that it does of those who have been born—thereby showing that God views them both the same way. For example, in Exodus 21:4 and 21:22 the same Hebrew word translated "child" or "children" is used, despite the fact that verse 4 refers to a postnatal child while verse 21 refers to an unborn life. The New Testament also uses the same Greek word for life before birth (Luke 1:41,44) as it does for life outside the womb (Acts 7:19). It is not surprising, therefore, to learn that the unborn are often described in the same ways as those who are born (Genesis 25:22-23; Job 31:15; Isaiah 44:2; Hosea 12:3). For that matter, the prophet Jeremiah notes that had his death been prenatal, the womb would have been his grave (Jeremiah 20:17); and the prebirth death of one of God's prophets cannot be equated with the death of a nonperson.

Scripture further espouses the fact that all human persons are the offspring of other human persons. After all, Genesis 1:24-25 decisively mandates that each "kind" within creation is to reproduce solely after its own "kind." The procreation of existing human persons, therefore, is limited solely to the generation of new human persons. In other words, via the reproductive process, it is impossible for existing persons to even produce a nonperson.

God's image in man (see Genesis 1:26; James 3:9) is particularly attacked by abortion. After all, abortion not only destroys the image of God in the fetus by killing the baby, but also disregards God's command to multiply His image in future generations by terminating the reproductive process. In the end, because the fetus results from two persons, each made in the image of God, Scripture indicates that he or she is also a person found in God's image.

The Bible overwhelmingly argues for the personhood of the prenatal fetus, while simultaneously denouncing the horrible murder of unborn humans (cf. Exodus 21:22-23).[2] When all the facts are in, abortion may have been legalized by the Supreme Court, but it cannot be viewed as anything less than a direct assault on the moral law of God.

The Devastating Consequences of Abortion

Abortion rights is unashamedly driven by a feminist agenda that claims to put the feelings and interests of the mother above anything else. Thus, *the right to choose* on the part of the mother overrides *the right to live* on the part of the unborn child. As a result,

> Appeals to Biblical morality, to the constitutional right to life, to scientific facts about the development of life in the womb, to the brutality of abortion techniques—these objective issues carry no weight with people whose worldview allows for no external absolutes, who accept no moral criteria beyond a woman's arbitrary choice, or who uncritically accept orthodox feminist party line.[3]

Dr. Larry Epperson explains that "the underlying reason people want to have the option of abortion is to maintain the 'sexual freedom' and personal convenience. Their demand for such 'rights' is so overwhelming that their solution to the unwanted consequences of sexual relations is not to stop promiscuity, but to kill the unborn children that result."[4]

Though women who choose to abort may be ignoring God's moral standards in the moment, they rarely escape the lifelong guilt and heartache that results from their tragic choice. They have been designed by God as nurturers (cf. 1 Timothy 2:15; Titus 2:4); they have God's law written on their conscience (cf. Romans 2:14-15); and they have often been manipulated into their decision by others (perhaps a boyfriend or husband). As a result, they are often scarred by feelings of regret and shame even if they do not know the Lord (cf. Psalm 32:3-4).

These woman generally desire healing, but do not know where to find it. Some become depressed and suicidal. "Compared to women who have not been pregnant in the prior year, deaths from suicide, accidents, and homicide are 248 percent higher in the year following an abortion, according to a new 13-year study of the entire population in Finland. The study also found that the majority of the extra deaths among women who had abortions were due to suicide."[5] Another study found that "among the most worrisome of these reactions is the increase of self-destructive behavior among aborted women. In a survey of over 100 women who had suffered from post-abortion trauma, fully 80 percent expressed feelings of 'self-hatred.' In the same study, 49 percent reported drug abuse and 39 percent began to use or increased their use of alcohol."[6] Though not comprehensive, reports like these illustrate the mental and emotional anguish that can follow an abortion.

Guilt and shame presuppose sin, and sin can only be remedied through the forgiveness found in the gospel of Jesus Christ. Although the mother has sinned against God and her child, there is real hope to be found in God's grace, just as there is for any sinner. As David exclaimed in Psalm 32:5-6, writing after his adultery with Bathsheba and murder of Uriah, "I acknowledged my sin to You, and my iniquity I did not hide; I said, 'I will confess my transgressions to the LORD.' And You forgave the guilt of my sin."

Abortion and the Church

How can the church help women who are either pregnant (and considering an abortion) or who have already terminated a pregnancy?

Most basically, the church should help educate women so that they do not make this decision in the first place. This includes teaching biblically on the topic, and making prolife resources available to those in the congregation (including information on adoption and postpartum support). Also, teaming up with a nearby Pregnancy Resource Center is a helpful way to offer additional counseling and support to women who have questions.

Pregnancy Resource Centers, for instance, often have ultrasound machines that can help expectant mothers meet their unborn babies—in the same way that my wife and I met our granddaughter before she was born. Among abortion-minded women who visited the Pregnancy Resource Center in North Hills, California in 2006, the non-ultrasound clients chose to abort 61 percent of the time. However, those who used ultrasound would abort only 24.5 percent of the time.[7] This is just one example of how a Pregnancy Resource Center can supplement the church's efforts to convince women that abortion is not the answer.

What can the church do for women who have already had an abortion? Obviously the ideal scenario is to have opportunity to counsel a pregnant mother before any irreversible decision has been made about the fetus. But even when it is too late, pastors and other Christians can still offer the hope of the gospel to a mother who desperately needs forgiveness and salvation. Though conversion cannot erase the memory and pain of a wrong choice, it does bring supernatural peace with God in knowing that all sin has been forgiven through Christ's sacrifice on the cross. Psalm 103:8-12 promises this to those who embrace God's grace:

> The LORD is compassionate and gracious,
> Slow to anger and abounding in lovingkindness.
> He will not always strive with us,
> Nor will He keep His anger forever.

He has not dealt with us according to our sins,
Nor rewarded us according to our iniquities.
For as high as the heavens are above the earth,
So great is His lovingkindness toward those who fear Him.
As far as the east is from the west,
So far has He removed our transgressions from us.

What about the church's response to the abortion rights movement? Grace Community Church believes that Christians should vigorously employ all legislative and legal means to end abortion. This includes our constitutional rights of speech, press, petition, and assembly. Yet even in the exercise of our legal rights we must be careful to demonstrate the love of Jesus Christ not only for the unborn but also for those who oppose us—seeing them not as the enemy, but as the mission field.

The church should never stoop to illegal or dishonest methods in order to stop abortion. Such is neither biblical (cf. Romans 13:1-7) nor honoring to the glorious name of Christ (2 Corinthians 10:3-4). Thus we would not sanction the use of violence to achieve God's purposes. Instead, we would emphasize the preaching of the gospel. After all, hope for true lasting change (at either the individual or national level) can only be found in the good news of Jesus Christ.

Planned Parenthood?

Birth Control, In Vitro Fertilization, and Surrogacy

Pastoral Perspective

This chapter is adapted from material our pastors and elders have assembled over the years on these issues. It is representative of the general position of Grace Community Church.

There is no question that bearing children pleases God. That is evident from Titus 2:3-5 and Paul's exhortation to young widows in 1 Timothy 5:14. In addition to the pleasures of intimate companionship (Proverbs 5:19), procreation is one of the primary purposes of marriage (Genesis 1:27). Hence Psalm 127:3-5 says children are gifts from God and those who have many of them are blessed. A big family means increased responsibility, but children raised in a godly way will influence the world for good and for God.

Nonetheless, nothing in Scripture prohibits married couples from practicing birth control, either for a limited time to delay childbearing, or permanently once they believe their family is complete.[1] At the same time, Christian couples should prayerfully consider their motives before the Lord, carefully evaluating their reasons for postponing or preventing pregnancy. As in every ethical decision believers make, reasons for using birth control should reflect a biblical worldview and should not simply be dictated by the default practice of the culture.

Though the use of birth control (in principle) is not forbidden in Scripture, not all methods of birth control are acceptable. Prolonged abstinence between a husband and wife is forbidden in 1 Corinthians 7:5—making it a biblically unacceptable form of birth control. On the flip side, any type of birth control method that would cause an abortion must also be rejected. Life begins at conception (meaning fertilization), and the intentional destruction of that life is tantamount to murder. Any form of birth control that destroys the fetus or fertilized ovum rather than preventing conception is therefore wrong. (For more on our position on abortion, see the previous chapter in this book.)

Other methods of birth control, including nonabortifacient oral contraceptives, condoms, and the common surgical procedures of tubal ligation or vasectomy pose no problem biblically. If both husband and wife are persuaded before God and in their own consciences that they should have no more children, Scripture does not prohibit them from carrying through with that decision.

In all of this, the husband must be especially aware of his responsibility to selflessly serve and cherish his wife (Ephesians 5:25-29). He should never coerce his wife into using any type of contraceptive method with which she is not entirely comfortable. Emotional, hormonal, and physical side-effects should all be considered as the husband and wife together determine what type of contraceptive method, if any, is right for them.

We agree with Albert Mohler, who writes:

> Evangelical couples may, at times, choose to use contraceptives in order to plan their families and enjoy the pleasures of the marital bed. The couple must consider all these issues with care, and must be truly open to the gift of children. The moral justification for using contraceptives must be clear in the couple's mind, and fully consistent with the couple's Christian commitments.[2]

What About "the Pill"?

There has been a good deal of debate in recent years as to whether or not the oral contraceptive pill (OCP, more commonly known as "the pill") can on rare occasions cause early abortions. If evidence shows that it does, we would necessarily reject the OCP as an ethical form of birth control.

In essence, the pill prevents pregnancy by fooling a woman's body into thinking it is pregnant. The most common type of birth control pill is the combined oral contraceptive (or COC), which consists of both estrogen and progestin. Together, these hormones work to prevent ovulation (thereby precluding the possibility that an egg is available to be fertilized) and to thicken the cervical mucous (thereby inhibiting the ability of the sperm to travel through the fallopian tubes). As a result of these two primary mechanisms of action, the pill is 99 percent effective in preventing fertilization.[3]

> Oral contraceptives are made up of two hormones which are present in minute quantities. These two hormones are estrogen and progesterone. The pill is begun on day five of the menstrual cycle while the levels of all hormones (FSH [follicle stimulating hormone], LH [luteinizing hormone], estrogen, and progesterone) are at their lowest. The pills are continued for a total of twenty-one days on a daily basis. The hormones in the pill are absorbed very readily and begin their effects immediately. These effects are identical to the effects of the naturally occurring hormones as the body is not able to distinguish between the two. The hormones in the pill affect the pituitary gland by suppressing the secretion of FSH and LH. This occurs because the pituitary gland senses that there is an adequate level of estrogen and progesterone in the body, and further production is not necessary. This inhibition of production of LH and FSH leads to prevention of egg maturation and ovulation. Without ovulation, obviously, pregnancy cannot occur. The prevention of ovulation, therefore, is how oral contraceptives prevent pregnancy.[4]

But once in a while ovulation *does* occur in women who take COCs, meaning that occasionally an egg (called a "breakthrough egg") *can* become fertilized. It is in these relatively rare circumstances that ethical questions arise regarding the pill. Specifically, does the pill inhibit the implantation of a fertilized egg in the uterus (by thinning the uterine lining and thereby creating what is called a "hostile endometrium")? If it does, this third mechanism of action would be potentially abortiofacient in that it might prevent an otherwise viable fertilized egg from implanting in the womb, resulting in its rejection by the mother's body.

Much debate, then, surrounds whether or not the pill does, in fact, inhibit or prevent implantation through the creation of a hostile endometrium. Arguments, sometimes more emotional than scientific, have been raised on both sides of the issue.[5]

But what are Christians to think about these things?

As those who are unwaveringly committed to the prolife position, and who believe that life begins at fertilization (and not after implantation), we nonetheless see no convincing scientific or medical evidence that would lead us to conclude that COCs, taken properly, do in fact cause abortions.

It is generally agreed that the endometrium thins during COC use *when ovulation is successfully prevented* (which is over 99 percent of the time). But does that thinning make the endometrium hostile when the first two mechanisms of action fail, and ovulation (and ultimately fertilization) does in fact occur?

Based on our understanding of the current medical literature, we see no reason to conclude that it does. To begin with, it remains somewhat uncertain to what degree a thinned endometrium affects the ability of the fertilized egg to implant. In fact,

> recent *microscopic* studies of the endometrium demonstrate that we cannot predict receptivity based on thinness or thickness [of] the uterine lining, raising new questions about the significance of observed endometrial thinning in COC cycles. Most obstetricians have delivered babies that were conceived while the mothers were taking OCPs. These babies have done

fine, and the risk of miscarriage or congenital abnormalities was no greater than for babies in the population at large.[6]

Secondly, and more importantly, there is good reason to question the assumption that the mother's endometrium remains thin (or "hostile") if fertilization does in fact take place (even during COC use). Medical evidence suggests that if and when fertilization occurs, significant hormonal changes take place in the mother's body which override the hormonal effects of the pill and result in a receptive endometrium.

> Once the egg has been fertilized, it normally takes five to seven days for it to continue its journey and implant in the uterus. During this time, estrogen and progesterone production have increased by virtue of the breakthrough ovulation. Wouldn't this counterbalance all the effects of the pill?[7]

In a 2005 article published for the Association of Prolife Physicians, James P. Johnston responds to such questions with an affirmative answer.

> The proponents of the "hostile endometrium theory" argue that OCs [oral contraceptives] are abortifacient based upon the third mechanism of action. The medical literature clearly supports the claim that the uterus becomes thinner and less glandular as a result of the OCs, however, the medical literature comes to this conclusion from non-ovulatory pill cycles. It is assumed that this finding in non-ovulatory pill cycles would prevent implantation of the embryo conceived in an ovulatory pill cycle, but this presumption is false. If a woman on OCs ovulates and conceives, everything changes: through the HCG's [human chorionic gonadotropin hormone] effect on the corpus luteum, and the corpus luteum's release of high levels of estrogen and progesterone, the uterus is able to nourish its new guest very well.
>
> It is noteworthy that in a normal menstrual cycle, on

the day of ovulation, the endometrium is not receptive to
implantation. If the embryo were to drop down through the
fallopian tubes into the uterus on that day, it could rightly be
called a "hostile endometrium." But following ovulation, the
corpus luteum transforms this hostile endometrium into a
receptive, nourishing bed, where the embryo will attach about
one week later after its trip through the fallopian tube, and
where the baby will continue to develop until birth.[8]

In other words, according to Johnston, the pill does not cause
a hostile endometrium if indeed fertilization takes place—since the
hormones released after fertilization are of far greater magnitude than
those found in the pill.[9] Thus, "if ovulation takes place, a completely
different hormonal milieu exists,"[10] resulting in a thickened endometrium that is ready to receive the fertilized egg.

This is essentially the same line of reasoning that Joel E. Goodnough employed in his 2001 article responding to those who claim
that the pill can prevent implantation:

> [Their] contention that it does cause abortions is speculative,
> being based primarily on the observation that the OCP creates
> an endometrium that appears to be hostile to implantation
> when it functions as it was designed to do—prevent ovula-
> tion. What is not clear is what happens to the endometrium
> when the OCP fails to do what it was designed to do and
> ovulation occurs. I have cited some studies that suggest that
> the endometrium is more normal when ovulation does occur
> on the OCP...
>
> [I]t is not possible, based on [current] studies, to con-
> clude that the OCP causes abortions. In fact, based on more
> recent studies, it appears that the OCP, when taken correctly,
> approaches 100% effectiveness in preventing ovulation.[11]

Having examined these issues extensively, our own medical expert
Michael Frields (a leading OB/GYN and member of Grace Community Church) has concluded that birth control pills are in no way an
abortive method of birth control. He writes:

Oral contraceptives act to prevent pregnancy by preventing ovulation which, in turn, precludes conception. This certainly meets the criterion for an acceptable method of birth control by acting prior to conception. While it is true that the oral contraceptive is not one hundred percent effective, and that a small number of pregnancies do occur even though the pill is taken correctly, studies have clearly demonstrated that pregnancies conceived while on the pill have no increased likelihood for miscarriage or other pregnancy related problems...

In summary, based on our understanding of the mechanism of action of the pill, it is an acceptable method of temporary birth control from a Biblical standpoint. Oral contraceptives are the most effective temporary method of birth control available today, as well as having a very high margin for safety if used according to current guidelines. If well tolerated, the pill is not only safe and effective, but also offers several health benefits.[12]

Dr. Frields's findings are consistent with those of other leading evangelical physicians. In 1999, a group of four prolife physicians produced an extended statement in which they contend that the alleged third mechanism of action (the creation of a hostile endometrium in which implantation would be inhibited) lacks credible evidence. Thus, they conclude that "there is no evidence that shows that the endometrial changes produced by COCs contribute to failure of implantation of conceptions, nor is there evidence that COCs cause an increased per pregnancy ratio of ectopics."[13]

An earlier document, entitled "Birth Control Pills: Contraceptive or Abortifacient" was produced in 1998 and signed by 21 prolife physicians who agreed that OCPs do not pose a threat of being abortifacient.[14] Similarly, a 2005 statement released by Focus on the Family's Physician Review Council indicated that, after two years of extended investigation and deliberation, "the majority of the physicians [on the council] feel that the pill does not have an abortifacient effect."[15]

On balance, other Christian organizations (such as the American Association of Pro-Life Obstetricians and Gynecologists and the Christian Medical and Dental Association) have taken a wait-and-see position, suggesting that more medical research is necessary before a final verdict can be reached.[16] These organizations respect the informed and conscientious positions held by physicians on both sides of the debate.

We recognize the fact that further research is still being done on this important issue. And we would encourage Christian married couples who are considering the use of COCs (or any other forms of birth control) to prayerfully consider their decision, to diligently study the issues for themselves, and to talk through their concerns with their doctor.

In summary, we do not see a compelling reason, given the current medical evidence, to categorically oppose the use of OCPs (and of COCs in particular). Nonetheless, we would never encourage a believer to violate his or her conscience. As noted earlier, we are deeply committed to the life of the unborn, and we respect other prolife Christian leaders who might disagree with our conclusions on this issue. At the same time, we would caution well-meaning but under-informed lay people from using emotionally charged speculation to judge others or to stir up unwarranted fears.

What About In Vitro Fertilization and Surrogacy?

What follows is a list of initial conclusions our pastoral staff has reached based on our conversations with evangelical doctors. All conclusions reflect the following biblical presuppositions:

- God opens and closes the womb according to His sovereign will (Genesis 29:31; 30:22; 1 Samuel 1:5-6; Psalm 127:3).

- It is acceptable for Christians to take advantage of existing medical technology as long as the specific methods do not violate the clear teaching of Scripture (cf. Romans 14).

- Life begins at conception (Psalm 51:5; 139:13-16).

- Abortion is not an option because it destroys human life (Genesis 9:6; Exodus 20:13).

- Physical intimacy between a husband and a wife is the means God designed to produce offspring (Genesis 2:24).

Initial Conclusions

Given those biblical presuppositions, here are ten initial conclusions:

1. All couples desiring to have children, whether naturally or with medical assistance, should carefully examine their motives to ensure that the desire to have a child has not become idolatry of the heart. This kind of self-examination should continue to take place even after children are born.

2. Neither in vitro fertilization nor surrogacy is a legitimate option for a single individual who is seeking to have a child without a biblical marriage.

3. Neither in vitro fertilization nor surrogacy is a legitimate option for a couple involved in an unbiblical union (e.g., a homosexual or lesbian relationship, or an unmarried man and woman who are living together).

4. Every embryo created between a husband and a wife—that is, every egg fertilized—should be allowed to be implanted.

5. A maximum of three eggs (preferably, only two) should be fertilized, since that is the greatest number the womb can reasonably sustain; when more than three are implanted, the additional embryos usually face death or serious defects.

6. If freezing is necessary as part of the in vitro process because of impending medical treatment (e.g., radiation or chemotherapy), the wife's eggs and the husband's sperm should be frozen separately.

7. If frozen fertilized eggs exist, they should be handled as

follows: (a) All of them (though not exceeding three at a time) should be implanted in the biological mother; (b) they should never be discarded or destroyed.

8. Scripture does not specifically address in vitro fertilization and surrogacy per se. However, as stated at the outset, physical intimacy between a husband and a wife is the means God designed to produce offspring. For this reason, we believe that Christians should not use methods that employ donated eggs or sperm from a third party. Nor should they use methods that utilize a third party as the carrier of a baby resulting from the implantation of a husband's sperm and his wife's egg (such as surrogacy). Though not exactly a parallel case, the disastrous ramifications of Abraham and Sarah's attempt to use Hagar as a third party in order to continue Abraham's family line in Genesis 16—particularly the tension that resulted between the two women—may serve as a warning for those intending to pursue methods involving a third party.

9. The increasing legal and custody issues surrounding surrogacy provide an additional warning to those considering a method such as surrogacy.

10. Along with various medical options, Christian couples should seriously consider adoption, which is both viable and God-honoring (cf. James 1:27).

Hope, Holiness, and Homosexuality
A Strategy for Ministering to Struggling Christians

John D. Street

One of the more significant challenges for Christians today is finding an effective, uncompromising, and yet compassionate ministry to gays and lesbians. Though it may be difficult to maintain a biblical balance in an ecclesiastical culture of extremes, it is vital for thinking Christians and biblical churches. On the one hand, there are churches that have rejected any notion of ministry to homosexuals and choose to rebuff them with disdain. On the other hand, there are churches that embrace and accept them into unquestioned fellowship. Both approaches are wrong. The former lacks Christlike love, and the latter biblical discernment. As we consider a right response, let's begin by looking at several specific examples.

Derek, after becoming a Christian, has come out of a full-blown homosexual lifestyle. He senses the weaknesses of his habituated body and the sinful tendencies of his heart and thought-life. But he insists that he desperately wants to be freed from their control and domination. Furthermore, he believes that Jesus Christ is the solution to his battle and the misery it has engendered, but he is having trouble making the connection between his newfound faith and the biblical solutions that will bring substantive and lasting change. Of grave concern is that Derek married a Christian wife not long after his conversion. His desperation makes him seem like a nearly drowning man barely clinging to an ocean dock at which the powerful currents of desire threaten to pull him away.

A second young man, Chas, is single and very effeminate; many people at church assume he is a homosexual because of his mannerisms. The way he dresses, walks, and talks is noticeably different than that of the other men at church. It is unmistakable that his closest friends are the single young ladies in the college and career group, although he has never expressed special romantic interest toward any one of them. Even though his topics of conversation are more feminine than masculine (clothes, style, haircuts, etc.), he has never confessed any homosexual tendencies to anyone. Yet the evidence seems convincing, and to make matters worse, he seems closed to discussing this issue with anyone.

Then there is a single, middle-aged woman, Rosie, who was supposedly converted after two decades of lesbian relationships. She has become very active in the women's ministry and Bible studies in the church. Rosie was never married and openly acknowledges that from the time she was a little girl she has never liked men. Her appearance is unmistakably masculine and she sports a short hairstyle. In recent years Rosie had been a semitruck driver for a local freight company. She proudly asserts, "I can do anything a man can do!" One of the pastor's wives has even been concerned about Rosie's interest in establishing a close relationship with her under the pretense of discipleship.

Cases like Derek, Chas, and Rosie are becoming more prevalent in the church. Increasingly, pastors and counselors are seeking guidance in ministering to professing Christians plagued with homosexual and lesbian desires that are "unnatural" (Romans 1:26).[1] Our purpose in this chapter is to provide the Christian reader with biblically accurate and effective ministry points for helping other Christians tempted with homosexual desires, and to provide descriptive parameters for addressing the "gay agenda" in our postmodern era.

It should be noted that I am using the descriptive term "Christian" with qualification. I fully understand that a person who *is* homosexual (gay or lesbian) or effeminate *is not* a true believer no matter how passionate their claim (cf. 1 Corinthians 6:9–11).[2] The gospel therefore must be the central discussion early in ministry to them. Unbelievers cannot be effectively counseled from Scripture unless they are first evangelized and respond in faith to Jesus Christ. Why? They are still slaves to sin, dead in their iniquities, having never been regenerated, transformed, or forgiven (cf. Romans 6:6,17-18; Ephesians 2:1-3; Titus 3:5-8). They do not live under the same biblical authority, nor are they indwelt by the Holy Spirit (1 Corinthians 6:19; Galatians 5:19-23). Because their soul is dead, they have an unresponsive and hostile heart when it comes to the truth of God's Word (Ephesians 2:5; cf. Romans 3:10-18). Many well-meaning Christians have stumbled here, trying to provide biblical help to homosexuals who were incapable of a heart-level spiritual response. This only leads to discouragement and frustration on the part of both. One vivid example of this comes from an unsaved pastor who finally came out of the closet about his homosexuality in what he called an "Open Letter to Family and Friends."

> This letter comes with a desire to break the silence of the last couple of years. A few of you have been attempting to contact me, and I have not responded for a variety of reasons. Nevertheless, the time has come to address a few things to clear the air over some obvious changes in my life and in the lives of my loved ones.
>
> You may feel that you never really knew me. That is an accurate statement indeed. The fact is that my life was devoted to one major goal over the last 25 years, that of escaping my sexual orientation. This required a great amount of duplicity, since I was never able or willing to disclose that to any of you.
>
> By the time I was sixteen, I promised God that I would do anything I could to find healing and to avoid disappointing my family. For me as a naive young man, this meant college,

seminary, marriage, and ministry. Through the years it came to mean countless hours in Christian counseling, support groups, books and seminars. I went through severe depression for weeks and months, despairing to the point of suicide. Day after day, year after year I studied, cried, prayed and memorized large portions of scripture. Many of you feel I haven't tried. To that I say God only knows the lengths to which I have gone to make myself thoroughly heterosexual.

I reached the limit in June…with an emotional breakdown, resignation from the ministry, and a huge shift in my personal life…I live with my partner…

I am sure that you have been incredulous over this. Many of you have prayed for me, a few have written. Some of you have called. I am truly sorry for the hurt I have caused, but that sorrow can never change who I am. My family continues to make adjustments. Your concerns for them have been greatly appreciated.

…I know you will practice separatist principles. Some of you will never speak to me again. I understand that. I don't ask you to agree with me or to accept me. Fundamental churches have no place for people like me, that is clear. Just know the facts, and that I am here. I have many dear folk who have stood with me in these difficult times.

I appreciate the memories that many of us share. Please know that I care about you and miss you.

He refers to the "countless hours in Christian counseling, support groups, books and seminars" that were ineffective for bringing about change.[3] Eventually it became apparent he had never surrendered his life to Jesus Christ as Savior. That realization is where true and lasting change begins. All the counsel and reading could not change his sinful heart because there had never been a genuine repentance unto salvation. To force Christian principles of moral behavior on an unbeliever only turns him into a Pharisee.

Even if extensive counsel is given to unbelievers, they cannot change themselves. Note how this man acknowledges "the lengths to which I have gone *to make myself* thoroughly heterosexual." Many homosexuals who claim to be Christians try unsuccessfully to do the same. But this can happen only as a direct result of the radical regenerating power of the Holy Spirit. Thus, Christians who counsel an unbelieving homosexual, as with any unbeliever, should focus their efforts on the gospel and a call to repent. Though such counsel may require persistence and patience over an extended period of time, no true change can take place until the unbeliever genuinely embraces Jesus Christ as Lord and Savior.

In all three of our introductory case scenarios each individual claimed to be Christian. As a Christian friend, I am fairly confident that Derek is a believer because he understands the gospel and his desire to change is so strong, evidenced by his deep remorse and repentance over his sin. He is responsive to biblical teaching and admonition. Chas's problem is more complicated. I have seen cases where some men were effeminate-acting heterosexuals who needed counsel on how to be more masculine in leadership, attitude, and action. They were open to some loving confrontation on how to act more in accord with biblical masculinity. But if Chas persists in being unresponsive to biblical counsel, there is reason to doubt that he possesses the teachable spirit that accompanies salvation. He is not compelled by the truth because there is nothing in his heart that resonates with it.

Then there is the sad case of Rosie. Once you understand her past as well as her attitude and actions with the other women at church, there is good reason to believe she is not a Christian. What is the difference with her case? It is her total disregard for biblical instruction and avoidance of God-appointed masculine leadership in the church. As an undershepherd of God's flock, I would be concerned that Rosie is a predatory female who has found God's flock to be unsuspecting prey for her illicit appetite. She has found that Christians tend to relax their discernment when another claims to be one of them. In fact, many will even take up her defense if anyone questions the genuineness of her faith. And yet, the warning of our Lord is clear:

> Not everyone who says to Me, "Lord, Lord," will enter the kingdom of heaven, but he who does the will of My Father who is in heaven will enter. Many will say to Me on that day, "Lord, Lord, did we not prophesy in Your name, and in Your name cast out demons, and in Your name perform many miracles?" And then I will declare to them, "I never knew you; depart from Me, you who practice lawlessness" (Matthew 7:21-23).

Rosie has a rebel's spirit. Some guilt-ridden homosexuals and lesbians have taken refuge in the church in order to salve their conscience (cf. Romans 2:15). Subsequently, in spite of their stumbling intentions to feel better, their strong desires are still dominated by depravity and they proceed to practice their lust among God's people. Women like Rosie often prey on Christian women who have unhappy marital relationships. She understands how a woman thinks and will often begin by being a strong but caring listener under the pretense of spiritual concern. Bible studies frequently turn into lengthy discussions on personal issues (something the husband often will not do with his wife). In a case like hers, the church needs protection and Rosie needs Christ. Like the "false teachers" mentioned by Peter who entice Christians to follow their "sensuality," Rosie could be full of sensual greed in her attempt to exploit the unhappy women of the church (2 Peter 2:1-10).

If Rosie is willing to surrender her life to the Lord Jesus Christ and become accountable to church leadership she will find that biblical obedience, with the enablement of the Holy Spirit, can bring real and lasting change. If you are reasonably sure that your friend's profession of faith in Christ is genuine, then serious ministry of the Word can begin to make changes in his or her life.

A Strategy for Ministering to Struggling Christians

After you are confident that your friend has a genuine desire to change and be obedient to Christ (like Derek), then it would be fruitful to take a careful inventory of their lifestyle and habits of thought. Frequently you will find that homosexuals grew up in a home characterized by one or more of the following: parental irresponsibility, molestation, absence of biblical role models (in the parents' marriage), and either a total lack of religious influence or a very harsh, demanding, legalistic upbringing.

Understanding the personal history of your friend will greatly affect the direction of your biblical counsel. For instance, as Chas grew up he was small in stature. He was often ostracized by other boys. Even though he tried very hard to be accepted, they excluded him. From his earliest memories he reluctantly gravitated to girls and learned to resign himself to an effeminate lifestyle. His thoughts were full of anger toward God for making him this way and he eventually revealed that he would purposefully exaggerate his feminine mannerisms out of spite, especially at church and around Christians. He had to repent of his deepseated anger toward God and acknowledge that God had not made a mistake by making him the way He did (cf. Psalm 5:4; 92:15; Isaiah 46:9-10). There are, after all, some great men in the Bible who were small in stature (cf. 1 Samuel 16:7; Luke 19:3). Through effective biblical discipleship, Chas came to recognize that at an early age—as his desire for acceptance among other young men was rebuffed—his cravings inverted and he responded sinfully. Understanding the personal history of your friend is imperative if you are going to dig out dominating and sinful motivations, thoughts, and desires.

Here are some helpful principles for when you disciple the Christian who is tempted by homosexuality:

1. Identity must be formed "in Christ"

The theological understanding of the Christian being "in Christ" is critical for those who struggle with homosexuality (Romans 8:1; cf. Galatians 3:26-29; Ephesians 1:1; Philippians 1:1; 2 Timothy 1:1).[4] Sometimes, early in discipleship, your counselees will express to you in so many words, "I am a homosexual." They have become convinced by their own fruitless struggle with their sexual weaknesses or by the world's relentless drumbeat that they are genetically hardwired this way and cannot change.[5] Of course, this is a cultural lie and it robs your counselees of hope.

Who they are "in Christ" must be the planet around which all their thoughts and actions orbit. This is more than just a metaphor, it has to do with how Christians view themselves—as undeserving sinners who enjoy the gracious provisions and righteousness of Christ in order to have full acceptance with God the Father. Gospel-centered counseling and discipleship is critical to establish early. When their thought-life is practiced "in Christ," it brings hope and change to thoughts, desires, and behaviors. They think and act in new ways and abandon homosexual and effeminate dress, words, and mannerisms. It is especially effective to faithfully teach the principles of Romans 6:1-14 while recalling the earlier context of Romans 1:24-27. How Christians view themselves and their position in Christ will greatly affect their change and growth in sanctification. A Christian tempted by homosexual (or lesbian) desires is not a homosexual, he or she is a *Christian!* This thought and all of its theological richness is vital to understand if your counselees are going to possess the perseverance to defeat this foe.

2. Confession must include the condition as well as the behavior of homosexuality

Change begins when you see the problem as God sees it. This is when your spiritual perception can honestly identify aspects of the inner and outer man in sin. It is when you realize that your life is an affront to God's holiness and you are crushed and broken because of it (Proverbs 28:13; James 4:8-10).

Some Christians, being more psychologically persuaded, advocate the misguided idea that homosexuality is a condition (caused by a chemical or genetic predisposition) that no one can help or change. Thus they say that although the *practice* of homosexuality is sinful, the *condition* is not. But no such distinction is made in Scripture. God does not just consider outward actions; He looks at the heart (cf. 1 Samuel 16:7; Psalm 7:9; Jeremiah 17:10). The Pharisees believed that as long as they did not actually commit adultery they were fine, but Jesus rebuked that idea and said that a man who lusts in his heart is already an adulterer (Matthew 5:28). God's view of the problem does not divide the internal from the external.

Both the condition and the behavior are "unnatural" and grievously sinful, and the only hope for true change *within and without* is Jesus Christ (Luke 5:32; 1 Corinthians 6:11). When homosexually oriented, the body's condition (biological urges) and behavior (thoughts, longings, and actions) are both in rebellion against God's plan and order. Upon realizing this, the truly regenerate heart will respond with heartfelt sorrow and confession to God, as specific thoughts, desires, and deeds are acknowledged as sinful before Him. Confession gives it an appropriate label and calls it what God calls it—sin! Repentance follows as the proof of genuine confession.

3. Repentance must involve a complete renunciation of homosexual sin

Christians who have a history of homosexual struggles are in a special category of sin in Scripture. Every Christian struggles with daily sin and the subtle ways it manifests itself in his or her life (cf. Romans 7:23-24).[6] These require continual confession and repentance. John Calvin said the Christian life is a race of repentance—not a race to attain repentance, but a race that is characterized by repentance. All Christians practice regular repentance from sins, but the homosexually tempted Christian has a particular sin that has been persistent and unrelenting for some time.

It is possible for some sins such as this to overshadow the Christian's life for an extended period. In biblical counseling we call these "life-dominating sins" in order to theologically distinguish them from individual differentiated sins. Life-dominating sins are sins that the Christian continues to commit because he feels powerless to change, even though he knows these sins are wrong (cf. Psalm 19:13; 119:133; Romans 6:12-13). Jay Adams has defined them well:

> When a man (as a man; a whole person) can be labeled fairly as a drunkard, homosexual, a drug addict, etc., he has a life-dominating problem. He is no longer merely a man, but the

Bible speaks of him as a certain kind of man (drunkard; liar; double-minded, etc.); i.e., a man characterized by or dominated by the particular problem that gives him his name. The Bible labels those with life-dominating problems.[7]

Change necessitates an initial far-reaching repentance for sins that have become life-dominating. Genuine repentance is a change of mind that is so complete that it leads to a change of life (Matthew 3:8; Luke 3:8; 2 Corinthians 7:10). So repentance from life-dominating homosexuality must be so comprehensive that it renounces the entire lifestyle. Every thought, motivation, desire, word, habit, and action that has facilitated homosexuality must be confessed before the Lord as sin. This may require more than one counseling appointment to achieve. Then bridges need to be burned in that person's life to make the repetition of the sin difficult (cf. Mark 9:42-50). If the person has friends (even so-called Christians) who encourage this sin, those friendships must end immediately. If the bridge is a co-worker or the work environment, the person needs to change jobs. Any pipeline that fuels the sin of homosexuality must be severed. Of course, the counselee must then focus on friends, activities, and thinking that will facilitate righteousness (cf. Colossians 3:5-11).

Confession and repentance do not end there. Every time and in whatever form this sensual sin raises its head, it must be struck down through confession and repentance. Confessional prayer is a critical tool for the homosexually enticed Christian.

4. God's original model for sexuality must be taught

Most people who seek biblical help for overcoming homosexual desires are well aware of the Bible's condemnation of homosexual sin (Genesis 18:20-21; Leviticus 18:22; 20:13; Deuteronomy 23:18; 1 Kings 14:24; 15:12; 22:46; 2 Kings 23:7; Romans 1:27; 1 Corinthians 6:9; 1 Timothy 1:8-11). Only those who have been infected with the pseudodoctrine of liberal theology (by "metropolitan churches" that advocate homosexuality and denounce the clear biblical teaching on this issue as "unloving") refuse to recognize that it is a sin.[8]

Though they accuse Bible-believing Christians of being homophobic, they themselves are theophobic (afraid of God). They are driven to rewrite what the Bible says about homosexuality because they fear what God says.

However, most struggling Christians who desire real help already know homosexuality is a serious offense against God. For them, I rarely need to rehearse the strong scriptural prohibitions against homosexuality. However, I would examine the prohibition passages in-depth if I believed the counselee had adopted a cavalier attitude toward what God's Word reveals on this subject.

A far more profitable approach has been careful instruction on God's original design for sexuality. This would include detailed theological instruction on the divinely instituted paradigm for sexual intimacy (in heterosexual marriage) and the importance of the gender distinctiveness of Adam and Eve. In Genesis 1:26-27, we see that the distinctive genders are plural (male and female), reflecting the plurality of the Godhead ("Let Us make man") and yet coming together into an essential unity of persons. God in relationship creates man in relationship, male and female, in perfect unity bearing His image (singular). Lesbian and homosexual relationships distort and destroy the reflective image of God that mankind in gender complement must have. Help your disciplee see the divine design and beauty of gender complementarianism, which is rightly exhibited in marriage (cf. Genesis 2:18-25).

Further instruction can be given on the creation mandate to "be fruitful and multiply, and fill the earth and subdue it" (Genesis 1:28). This mandate was not given to two men or two women, but to a man and a woman. Without artificial means, homosexual or lesbian couples cannot procreate or fulfill God's command. Such can only be naturally and righteously fulfilled through monogamous heterosexual marriage.

Two people of the same gender can be close friends, but it is impossible for them to enjoy the depth of companionship that God intended for a husband and wife in marriage. Eve was created as the effective counterpart to Adam in Genesis 2:18. The word "suitable" in that passage refers to her being made to correspond to Adam and thereby complement him in every way. God designed the male and female relationship, when living righteously as a husband and wife, for rich companionship. This is something homosexual relationships can never replicate.

Ultimately, every homosexual and lesbian relationship must borrow from God's original design to survive—because every same-sex relationship has a dominant (male) role and submissive (female) role. Even in their sinful rejection of God's original mandate, homosexuals tacitly give tribute to the "natural" created design of complementary gender roles.

5. Sexual relationships must be viewed as a matter of worship

Any perversion of God's creation order in sexual relationships demonstrates idolatry. All sexual sin comes from a covetous heart that worships something other than the God of glory. The apostle Paul warns in Colossians 3:5, "Consider the members of your earthly body as dead to immorality, impurity, passion, evil desire, and greed." Each of these terms is directly related to sexual sins. Then he adds, "...which amounts to idolatry." In Christ, Christians are dead to these evils, but the warning Paul gave assumed his readers still struggled with them at times. Hence, they needed to think rightly about their earthly bodies being freed from such enslavements. Prior to salvation they were in bondage to sexual sins. But death frees slaves. Since Paul's readers had died with Christ and been freed, they needed to understand that to return to such sins was to return to slavery and wholesale idolatry.

Christians who surrender to homosexual and lesbian temptations are bowing their heart to the idol of sexual greed (cf. Ephesians 5:3). It is false worship. Therefore it is imperative they return and worship the true and living Lord in heartfelt obedience. Once this is understood and the right type of worship is restored there will be a deep satisfaction that comes from a new and vibrant life surrendered to the Savior.

THE RIGHT TO DIE AND THE RIGHT TO KILL

Euthanasia, Suicide, and Capital Punishment

PASTORAL PERSPECTIVE

This chapter is adapted from material that our pastors and elders have assembled over the years on these issues. It is representative of the general position of Grace Community Church.

Euthanasia, suicide, and capital punishment are related on at least two fronts. First, they each involve an intentionally premature death—meaning that death is actively induced rather than allowed to naturally occur. Second, they are all controversial subjects—especially euthanasia (including physician-assisted suicide) and capital punishment (government-mandated execution). Many Americans, including Protestants, hold differing views on whether or not "mercy killing" should become legal, and whether the death penalty should remain so.

According to recent worldwide statistics, each year roughly one million people kill themselves by intentionally committing suicide, averaging out to one suicide every 40 seconds. Significantly, that number is higher than those who are murdered or killed in combat. Moreover, it is estimated that unsuccessful suicide attempts are up to 20 times more frequent than completed suicides. Based on such estimates, a suicide is attempted every 2 seconds. Around the world, suicide is among the top three causes of death among people ages 15 to 44; and even in the United States, the number of suicides (over 32,500 in 2005) is nearly double that of homicides (around 18,000 in 2005).[1]

Physician-assisted suicide, though legal in some countries, is illegal in the United States except in the states of Oregon and Washington, where the Death with Dignity Act was passed in 1994. On the flip side, capital punishment is legal in 38 states, though it has been abolished in over 90 nations worldwide. In 2007, over 1,200 people (and probably many more) were executed in 24 countries, with China, Iran, Saudi Arabia, and Pakistan leading the world in total number of executions. That same year, 42 convicted criminals were put to death in the United States.[2]

Though statistics like these are sobering, the issues at hand sometimes hit much closer to home when a loved one is on life support, or a friend is battling with bouts of severe depression, or a proposition on the ballot involves the death penalty. So what are believers to think about such things? And how can pastors and church leaders help their people process these matters in a way that is both thoughtful and biblical? Our hope is that the brief snapshots presented in this chapter will provide a helpful starting point for thinking clearly about these controversial and timely issues.

Euthanasia

Euthanasia involves a deliberate medical act or omission taken by oneself, one's doctor, or a third party for the intent purpose of causing one's death, and successfully causing that death. It is believed by proponents of euthanasia that the death being caused is for the good of the person who is being put to death (which is why euthanasia is sometimes called "mercy killing").[3]

Active euthanasia occurs when a person takes proactive steps to *cause* his own death or the death of another. With active euthanasia, the medical reason for death is not sickness or injury, but rather the specific action taken to terminate life.

Passive euthanasia takes place when available medical treatment that could clearly enable a person to live significantly longer is deliberately withheld or withdrawn. The intent of passive euthanasia is to cause a person's death at a time when natural death is not imminent.

Letting die (which is distinct from *euthanasia*) involves the withholding or withdrawing of life-prolonging and life-sustaining medications and technologies from an irreversibly ill patient with whom death is imminent even with treatment. The intention of "letting die" is not to bring about death but to enhance the well-being of the patient by avoiding useless prolonging of the dying process.

The difference between passive euthanasia and letting die, then, is this: With passive euthanasia, death is not imminent and medical treatment could clearly enable a person to live significantly longer; but with letting die the patient's death is imminent even with treatment (i.e., medical technologies can no longer prevent death). Whereas the former seeks to cause a person's death, the latter seeks to "enhance" the well-being of the patient by avoiding the prolongation of the dying process.

In thinking through a biblical response, we must remember that though death is inevitable, its timing ultimately rests in the hands of God (Deuteronomy 32:39; 1 Samuel 2:6; Hebrews 9:27). Life is a gift from God, and everyone has an obligation to value his own life and the lives of others regardless of the circumstances.

Because Scripture prohibits murder and suicide (Genesis 9:6; Exodus 20:13; Deuteronomy 5:17), euthanasia (either active or passive) is never an acceptable option for the believer. In addition to violating the prohibition of suicide, the act of killing oneself is the ultimate expression of selfishness.

On the other hand, in the case that the patient is irreversibly terminal and death is imminent regardless of available medical treatment, it is acceptable for the patient or—if the patient is unconscious—a legally authorized third party (e.g., a spouse or family member) to choose to have life-sustaining medication or support systems withheld or removed. In such circumstances, the patient would die shortly thereafter by natural means.

Thus, although Scripture forbids all forms of euthanasia (because Scripture forbids murder), we believe that letting die is an acceptable option when death is both imminent and inevitable.

Believers and their loved ones may want to consider creating a living will that indicates an individual's wishes regarding medical treatment in order to guide medical personnel in the event that he or she is unable to make decisions or choose treatment options.

As a helpful aside, Dr. Keith Essex, a professor at The Master's Seminary, provides four biblical guidelines regarding death:

> First, death is inevitable (Eccl 3:2). Therefore, each person should make preparations for death. With the present legal climate, it is imperative that each believer have an advanced medical directive. A durable power of attorney is better than a living will. The surrogate chosen should have the same Christian perspective as the believer.
>
> Second, death is an enemy (1 Cor 15:26). Therefore, when the hope of recovery through medical treatment remains a possibility, the believer should take advantage of every opportunity to forestall death so that he can continue to serve the Lord.
>
> Third, dying is a process (Heb 11:21, 22). Therefore, when it is reasonably certain that a patient's disease is incurable and terminal, measures designed to control physical pain, to provide food and water, to give regular hygienic care, and to ensure personal interaction and mental/spiritual stimulation should be instituted. "Letting die" is not to be equated with "passive euthanasia."
>
> Fourth, suffering is a part of present earthly life and death (Rom 8:18; 2 Cor 4:17-18; 1 Pet 5:9-10). Therefore, the Christian will patiently endure any pain, especially at the end of life. Pain will not become the reason to commit the unbiblical act of euthanasia.[4]

Later, Dr. Essex concludes with this pastoral exhortation:

> First, it is imperative that we show compassion to the dying. The advocates of euthanasia assert that they wish to show

mercy by killing those in pain or by allowing them to kill themselves. But this supposed expression of mercy defies the instruction of the God of all mercies (Ps 119:156)! Instead of mercy killing, Christians need to exhibit mercy living as we pray for, visit, and care for the dying among us. Second, to die well, believers must trust God. It is not euthanasia that is the good death! Rather, it is the Christian who maintains his faith strong in the Lord even unto death and leaves this life with joy who truly dies well.[5]

Suicide

Suicide is a serious sin of self-murder (Exodus 20:13; 21:23), but it can be forgiven like any other sin. And Scripture says clearly that those redeemed by God have been forgiven of all their sins—past, present, and future (Colossians 2:13-14). Paul says in Romans 8:38-39 that nothing can separate us from the love of God in Christ Jesus.

So if a true Christian were to commit suicide in a time of extreme weakness, he or she would be received into heaven (cf. Jude 24). At the same time, however, an act of such selfishness or hopelessness would not normally characterize a true believer, since God's children are defined repeatedly in Scripture as those who have hope (Acts 24:15; Romans 5:2-5; 8:24; 2 Corinthians 1:10) and purpose in life (Luke 9:23-25; Romans 8:28; Colossians 1:29). Furthermore, suicide is often the ultimate evidence of a heart that rejects the lordship of Jesus Christ because it is an act in which the sinner takes his life completely into his own hands rather than submitting it to God's will. Thus, although it may be possible for a true believer to commit suicide, we believe it to be an unusual occurrence. Someone who is considering suicide should be urged, above all, to examine himself to see whether he is in the faith (2 Corinthians 13:5).

The Bible makes it clear that God alone is the one authorized to give and take life (Deuteronomy 32:39; 1 Samuel 2:6). Thus, when suicide is mentioned in Scripture it is presented in a context of judgment, shame, and sin—as seen especially in the suicides of Saul

(1 Samuel 31:4-5) and Judas (Matthew 27:5). Other examples include Abimelech (Judges 9:54), Ahithophel (2 Samuel 17:23), Zimri (1 Kings 16:18-19), and nearly the Philippian jailor (Acts 16:27-28). Never does the Bible condone suicide as that which is honorable, noble, or right.[6] The act of self-murder is an offense to God because it violates the image of God in man (Genesis 1:27; 9:6), and because it essentially blames God for difficult circumstances while simultaneously failing to trust Him for deliverance.

To be clear, however, suicide is *not* the unpardonable sin. That sin, which Matthew 12:30-32 describes as the blasphemy of the Holy Spirit, relates to a level of such willful rejection and hard-heartedness that repentance is no longer possible (cf. Hebrews 6:4-6; 10:29).[7] Suicide is not in the context of those passages in Scripture that address the unpardonable sin.

Believers who express feelings of deep discouragement, depression, or even hopelessness should be encouraged to find their hope in God (Psalm 42:11; 62:5-8; 130:5-7; 1 Timothy 6:17; 1 Peter 1:13). God's response to Elijah's despair (in 1 Kings 19) is instructive in this regard, as the Lord emphasized both His greatness (through a stunning display of natural phenomena) and His gentleness (through a still, small voice). Believers who feel hopeless must be reminded of both the sovereign greatness and the parental kindness of God.

They should also be made aware of the fact that depression is often the fruit of underlying sin issues, such as anxiety, unmet expectations (a form of selfishness and pride), or guilt (Psalm 32:3-4). Though medications may sometimes be involved (per the determination of a medical doctor), counselees should understand that drugs are never a cure for deeper heart issues. The Scriptures alone are sufficient for addressing the issues of the heart (2 Timothy 3:16-17; Hebrews 4:12; 2 Peter 1:3). Those who look for ultimate answers in places other than God's Word will find themselves disappointed.

From a counseling perspective, each situation must be handled using biblical principles and prayerful wisdom on a case-by-case basis (1 Thessalonians 5:14). Some counselees may be threatening to commit suicide simply to manipulate others or gain attention. If so, they may need to be directly rebuked. Others, however, may be sincerely struggling with feelings of hopelessness and depression, and need to be comforted.

In every case, counselees (both those who profess Christ and those who do not) need to be pointed to the truth and hope of the gospel. They must also be reminded that suicide is a sin that is never warranted, nor is it ever the right solution to whatever problem they may be facing. Even in the darkest of trials, believers are called to confidently trust in God and prayerfully rely on Him for strength and joy (Matthew 6:25-34; Romans 8:28; James 1:2-3).

Capital Punishment

There is no question God has authorized governments to exercise capital punishment. The principle is established in Genesis 9:6, implicitly upheld by Christ in Matthew 26:52 (where Peter is warned of the consequences of murder), and reiterated by the apostle Paul in Romans 13:4 (cf. Acts 25:11, where Paul indicates he understands some crimes are worthy of death).

Under the Old Testament theocracy, God prescribed the death penalty for crimes such as murder, blasphemy, witchcraft, false prophecy, rape, homosexuality, kidnapping, and idolatry. The death penalty was very public and administered swiftly, though not without due process. The purpose was not only to bring retribution upon the guilty party, but also to deter others from similar crimes. Thus, capital punishment as instituted under the Mosaic law was a key part of the protection and purification of Jewish society.

New Testament believers are not under the specific civil mandates of the Mosaic law code. But the *principle* of capital punishment (as a consequence for murder specifically) was instituted by God long before Moses (to Noah in Genesis 9:6), and is reiterated by Paul in Romans 13. Thus, the New Testament underscores a government's God-given right to impose the death penalty for crimes worthy of death.

Romans 13 says that the government is established by God (verse

1), by His divine ordinance (verse 2), for the purpose of restraining evil and promoting good (verse 3). Thus, government is a minister of God (verse 4), which is vested with the authority to punish evil (up to and including the use of the "sword" or death penalty). Part of government's divine mandate is to protect its citizens by making evildoers afraid of the consequences that come from acting wickedly. In a fallen world, the threat of punishment is a necessary part of deterring crime and keeping the peace. As Robert Culver points out:

> What must not be lost sight of is that unpleasant as is the task of the jailor and the use of the whip, the cell, the noose, the guillotine, these things stand behind the stability of civilized society, and they stand there necessarily, for God has declared it so, in harmony with reality, rather than with apostate sociological opinion. Government, with its coercive powers is a social necessity, but one determined by the Creator, not by the statistical tables of some university social research staff! No society can successfully vote fines, imprisonment, corporeal and capital punishment away permanently. The society which tries has lost touch with realities of man (his fallen sinful state), realities of the world, and the truth of divine revelation in nature, man's conscience, and the Bible.[8]

By divine design, civil punishment exists to deter wickedness. To the degree that government fails to enforce just consequences for evildoing, it threatens both the national stability of its society and the individual security of its citizens.

Critics may claim capital punishment is hateful and destructive, but it is actually an outworking of God's common grace to humanity, enabling sinful societies to maintain civil order and deter criminal activity. When executed properly, capital punishment serves as a terror to wrongdoers, restraining depraved sinners from doing what they would otherwise be prone to do (cf. Romans 3:10-20), and thereby saving lives. On the other hand, when blood is shed and remains unrequited, that nation comes under the judgment of God (Genesis 4:9-11;

9:6; 42:22; Joshua 2:19; 2 Samuel 4:11; Ezekiel 7:20-27; 18:10-13). We believe the current level of moral decadence in our own nation is partly the result of an inconsistent and often ineffective practice of capital punishment. If perpetrators were dealt with properly, potential criminals would be deterred, and the number of unlawful activities would decrease.

This does not mean, of course, that individual Christians should ever take the law into their own hands. Individual believers are called to forgive those who hurt them (Matthew 5:38-45), and to trust that God will bring vengeance in His own time (Romans 12:14-21). David's unwillingness to kill Saul is a wonderful example in this regard (1 Samuel 24:1-22; 26:1-25). Nonetheless, it is the corporate responsibility of the civil government to enforce the law and to punish wrongdoers in keeping with the nature of their crimes. Christians who serve in law enforcement, civil government, or even on a jury have a God-given responsibility to uphold justice and oppose corruption. On the flip side, believers are to be submissive to civil government as exemplary citizens (1 Peter 2:13-20). They are to obey the law at all times, unless doing so would require them to violate a clear command of God (Acts 5:29).

In closing, some might ask how we can hold to a pro-life ethic (one that opposes abortion, euthanasia, and suicide) and yet support the government's right to exercise capital punishment (specifically as a consequence for murder). John Feinberg and Paul Feinberg provide a helpful response to this question:

> Can one consistently argue against abortion and euthanasia and espouse capital punishment? We think so on at least three grounds: a sanctity of life ethic, a demand to treat all persons justly, and a commitment to non-consequentialist ethics. Given a sanctity of life ethic, human life is sacred and must be protected. Hence, abortion and euthanasia are ruled out. Execution of murderers underscores the sanctity of life and the seriousness of taking the life of others. As to justice, the unborn, the aged, and the infirm have done

nothing deserving of death. The convicted murderer has. Justice demands rejecting abortion and euthanasia and executing murderers. Finally, on a non-consequentialist theory of ethics such as ours, God prescribes the protection of the innocent and the punishment of those who take life. If one follows those divine commands, he will have to reject abortion and euthanasia and favor capital punishment.[9]

Part 3

POLITICS
AND ACTIVISM

GOD, GOVERNMENT, AND THE GOSPEL

How Should Christians Think About Political Activism?[1]

JOHN MACARTHUR

As I write this chapter, our nation is on the brink of another presidential election. Not surprisingly, the U.S. political scene has reached a fevered pitch. From conventions to campaign ads, American televisions, radios, and newspapers echo the emotional upsurge we've come to expect every four years. Water-cooler conversations about sports and movies have now been replaced with endless discussions about economic policy, public education, and international affairs. The election is at the forefront of everyone's thinking as awareness and activism sweep the nation.

As is so often the case, much of the evangelical church has eagerly jumped on the political bandwagon. Pulpits resound with accolades for one or the other candidate and with approval or disdain for certain bills and plans. Committees and coalitions have been formed, pledging to protect the Ten Commandments and denounce any advance by the "immoral minority." Some even suggest that to be a Christian means you must be a Republican and not a Democrat, and that not to vote is a serious sin. After all, they say, good citizenship implies political involvement.

Such political preoccupations are somewhat ironic considering the dominant premillennial eschatology of conservative evangelicalism. Our end-times theology tells us that until Christ returns, nothing can or will fix this crumbling world system. Yet our political practice suggests we are desperately trying to fix it nonetheless.

In just a short time, this current election will be over—a soon-forgotten part of the history of the democratic process in our nation. But it will not be long until new issues, new policies, and new candidates arise. When they do, how should Christians respond? In this chapter, we will explore five biblical principles Christians should consider in thinking rightly about government and political activism.

Thinking Rightly About Government

1. Our Commission Is the Gospel

Though you might not know it during election season, true Christianity is more concerned with saving souls than it is with gaining votes. The Great Commission is not a call to effect policy change, but a command to "go therefore and make disciples of all the nations, baptizing them in the name of the Father and the Son and the Holy Spirit, teaching them to observe all that I [Jesus Christ] commanded you; and lo, I am with you always, even to the end of the age" (Matthew 28:19-20). Rather than concentrating on political issues and debates, believers should be consumed with their responsibility as Christ's ambassadors. That is the church's mandate. When other priorities and pursuits crowd out the Great Commission, both the message and the mission get confused.

The term *evangelical* comes from the Greek word that means "gospel" or "good news." It was coined by Martin Luther to refer to Protestants as those who were defined by the gospel of grace. Sadly, five centuries later, evangelicalism is more often associated with partisan politics, at least in the eyes of the world, than it is with the good news of salvation. Such is indicative of the misplaced priorities that have plagued American evangelicalism for decades. Rather than focusing on the God-given priority of evangelism (from the same Greek word that means "evangelical"), American evangelicalism has spent billions of dollars and millions of man hours fighting to legislate morality. Not only is it a battle we cannot win (since legislated morality cannot change the sinful hearts that make up a depraved society), it is also a battle we have not been called to fight.

Only the gospel, through the power of the Spirit, can effect real change in society—since it transforms sinners from the inside out. After all, there are no Christian countries, only Christian individuals. Hence, our commission is to proclaim that gospel faithfully in whatever context God puts us. When we allow ourselves to get distracted by politics, we inevitably neglect our responsibility to preach the gospel.

Political activism can also tempt us to blur the lines regarding our mission field. Those in an opposing political party become "enemies" rather than lost souls who need Christ preached to them with love and compassion. Those who share our political convictions are embraced as "brothers and sisters" even though they may also be lost souls who need Christ. Ungodly partnerships can develop when true Christians join hands with cult groups and other unbelievers based on shared political ideologies. And unbiblical perspectives can be adopted, based on maintaining the party line, even when those views don't square with Scripture.

Though He was talking specifically about money, Jesus' statement that "no one can serve two masters" (Matthew 6:24) serves as an appropriate warning for those who attempt to mix biblical Christianity with political activism. The two are not the same, and in fact are often at odds. In many cases, evangelical pastors, leaders, and lay people need to refocus their efforts on Christ's command to tell the world about Him. If our highest aim is to glorify God, we will make His priorities our priorities and embrace the mission He has given us to obey.

2. Our Confidence Is in God

In God we trust. Those four words are minted on U.S. coins, printed on U.S. dollar bills, and etched in the walls of thousands of courtrooms across our nation. To many Americans, the slogan is nothing more than the vestige of a day gone by. But for us, as Bible-believing Christians, that phrase is a way of life.

What does that mean for believers when it comes to politics?

For starters, it means we can trust God regarding both national and foreign affairs. No matter who is in the White House, the Congress, or the courtroom, God is on His throne. He is the one of whom Paul exclaimed, "He who is the blessed and only Sovereign, the King of kings and Lord of lords, who alone possesses immortality and dwells in unapproachable light, whom no man has seen or can see. To Him be honor and eternal dominion! Amen" (1 Timothy 6:15-16).

A quick survey of Scripture reveals that God is sovereign over all the affairs of this world. He is sovereign over Satan and sin (Job 1:12; 2:6; Luke 5:21; 22:31), over all governments and military powers (2 Chronicles 20:6; Romans 13:2); over nature and natural disasters (Psalm 107:29; Nahum 1:3-6); over sickness and disease (John 9:3; 11:4; Revelation 21:4), and over every human being (Acts 13:48; Romans 9:17-18), including you and me (Proverbs 16:9; 19:21; James 4:13-15). Put simply, God is in control. He does "whatever He pleases" (Psalm 115:3), and "works all things after the counsel of His will" (Ephesians 1:11).

God's sovereignty does not excuse human sinfulness or irresponsibility. But it should give Christians great reason to hope when they see the society growing more and more wicked. It should relieve them of anxiety and worry (cf. Matthew 6:25ff; Philippians 4:6), as well as the misguided notion that it is their responsibility to effect political change. The Lord is directing our nation within His providential purposes for His glorious ends. And He is doing the same with every other earthly government.

God has already revealed how this world will end. In its discussion of the last days, the Bible is clear that society will continue to get worse until the return of Christ (2 Thessalonians 2:7-12; 1 Timothy 4:1-5; 2 Timothy 3:1-5; 2 Peter 3:3). Yet many evangelicals approach politics as if the degradation of society is something they can stop with legislation. The truth is that no society will ever be truly made right until

Christ comes and sets up His kingdom (Isaiah 9:7; Jeremiah 23:5-6; Daniel 2:24; 7:14; Luke 1:32-33; Revelation 5:10; 20:6). Until then, believers should not be surprised to see morally-conservative political efforts fail, or to realize that such failures are part of God's sovereign plan.

Instead of political activism, a far better strategy for Christians is to focus on being faithful to what God has actually called them to do within their own sphere of influence—exalting the Savior (1 Corinthians 10:31; Colossians 3:17), encouraging the saints (Hebrews 3:13; 10:24-25), evangelizing the lost (Acts 1:8; 1 Corinthians 9:19-23; 1 Peter 3:15), and exhibiting godly conduct (1 Thessalonians 4:11; 2 Thessalonians 3:12; 1 Timothy 2:2). National and international affairs, on the other hand, can be entrusted to God. This is not to say that American Christians should not vote, but that in voting they should realize that God has already determined the outcome of every election. Whatever that outcome may be, believers can be absolutely confident that it accords perfectly with God's sovereign purposes for the future of both our nation and our world.

3. Our Charge Is to Submit

No discussion of politics would be complete without a reminder that Christians are commanded to willingly submit themselves to the governing authorities. In so doing, we follow both the command of Scripture and the example of Christ and the apostles.

Our Savior came into a world where slavery abounded, dictators dominated, heavy taxes were the norm, and the followers of God were frequently persecuted. The people of Jesus' day had no democratic process, nor did they possess many of the liberties we take for granted in this nation. But how did Jesus respond to these circumstances? He told His listeners, "Render to Caesar the things that are Caesar's; and to God the things that are God's" (Matthew 22:21). He did not call upon angelic armies to bring down oppressive governments or attempt to establish a new political order. He did not set up any kind of political administration, nor did He organize public protests against Rome. His ministry was not focused on those things, but instead was ever aimed at the hearts of individual sinners who were in desperate need of God's grace (Mark 10:42-45). Jesus did not lead civil rights demonstrations. Rather, He preached the good news of forgiveness and salvation. The Lord did not launch a new political order, but a spiritual one—namely, the church. Christians have been called to follow His lead.

So how can believers balance the priority of God's kingdom with the desire to be good citizens on earth? Politics and social activism are not the answer. After all, God has called His people to just two foundational civic responsibilities. The first is in Romans 13:1: "Every person is to be in subjection to the governing authorities." The second is in Romans 13:7: "Render to all what is due them: tax to whom tax is due; custom to whom custom; fear to whom fear; honor to whom honor." The sum of our civil duty, then, is to submit and pay taxes. Beyond that we should focus on those things that are of eternal value. Political activism may seem significant in the moment, but it pales next to kingdom priorities (Matthew 6:33).

The apostle Paul lived in a day under Roman control and dominion, in which Christians were viewed with suspicion and often greeted with persecution and suffering. Yet the right response was not retaliation, but deference and compliance. In Romans 13:1 Paul established this fundamental principle: as Christians we are to obey our civil authorities no matter whom they may be. Believers have a God-given duty to submit to the government, even when the ruler is as wicked as Nero.

The apostle Peter, similarly, instructed his readers to submit to the governing authorities: "Keep your behavior excellent among the Gentiles, so that in the thing in which they slander you as evildoers, they may because of your good deeds, as they observe them, glorify God in the day of visitation" (1 Peter 2:12). In other words, "Outsiders may say evil about you, but make sure it is a lie." But how can we live righteously in a society that hates us? Verses 13-15 continue, "Submit yourselves for the Lord's sake to every human institution, whether to a king as the one in authority, or to governors as sent by him for the punishment of evildoers and the praise of those who do right. For such is the will of God that by doing right you may silence the ignorance of foolish men." When Christian citizenship is marked by exemplary behavior, it silences the ridicule of unbelievers.

As believers, we have the weighty responsibility of living out the Christian faith with consistency and integrity. Our allegiance and submission to the Lord (Romans 12:1-2) should motivate us to be exemplary citizens. We should never garner a reputation for trouble-making or for demeaning those who are in authority. Though we are called to boldly denounce unrighteousness and immorality, we must also give honor and respect to those whom God has placed over us. This biblical pattern applies to every Christian living at any time in any place. We are called to submit.

4. Our Commitment Is to Pray

In addition to submitting to the laws of our land, we are commanded to pray for those in authority over us. Even those whom we consider political "opponents" are to receive our prayers on their behalf. It was during Nero's reign that Paul told Timothy, "I urge that entreaties and prayers, petitions and thanksgivings, be made on behalf of all men, for kings and all who are in authority" (1 Timothy 2:1-2). Paul prayed for the very king who would eventually authorize his execution. And he instructed Timothy to do the same.

The apostle Paul continues by delineating two aspects of a Christian's prayer for government authorities. First, believers should pray for those in authority over them "so that we may lead a tranquil and quiet life in all godliness and dignity" (verse 2). An immediate by-product of praying for our leaders is that it removes feelings of anger and resistance toward them. It prompts us to seek peace rather than to rebel or overreact—to lead lives that are tranquil, quiet, godly, and dignified. As Paul told Titus: "Remind them to be subject to rulers, to authorities, to be obedient, to be ready for every good deed, to malign no one, to be peaceable, gentle, showing every consideration for all men" (Titus 3:1-2). When our leaders do something we don't like, our first response should be to pray, not protest.

Second, Christians should pray for the salvation of their leaders. Speaking of such prayers, Paul wrote,

> This is good and acceptable in the sight of God our Savior, who desires all men to be saved and come to the knowledge of the truth. For there is one God, and one mediator also between God and men, the man Christ Jesus, who gave Himself as a ransom for all, the testimony given at the proper time...Therefore I want the men in every place to pray, lifting up holy hands, without wrath and dissension (1 Timothy 2:3-6,8).

Praying for the salvation of our leaders is good in the sight of God. The salvation of souls is in keeping with God's gracious nature and His sovereign purposes; it is the reason Christ died on the cross. When we pray for our nation, we must not limit our prayers to policy decisions and other temporal issues. We must also pray for the souls of those in government and civil service, that by God's grace they might be saved through faith in Christ.

One final point in this regard comes from Paul's use of the word "thanksgivings" in verse 1. Thanks to the freedom of speech we enjoy, Americans love to openly criticize our government—from court decisions and elected officials to police officers and IRS agents. But the attitude Paul expressed here was one of thanksgiving, not bitterness or resentment. We must remember that God is the one who appoints those in positions of authority (Romans 13:1). To complain about them is ultimately to complain against God.

5. Our Citizenship Is in Heaven

Finally, believers must not forget that though we currently dwell in this country, our true citizenship is in heaven. We are in the world, but not of the world. Our ultimate allegiance is to the Lord. We follow His directions, commandments, and standards as revealed to us in His Word and energized in us by His Holy Spirit. We live for eternal matters, operating with a wholly different set of priorities than those in the world around us. Though we now reside in an earthly kingdom, our resources and efforts are primarily focused on advancing the work of an eternal kingdom (cf. Matthew 6:33).

Paul was a Jew by ethnic heritage and a Roman by earthly citizenship. But he was unambiguous about where his ultimate allegiance was placed. As he wrote to the Philippians:

> Our citizenship is in heaven, from which also we eagerly wait for a Savior, the Lord Jesus Christ; who will transform the body of our humble state into conformity with the body of His glory, by the exertion of the power that He has even to subject all things to Himself (Philippians 3:20-21).

Our identity, priorities, and mission are not defined by our citizenship on earth, but in heaven, where our Savior awaits (Acts 1:11; 1 Thessalonians 4:16), and our fellow countrymen dwell (Hebrews 12:23). It is there that our names are recorded (Luke 10:20; Revelation 13:8), and our treasure is stored (Matthew 5:12; 6:20; 1 Peter 1:4). Though we live in this world, we do so as servants and ambassadors of our heavenly King, Jesus Christ. Thus, when we focus on spiritual pursuits rather than political ones, we are living in a way that is consistent with our true citizenship.

If space permitted, we could recount the numerous failed attempts believers have made throughout church history to Christianize government through political means. Time and time again, Christian political efforts have resulted in, at most, some immediate political gains. But these gains are only external, lacking any power to change the heart of the non-Christian society that surrounds us. And history has shown that these gains are also always temporary, eventually resulting in greater spiritual confusion and moral decline.

Getting Back to Our Primary Mission

While American Christians have been given a voice in our nation's affairs, a voice that we should exercise, we must remember that our allegiance is first in heaven and only second to our earthly government.

Our primary concern, then, should be saving souls rather than gaining votes. Rather than being consumed with political debates, we should be consumed with our responsibility as Christ's ambassadors. These are the efforts and activities that have eternal value. And while we preoccupy ourselves with the spiritual rather than the political, we can rest in knowing that He is sovereign over the governments and affairs of this world.

One day Jesus Christ will return. When He does, He will establish His kingdom, the perfect government in which He will rule with absolute equity and justice. As His servants, we will have the joy of participating in His flawless and incorruptible administration. In fact, we will reign with Him as we worship Him in His resplendent glory.

In the meantime, we would do well to remember that our primary mission is to preach the gospel and not to instigate political change. Though we submit to and pray for the governing authorities whom God has placed over us, we do so remembering that our true citizenship is in heaven. In John 18:36, Jesus told Pilate: "My kingdom is not of this world. If My kingdom were of this world, then My servants would be fighting…but as it is, My kingdom is not of this realm." The church must live in light of this, at least until our King returns and tells us otherwise.

Faith, Fidelity, and the Free Market
Biblical Living in a Secular Economy

Jonathan Rourke

Political advisor James Carville coined the phrase "It's the economy, stupid" as a slogan for Bill Clinton's 1992 run at the White House. The phrase was intended to separate his candidate from incumbent George H.W. Bush, who had watched the American economy drift into a recession. The effective campaign eventually led to Bill Clinton's inauguration as president, underscoring the fact that people care far more about economic issues than moral ones. If there is one thing that people on both sides of the political aisle agree on, it is the importance of the economy in general, and how it affects personal wealth in particular.

The purpose of any economy is to manage scarcity. Resources are limited and demand exceeds supply, so currency was invented to regulate the distribution and acquisition of goods. In modern society, that currency is *money* (or increasingly, credit).

In this chapter we will focus both on how Christians should view their relationship to the economy in general, and on how they should think about their own personal wealth in particular. The first goal is to show that God owns all money and that man reveals the true nature of his heart in his stewardship of that money; the second is to outline the responsibility of the Christian in the economy as he works, plans, and gives.

God Is the Owner of All Money

The Bible is not silent on the issue of money; far from it. Jesus said more about money in His parables then about heaven and hell; and the topic of money or business formed the basis for many of Jesus' illustrations. All money is God's money (Psalm 50:10-12). We are merely stewards of what He has given us. In ancient Israel, wealth could not be stored up by any one family or tribe for too long because every 50 years, during the year of Jubilee (Leviticus 25), all property was returned to its original owner, and slaves were given freedom.

The acquisition of wealth is a gift from God and not something for which believers can take credit. Deuteronomy 8:17-18, directed to Old Testament Israel, makes this clear, because "otherwise, you may say in your heart, 'My power and the strength of my hand made me this wealth. But you shall remember the Lord your God, for it is He who is giving you power to make wealth, that He may confirm His covenant which He swore to your fathers, as it is this day.'"

Man Is the Steward of God's Money

It is important to remember that money itself is not evil, and possessing it is likewise not evil. Morality is introduced in how people think about and use money. Like any other common grace that God gives to all mankind, it can be used for God's glory, or abused for selfish and sinful ends.

A number of godly individuals throughout biblical history have been materially wealthy. Adam was rich, lacking nothing in the Garden of Eden; and even after his sin-induced exile he enjoyed the earth's abundant resources without competition. Noah was similarly wealthy, in the sense that after the Flood the entire earth was his to possess and populate. Job, Abraham, Lot, Isaac, and Jacob all possessed a great wealth of flocks and herds along with the infrastructure to raise them.

Joseph, Moses, Daniel, and others, though living in foreign lands, were given significant responsibility and the wealth that attended such privilege. Saul, David, Solomon, and even the kings of Israel who followed until the captivity would have enjoyed massive financial resources. Jesus never condemned the rich for having money, but only warned them that their wealth could cause them to become self-reliant and therefore hinder them from entering the kingdom of heaven (Matthew 19:23-24).

On the other hand, it is not necessarily a sign of God's displeasure to be lacking financial resources. There will always be poor people because everyone is entrusted with different amounts of money (Mark 14:7). Jesus was poor, not just during His teaching ministry, but for most of His upbringing. In fact, when He was taken to the Temple as an infant, the family's sacrifice was that of a poor family, namely "a pair of turtledoves or two young pigeons" (Luke 2:24; cf. Leviticus 12:1-8). The apostle Paul likewise experienced poverty, as did other faithful saints (Philippians 4:10-14; cf. Acts 11:29). Those who teach that economic abundance is a sure sign of spiritual blessing or maturity confuse the fact that earthly riches and eternal rewards are two different things (Matthew 6:19-24; Luke 12:13-21), and that gold and godliness do not always go together (1 Timothy 6:5-10,17-19).

Nonetheless, it is not desirable for Christians to be completely ignorant of the economic forces at work in our culture. In 11 of His 39 parables, Jesus showed a familiarity with a variety of economic concepts: investing (Matthew 13:44-45), saving (Matthew 13:52), debt (Matthew 18:23-35), wage structures (Matthew 20:1-16), leasing (Matthew 21:33-46), banking (Matthew 25:14-30), debt cancellation (Luke 7:41-43), accumulating reserves (Luke 12:16-21), cost analysis (Luke 14:28-30), estate planning (Luke 15:11-32), and brokering complex deals (Luke 16:1-12). The Bible does not place a premium on ignorance; thus, believers should have a basic understanding of and appreciation for economic principles and practices. The danger comes when understanding and appreciation turn into obsession and anxiety.

Stewardship Reveals the Heart

While an awareness of the economic forces at work in the culture is good, conformity to the motives or mindsets of culture is evil (Romans 12:1-2). First Timothy 6:9-10 warns that "those who want to get rich fall into temptation and a snare and many foolish and harmful desires which plunge men into ruin and destruction. For the love of money is a root of all sorts of evil, and some by longing for it have wandered away from the faith and pierced themselves with many griefs." Snaring temptations await those who long for money and the material possessions money can buy. Notice that the heart is the focus, not money. When the greedy heart lusts after money, it is quickly shot through with arrows of grief.

The apostle Paul lists greed in Romans 1:29-30 alongside other sins such as murder. Proverbs 11:6 says that "the righteousness of the upright will deliver them, but the treacherous will be caught by their own greed." Though greedy people may accumulate a great amount of worldly wealth, Jesus had this to say about them: "Not even when one has an abundance does his life consist of his possessions" (Luke 12:15). Our world may be impressed by the size of someone's bank account, but God isn't. He is concerned with the heart (1 Samuel 16:7; Jeremiah 17:10; Acts 5:1-11). While wealth cannot make people spiritual, it can reveal their spiritual priorities. As Jesus said, "Where your treasure is, there your heart will be also" (Matthew 6:21).

Stewardship Is a Spiritual Issue

Greed is antithetical to the Christian walk. Paul warns believers to "consider the members of your earthly body as dead to immorality, impurity, passion, evil desire, and greed, which amounts to idolatry" (Colossians 3:5). Greed is idolatry. Material wealth can become an idol that is worshipped instead of God, as the perceived source of all that is needed, loved, and desired.

Materialism is not about how much you possess, but your disposition toward it. This is about your attitude, not your net worth. Paul told Timothy, "Instruct those who are rich in this present world not to be conceited or to fix their hope on the uncertainty of riches, but on God, who richly supplies us with all things to enjoy. Instruct them to do good, to be rich in good works, to be generous and ready to share, storing up for themselves the treasure of a good foundation for the future, so that they may take hold of that which is life indeed" (1 Timothy 6:17-19). Timothy was not instructed to rebuke or neglect the rich, nor was he to redistribute their wealth so everyone was equal. Rather, he was to instruct them from the Scriptures on how to best use their wealth to the glory of God.

The Biblical Responsibility for Stewardship

Scripture provides believers with three basic criteria for approaching financial stewardship in a way that honors the Lord.

Be a Faithful Worker

When God created man, work was a significant part of his daily responsibility. The book of Genesis records the fact that God took Adam and placed him in the Garden of Eden "to cultivate it and keep it" (Genesis 2:15). Adam's dominion on the earth began with a job, not a hammock.

A strong work ethic is a biblical work ethic. The Christian's attitude at work will testify to the power of the gospel in his or her life. Ephesians 6:5 demands that every employee, even slaves, must "be obedient to those who are your masters according to the flesh, with fear and trembling, in the sincerity of your heart, as to Christ." To work hard for your boss is to work hard for the Lord. Even a world that is hostile to the gospel is welcoming to hard workers. Though your boss may not initially respect your faith, he will respect your diligent work ethic. As a result, your hard work will give you greater opportunities to share the gospel in your workplace.

Hard work, under normal circumstances, will also produce material wealth and garner the respect of those around you. When Paul wrote to the church in Thessalonica he summarized their responsibilities before a hostile world. They were to mind their own business and work with their hands "so that your daily life may win the respect of outsiders and so that you will not be dependent on anybody" (1 Thessalonians 4:12 NIV). Some of them had become lazy, unruly, and undisciplined (2 Thessalonians 3:11), and they needed to get back to work. Paul uses very strong language in his direct exhortation: "Such persons we command and exhort in the Lord Jesus Christ to work in quiet fashion and eat their own bread" (2 Thessalonians 3:12). If the Christian adult is not working, he is outside the express will of God and should not be surprised that he experiences need. (Note that, within Christian families, the husband and father is primarily tasked with earning a living outside the home [1 Timothy 5:8]; while the wife and mother is primarily tasked with being a homemaker [1 Timothy 5:14; Titus 2:4-5]. In neither case is laziness or idleness acceptable.)

The book of Proverbs reveals the axiomatic truths regarding the acquisition of wealth. From just a surface reading, it is promised that in all labor there is profit, but those who waste time will suffer want (14:23). Proverbs 28:19-20 says, "He who tills his land will have plenty of food, but he who follows empty pursuits will have poverty in plenty. A faithful man will abound with blessings, but he who makes haste to be rich will not go unpunished." The general principle is that the one who works diligently will have plenty of food for himself and his dependents. Beyond this he is blessed with an abundance of good things from the hand of God as a reward for his diligence. The contrast is stark for the one who chases foolish, get-rich-quick schemes. He is not just poor, but he is punished with poverty in plenty (Proverbs 20:4).

There is an old saying, "Work smarter, not harder." In our culture the phrase should probably be "Work harder *and* smarter." Often people face economic hardship not only because of foolish choices, but because they are unwilling to work as hard as they should. If you work diligently to do the best job possible regardless of how long it takes, the Bible teaches that as a general rule, money will not be an issue.

Be a Careful Planner

One of the reasons diligent workers have more money is because they do not have as much time to spend it. But what are they to do with the resources they accumulate? This brings up a second practical criterion regarding Christians and the economy. Beyond being faithful workers, believers must also be diligent planners. Careful planning involves at least six considerations:

1. Don't be consumed by consumption. The modern culture is one of consumption. Experts say 70 percent of the American economy relies on the shopping that Americans do. Being a consumer is not wrong, but remember the foolish man is the one who consumes everything he gets and leaves nothing for the future (Proverbs 21:20). There is no reasonable excuse for spending everything you make, or worse yet, spending on average more than you make and leaving yourself burdened with debt. Biblical wisdom calls for living within your means.

2. Don't borrow yourself into bondage. You may be familiar with the verse, "Neither a borrower nor a lender be." However, it is not a verse from Scripture, but fatherly advice from Polonius in Shakespeare's *Hamlet* (Act I, Scene 3). One verse in Scripture that does address debt is Proverbs 22:7, where the borrower is warned that borrowing and servitude go hand in hand. The more you owe others, the more they will control your life. How sad it is when Christians cannot voluntarily give money to ministry because it involuntarily goes to creditors.

In the Old Testament, God gave laws to govern the lending industry in Israel, especially the issue of interest rates (Leviticus 25:36-37). Originally the Jews were instructed that if they lent money *to each other* the loans had to be free of interest (Exodus 22:25), though they could charge interest to Gentiles. When the psalmist offers practical examples of those who are right before God, he includes the person who "does not put out his money at interest" (Psalm 15:5). Ezekiel's portrait of a righteous man also includes the fact that he lends to the poor without interest (Ezekiel 18:8,13,17).

However, even in Jewish society corruption quickly surfaced. Ezekiel condemned Israel for her abominable behavior: "You have taken interest and profits, and you have injured your neighbors for gain by oppression" (22:12). Jesus took the Old Testament restrictions about lending out money for interest and extended them even further. According to His teaching, there is nothing particularly commendable about lending money to others so that you can gain something in return, since even unbelievers do that. Instead, His instruction was to "lend, expecting nothing in return; and your reward will be great" (Luke 6:34-35). The Lord's words must be taken to heart as specific opportunities arise to lend money directly to others, especially within the church.

The Bible then does not prohibit reasonable lending or responsible borrowing, provided it is not motivated by greed or materialism, and is preceded by prayerful planning and wise counsel.

3. Don't cosign your way into a corner. Another caution involves surety. The general biblical principle is that the believer should not cosign for someone else. The wise person will not be held accountable for the debt of others. The instruction from God is clear that you should never take on the debt obligations of a stranger or even a neighbor. It is true that, in the narrative of Joseph and his brothers, Judah offers himself as surety to guarantee the safe return of his youngest brother Benjamin (Genesis 43:9). However, as it relates to money matters, Solomon offered a stern warning in Proverbs 6:1-5. If you are on the hook for someone else's liabilities, the wisest thing to do is go and free yourself from that obligation. To do so is to deliver yourself like an animal from a hunter (Proverbs 6:5), and it should be of such priority that until it is resolved you "give no sleep to your eyes, nor slumber to your eyelids" (Proverbs 6:4; cf. Proverbs 20:13; 27:13). Even in the case of a relative or close friend, it is best to say no to cosigning. It is not worth risking a ruined relationship with them, not to mention your own financial hardship, should they find themselves forced to default on the loan. If the professional lender who makes a living lending money does not believe they are a good risk, then we should be careful to think otherwise.

4. Don't sell your soul for success. Proverbs 28:19-20 warns against the temptation to acquire money hastily through "empty pursuits." This carries the connotation of vain or frivolous pursuits with no clear outcome in mind. Such speculative approaches to getting more money would include gambling, multilevel marketing schemes, and deceptive business practices that take advantage of the ignorance of others.

Proverbs 12:11-12 says, "He who tills his land will have plenty of bread, but he who pursues worthless things lacks sense. The wicked man desires the booty of evil men, but the root of the righteous yields fruit." Throughout the book of Proverbs, wicked men are identified as those who have become wealthy by such corruption as fraud (13:11), receiving bribes (15:27), using deceptive measuring instruments (20:10,23), and even extorting money from orphans (23:10; cf. 22:23,28; Jeremiah 22:3; Zechariah 7:10). Clearly anyone involved in such practices will be subject to the punishment of God.

Financial stability is based on hard work and a growing knowledge of your chosen field of labor. Proverbs 24:3-4 says, "By wisdom a house is built, and by understanding it is established; and by knowledge the rooms are filled with all precious and pleasant riches." It is wisdom, understanding, and knowledge that work together to form a strong financial foundation on which to build any business or career. There is no promise made for those who want to build wealth through scheming, manipulation, or dishonesty.

5. Don't confuse risk with recklessness. Rank speculation is different from calculated risk-taking and responsible investing. It is appropriate to invest and even to take reasonable risks. There is no virtue in being paralyzed by doubt and fear after conducting due diligence. Ecclesiastes 11:4 warns that if you fear the wind you will never have the courage to sow your seed, and if you fear the clouds, you will never set out to harvest lest it rain on you. The fact is no one can ever be completely confident that an investment will bring profitable returns. If a person wants to increase their investments in a responsible and proactive way, it will necessarily involve careful planning, wise stewardship, and sensible risk-taking.

Risk-taking must be calculated and careful, not reckless. After all, "the plans of the diligent lead surely to advantage, but everyone who is hasty comes surely to poverty" (Proverbs 21:5). Hard work, diligent planning, and a refusal to be dishonest coincide with the blessing of God to make our wealth a fortress against the troubles of life (Proverbs 10:15,22). We can become the confident man of Proverbs 27:25-27, who is secure in his provision and prepared for the coming winter.

6. Don't neglect to prepare and protect. Preparation for disaster is no small matter. Unless an individual already has a sizeable fortune, he must rely on protection from others. Of course, the Christian's ultimate confidence is in God, and not in the uncertainty of material wealth (1 Timothy 6:17; cf. 4:10).

A major insurance company uses the slogan "We get you back where you belong." The idea of being insured is a relatively new concept. In Bible times, people did not have the safeguards we enjoy today. Job, for example, lost all he had in less than a day, being left with nothing but a few foolish friends and a nagging wife. And if God had not revealed the coming seven-year famine to Joseph, such that he could prepare for the future, many lives in Egypt and the surrounding nations would have been lost.

Nonetheless, it is not unbiblical or unwise to insure your goods, diversify your investments, and hedge your exposure in light of the possibility of future downturns. On the contrary it is wise, and a characteristic of those who prosper over the long term. This forms the basis of the wise council in Proverbs 27:23-24: "Know well the condition of your flocks, and pay attention to your herds; for riches are not forever, nor does a crown endure to all generations." Through active awareness of what he owned, the ancient flock-owner could be well prepared for the future. The wise planner today will likewise prepare for the future, avoiding unnecessary exposure to possible financial ruin through the use of insurance and other legal means. In all of this, again, Christians must realize that their ultimate security is in God; and that, having done everything to be responsible, they can rest in knowing that God is in control of all things, including their physical and financial needs (Matthew 6:25-34; Philippians 4:6).

Working hard to increase your income and planning carefully to avoid pitfalls are just two of the three principles Christians must consider in thinking rightly about finances. The third is perhaps the most important. If you want to be please God with your wealth, you must be a faithful worker, a careful planner, *and* a generous giver.

Be a Generous Giver

Lionel Robbins defined economics as "the study of the use of scarce resources which have alternative uses." This definition is most appropriate for the Christian because unlike the rest of the world, we have an alternative use for our money that has eternal significance. If appropriated correctly, this heavenly perspective on earthly wealth will help believers successfully navigate the narrow strait between the banks of need and greed.

The statistics on giving in America are impressive—*impressively weak,* that is. Donations to ministry are in a downward trend. Both the net amount of dollars contributed and the percentage of per capita income are decreasing. In 2004, an average of only 2.5 percent of the gross income of evangelical Christians was given to ministry. In Los Angeles County the median income is approximately $65,000 according to 2008 government statistics, so that amounts to a mere $31 of giving per week. For the sake of contrast, charitable giving was at an average of 3.3 percent during the Great Depression.

One-third of born-again Christians in America say they cannot give because they are too encumbered by debt. At the moment, consumer debt tops 2.5 trillion dollars, with the average American making installment payments on over $8,500 worth of consumer debt. Add to that the fact that the average college student leaves school with massive debt, and it is no wonder why so many people feel crushed under a hopeless burden of financial obligations.

When Jesus taught on the subject of money, it was always countercultural and counterintuitive:

> Do not store up for yourselves treasures on earth, where moth
> and rust destroy, and where thieves break in and steal…

No one can serve two masters...you cannot serve God and wealth...Do not worry then, saying "What will we eat?" or "What will we drink?" or "What will we wear for clothing?" For the Gentiles eagerly seek all these things; for your heavenly Father knows that you need all these things (Matthew 6:19,24,31-32).

The Lord's point was that materialism and Christianity are incongruent. The question then is how can we, as believers, worship God with our financial resources while at the same time rejecting temptations that lead to idolatry and covetousness? The answer is found in giving to the Lord and His purposes. When we give our money to the work of the gospel, we not only demonstrate our heartfelt love for God (2 Corinthians 9:7), we also store up for ourselves treasure in heaven (Matthew 6:16-24).

Giving to the Lord helps Christians overcome the temptation to hoard their riches (Matthew 6:19-21). Those who are successful at acquiring financial wealth are immediately presented with the temptation to greedily stockpile it. To give is to counteract this temptation by considering the needs of others rather than being consumed by self-indulgence. Moreover, stockpiling wealth is risky business, since earthly riches have a way of disappearing. Giving, then, is also a means to invest in eternal things, amassing a treasure in heaven that can never be lost. It therefore repositions the heart from being focused on the things of this earth to the things of God.

Second, giving to the Lord helps Christians overcome the temptation to forget Him (Matthew 6:22-24). In Proverbs 30:9 the writer asks God to protect him from both the trials that attend abject poverty and the deceptive comfort that comes from wealth. The danger in the latter is that he will forget God and become too dependent on himself and his money. In Matthew 6, Jesus reminds us that the eye is to be clear and seeing properly. If the spiritual eye is functioning rightly, then it will direct the believer in the righteous path regarding money. It will cause him to always see God as the provider of wealth and the one to be honored by it. Since no one can serve both God and money, the act of regularly giving money to the Lord demonstrates who our true Master is.

Third, giving to the Lord helps Christians overcome the temptation to be anxious by reminding them that God is in control and that His kingdom is their highest priority (Matthew 6:25-34). "Be anxious for nothing," Paul told the Philippians, "but in everything by prayer and supplication with thanksgiving let your requests be made known to God. And the peace of God, which surpasses all comprehension, will guard your hearts and your minds in Christ Jesus" (Philippians 4:6-7). Just a few verses later, Paul explained that he had learned to be content in whatever financial circumstances he found himself (verses 10-13). Often, financial anxiety comes from trying to live beyond our means. The one who gives learns to be content and thankful for whatever lifestyle God has provided, even if it is a modest one (1 Timothy 6:7; Hebrews 13:5). Solomon offers a number of vivid contrasts throughout the book of Proverbs (Proverbs 15:16-17; 16:8,19; 17:1; 19:1; 28:6), informing the reader that financial poverty—if accompanied by the fear of God, love, righteousness, humility, quietness, and integrity— is far better than economic wealth accompanied by turmoil, hatred, injustice, pride, strife, perversion, and a crooked spirit.

Dollars and Sense

By God's grace, the Scriptures contain a great deal of doctrinal and practical instruction regarding money and wealth. The biblical standard is clear, and we are wise to heed it. All belongs to God, and we are therefore stewards of His resources. Our attitude toward money reveals the priorities and passions of our hearts, and reminds us that how we think about wealth is ultimately a spiritual issue. There is however nothing inherently wrong with making money and using it wisely. With that in mind, the Christian will position himself in a place of blessing if he works faithfully, plans carefully, and gives generously.

GOD'S CARBON FOOTPRINT

Global Warming and the Environmental Movement

PASTORAL PERSPECTIVE

This chapter is an expansion of material our pastors and elders have assembled over the years on this issue. It is representative of the general position of Grace Community Church.

Recently, our church received a magazine published by a leading evangelical university. The cover was entirely green, with bold white and green letters exclaiming, "The Greening of Evangelicals."[1] The subhead noted, "A growing number of Christians are embracing the 'creation care' movement. It's not a bandwagon, they say. It's biblical." Inside, a full eight pages were devoted to the subject. Again, the claim was made that protecting the environment is a biblical mandate—"a growing number of Christians are warming to the idea of 'creation care'—the notion that the Bible commands us to conserve and protect the environment." Several of the university's faculty and staff were interviewed in the article. Their comments underscore the idea that protecting the planet is a matter of biblical stewardship:

> We were given a mandate in Scripture to care for creation, and that never went away. When you measure how many

tons of carbon dioxide we pump into the atmosphere every day, and then—in a sense—belittle that fact or disregard it as being not much, then I really think it's like an ostrich with its head in the sand...

At the end of the day, the fact that we waste and pollute might be a small matter, but Christ himself, in the parable of the dishonest steward in Luke 16, said that those who are unfaithful in small things will not be entrusted with big things...

We do not have infinite supplies of oil, aluminum, paper and so on. So if we can use these things more wisely, that's part of the Genesis mandate: Be good stewards of what I've given to you...

[Our school] recognizes the importance of being good stewards of God's creation, not because it is politically correct, but because God calls us to that kind of management of his creation.

The article goes on to note that the students at this university are taking small steps to preserve and protect the environment, such as turning off the lights when exiting a room, putting computers on standby when not in use, and recycling plastic bottles. The school's president even drives a hybrid SUV as "a small gesture intended to make a statement about the importance of environmental stewardship."

Throughout the article, readers are repeatedly reminded that the Christian's "ecological responsibility" is something that God mandated for believers in His Word. The conspicuous irony is that the eight-page spread contains hardly any references to the Bible. A general reference is made to Luke 16, and Genesis 1:28 and 2:15 are each mentioned in passing. But no Scripture is actually quoted or explained in the article.

It is one thing to claim to be biblical. It is another to actually support that claim. Before we as Christians rush to embrace the environmentalist mind-set that is impacting many in evangelicalism these days, we would do well to consider the example set by the noble Bereans, examining the Scriptures to see whether these things are so.

Are Christians to Care for Creation?

We affirm that Christians have a responsibility to care for every resource God has provided for us. With regard to natural resources, that principle was illustrated in the Old Testament when God put Israel in the Promised Land and commanded the people to let the soil rest every seventh year:

> You shall sow your land for six years and gather in its yield, but on the seventh year you shall let it rest and lie fallow, so that the needy of your people may eat; and whatever they leave the beast of the field may eat. You are to do the same with your vineyard and your olive grove (Exodus 23:10-11; cf. Leviticus 25:1-7).

God gave that command because He did not want the people to exploit the land and extract all its life. Allowing the land to rest every seven years ensured that it was replenished and would continue to provide in the future. (God similarly commanded the people to treat their animals without abuse [Deuteronomy 25:4; Proverbs 12:10]).

When the Lord gave the Israelites the Mosaic law, He warned them that if they apostatized, He would remove them from the land (Deuteronomy 28). Sadly, the children of Israel did just that and came under God's judgment—the northern tribes fell to Assyria in 722 B.C., and the southern tribes to Babylon in 605 B.C. In fact, God designated the Babylonian captivity as a 70-year captivity so the land could rest and make up for all the Sabbath years that Israel violated (cf. Leviticus 26:33-35; 2 Chronicles 36:17-21).

So, we agree that believers must not be reckless, abusive, or irresponsible with any of the wonderful resources God has given us. Moreover, we are commanded to show love and care to the people around us (Philippians 2:1-5), as well as willingly submit to government rules and regulations (Romans 13:1-7). Such principles will necessarily affect how we interact with our surroundings.

But all of that, in fact, has very little to do with today's environmental movement or the global warming craze that goes with it. The environmental movement is consumed with trying to preserve the planet forever. But we know that isn't in God's plan.

The earth we inhabit is not a permanent planet. It is, frankly, a disposable planet—it is going to have a very short life. Contrary to the teachings of evolutionary theory, the earth was created less than 10,000 years ago, and its end may be very close at hand. When God's purposes for it are fulfilled, He will destroy it with fire and create a new earth (2 Peter 3:7-13; Revelation 21:1).

This earth was never ever intended to be a permanent planet—it is not eternal. We do not have to worry about it being around tens of thousands, or millions, of years from now because God is going to create a new heaven and a new earth. Understanding this fact is important to holding in balance our freedom to use, and responsibility to care for, the earth.

Christians, Climates, and Conservation

In light of the temporal nature of this earth, what should Bible-believing Christians think about global warming and the environmentalist movement that undergirds it?

The goal of this chapter is not to examine the scientific data (about which there is considerable debate, at least regarding the implications of recent findings[2]). Rather, our intention is to look to the Scriptures for guidance in thinking through the issue in a way that really is *biblical*. The Word of God, not scientific hypotheses or popular opinions, must be our authority on these matters. *Special* revelation (in Scripture) has been given to us to help us understand and rightly approach *general* revelation (in creation)—meaning that in His Word, the Creator has revealed for us all we need to know for life and godliness (2 Peter 1:3,19).

With that in mind, here are five considerations—derived from Scripture—which can help us develop a framework for thinking about global warming in a way that is distinctly biblical.

1. We Must Rightly Divide the Text

It has become increasingly popular in evangelical circles to take verses (or parts of verses) out of context in order to make them mean something they don't really mean. The apostle Peter warned of those who would "distort" the meaning of "the Scriptures" (2 Peter 3:16), and Paul instructed Timothy to "be diligent to present yourself approved to God as a workman who does not need to be ashamed, accurately handling the word of truth" (2 Timothy 2:15). All believers are to carefully examine any message that claims divine authority (1 Thessalonians 5:20-22; 1 John 4), looking to see if it corresponds to what Scripture really says (Acts 17:11). Christians, and teachers especially (James 3:1), must be careful to rightly divide the text. Taking verses out of context makes Scripture mean something it was never intended to mean, and thus ascribes to God that which God did not actually say. Such is a dangerous practice (Deuteronomy 12:32; Proverbs 30:6; Revelation 22:18-19).

This is one of the primary concerns we have with much of the evangelical literature written about protecting the environment. Isaiah 24:4-6 is one passage that is sometimes used to defend a pro-global-warming perspective. The verses read:

> The earth mourns and withers, the world fades and withers, the exalted of the people of the earth fade away. The earth is also polluted by its inhabitants, for they transgressed laws, violated statutes, broke the everlasting covenant. Therefore, a curse devours the earth, and those who live in it are held guilty. Therefore, the inhabitants of the earth are burned, and few men are left.

Some climate-concerned Christians have interpreted these verses as referring to the devastating effects of global warming. From a superficial reading of these verses, the passage might seem like a good fit. The pollution of the earth's inhabitants not only evidences their guilt, but also leads to massive heat-related destruction and subsequent population decline.

But those who use these verses to affirm the occurrence of global warming fail to consider the context. Most obviously, verses 1-3 indicate that God is the one who causes the happenings in verses 4-6. Verse 1 says, "Behold, the Lord lays the earth waste, devastates it, distorts its surface and scatters its inhabitants." And verse 3 notes that it is according to the word "the Lord has spoken." If Isaiah 24:4-6 refers to the current climate controversy, then verses 1-3 make God responsible for the rising temperatures.

Moreover, verse 5 speaks of *moral* pollution (not smog or carbon emissions), as defined by the next phrase: "for they transgressed laws, violated statutes, broke the everlasting covenant." In other words, mankind's sin (against God) will result in His fiery judgment. Finally, these verses must be interpreted in an apocalyptic context. The parallels with other apocalyptic texts (such as Revelation 6, 8–9, 16) take this particular passage out of the realm of current events and put it squarely into a category of future prophetic judgment. In fact, the entire section of Isaiah 24:1–27:13 is apocalyptic.

In any case, this is just one example of how scriptures can be taken out of context to mean something that the Spirit never intended. (Along those lines, we would caution those who take the stewardship passages in the New Testament and apply them to issues that go far beyond the intent of the text. We would also caution those who might try to apply texts aimed solely at Old Testament Israel to New Testament Christians.) The bottom line is that we must be careful not to impose our views on Scripture, but rather, we must allow the Bible to determine our beliefs.

2. We Must Remember Whom We Worship

There is no doubt that the glories of nature reveal the glory of God (Psalm 19:1-6). He created the world in such magnificent splendor that His creative hand is seen at every turn. The vastness of the ocean (Job 38:16), the beauty of the stars (Psalm 8:1-4), the majesty of the mountains (Psalm 65:5-9), the wonder of the rain (Psalm 147:7-8)—these and so much more point to the awesome handiwork of the Creator.

Though cursed through the Fall, God's creative work is still resplendent. The problem comes when fallen man rejects the Creator, and instead worships the creation. The apostle Paul warned of this in Romans 1:20-25:

> Since the creation of the world His invisible attributes, His eternal power and divine nature, have been clearly seen, being understood through what has been made, so that they are without excuse. For even though they knew God, they did not honor Him as God or give thanks, but they became futile in their speculations, and their foolish heart was darkened. Professing to be wise, they became fools, and exchanged the glory of the incorruptible God for an image in the form of corruptible man and of birds and four-footed animals and crawling creatures. Therefore God gave them over in the lusts of their hearts to impurity, so that their bodies would be dishonored among them. For they exchanged the truth of God for a lie, and worshiped and served the creature rather than the Creator, who is blessed forever. Amen.

In many ways, these verses describe those in the secular environmentalist movement today. Instead of worshipping Father God, they worship "Mother Nature." They exchange praise for the Creator with praise for His creation (cf. Deuteronomy 4:16-18).

Though evangelicals can and should appreciate the creation, glorifying God as a result of it, they must be careful not to adopt the secular, naturalistic, evolutionary mind-set that characterizes our world. Nature can be inadvertently idolized when conserving it is given a higher priority than obeying the clear commands of the New Testament—starting with the greatest commandment, which is to love the Lord God wholeheartedly (Mark 12:29-30). As Isaiah 42:5,8 reminds us:

> Thus says God the LORD, who created the heavens and stretched them out, who spread out the earth and its offspring, who gives breath to the people on it and spirit to those who walk in it…"I am the LORD, that is My name; I will not give My glory to another."

3. We Must Rightly Understand the Creation Mandate

In Genesis 1:28, God commanded Adam to "subdue" the earth and "rule" over it. This included the responsibility to "cultivate" the earth (Genesis 2:15), as well as the authority to name the animals (2:19-20). The earth was created for mankind, and not vice versa (cf. Genesis 8:21–9:3). Hence, man was to make use of the earth's natural resources as he worked to tend and tame his world.

The dual tasks of subduing and cultivating became increasingly difficult after the Fall, since the creation—which was originally created perfect (Genesis 1:31)—came under God's curse (Genesis 3:17-19; Romans 8:20-22; cf. Revelation 22:3). We are still experiencing the effects of the Fall today. The ground no longer yields its fruit so easily (Genesis 3:19), animals view mankind with terror and suspicion (Genesis 9:2), and death for all remains a constant threat (Romans 5:12ff). Though creation is no longer man's willing subject (cf. Hebrews 2:5-8), God's mandate to subdue the earth has not changed (Genesis 9:1-3).

The commands found in Genesis 1:28 and 2:15 (cf. Genesis 9:1-3) give broad details as to how man is to subdue and cultivate the earth— by populating it and using its natural resources for his own preservation and advancement (cf. Psalm 115:16). Though some have attempted to read specific environmentalist concerns into these texts, their interpretations reflect their own biases and read more into the text than is actually there. (Ironically, many of these same people refuse to take Genesis 1–2 literally, yet they appeal to these chapters to support an environmentalist agenda.)

Because the creation mandate commands human beings to be fruitful and multiply (Genesis 1:28), to dominate the earth (1:28), to cultivate the earth (2:15), and to use both plant and animal resources for food (1:29; 9:1-3), we would necessarily reject any conservationist position that opposes population growth, gives a higher priority to environmental concerns than to the well-being of human beings, unduly restricts the cultivation of the earth for food, or mandates a vegetarian diet. Environmentally minded evangelicals often cite the creation mandate of Genesis to support their views; but in so doing, they must be careful not to inadvertently violate the very commands to which they appeal. Policies that stifle legitimate opportunities to subdue and cultivate the earth and its resources run contrary to, not parallel with, the Genesis mandate.

4. We Must Define Sin and Salvation Accurately

On February 14, 2005, the National Council of Churches USA published a document entitled, "God's Earth Is Sacred: An Open Letter to Church and Society in the United States."[3] The letter calls on Christians to repent of their "social and ecological sins." According to the letter, citing Ecumenical Patriarch Bartholomew,

> [T]o commit a crime against the natural world is a sin…for humans to degrade the integrity of Earth by causing changes in its climate, by stripping the Earth of its natural forests, or destroying its wetlands…for humans to contaminate the Earth's waters, its land, its air, and its life, with poisonous substances…these are sins.

The document goes on to assert that too many Christians have bought into "a false gospel that we continue to live out in our daily habits—a gospel that proclaims that God cares for the salvation of humans only and that our human calling is to exploit Earth for our own ends alone." In recounting the sins that must be repented from, the authors state the following: "We confess that instead of living and proclaiming this salvation through our very lives and worship, we have abused and exploited the Earth and people on the margins of power and privilege, altering climates, extinguishing species, and jeopardizing Earth's capacity to sustain life as we know and love it."

But such statements reflect a view of sin, salvation, and the gospel that is far different than that presented in the New Testament. The biblical gospel centers on the death, burial, and resurrection of Christ (1 Corinthians 15:3-4) as the sole means (John 14:6; Acts 4:12) through which individual sinners (rebels against God's moral law—Romans 3:10-18,23) can be reconciled to God (2 Corinthians 5:17-21;

Colossians 1:21-22). It is the power of God for salvation to everyone who believes (Romans 1:16), such that those who believe in the Lord Jesus Christ will be saved (Acts 16:31). As Paul explained to the Romans, "If you confess with your mouth Jesus as Lord, and believe in your heart that God raised Him from the dead, you will be saved; for with the heart a person believes, resulting in righteousness, and with the mouth he confesses, resulting in salvation" (Romans 10:9-10).

Nowhere in the New Testament are sin, salvation, or the gospel ever defined in terms of corporate (or even individual) ecological responsibility. Rather than being consumed with the things of this earth, believers are commanded to focus on the life to come. The apostle Peter, speaking of the destruction of this earth, vividly makes the point:

> The day of the Lord will come like a thief, in which the heavens will pass away with a roar and the elements will be destroyed with an intense heat, and the earth and its works will be burned up. Since all these things are to be destroyed in this way, what sort of people ought you to be in holy conduct and godliness, looking for and hastening the coming of the day of God, because of which the heavens will be destroyed by burning, and the elements will melt with intense heat! But according to His promise we are looking for new heavens and a new earth, in which righteousness dwells (2 Peter 3:10-13).

As Christians, we are not called to focus our resources on preserving this current planet. Instead, we are to keep our eyes on Christ (Hebrews 12:1-2) as we anticipate the world to come (Philippians 3:20; Hebrews 11:13-16), living this life in holy conduct and godliness (cf. 1 Corinthians 6:9; Ephesians 5:5). When the National Council of Churches suggests that "in this most critical moment in Earth's history, we are convinced that *the central moral imperative* of our time is the care for Earth as God's creation,"[4] we could not disagree more.

The central moral imperative for the church in this age was articulated by Christ Himself in the Great Commission:

> Go therefore and make disciples of all the nations, baptizing
> them in the name of the Father and the Son and the Holy
> Spirit, teaching them to observe all that I commanded you;
> and lo, I am with you always, even to the end of the age
> (Matthew 28:19-20).

We are to take the true gospel (that individual sinners can be reconciled to God through faith in Christ) to lost and dying souls. Saving the world, for Christians, is not about saving the planet, but the lost. Moreover, the greatest legacy we can leave the next generation is not a greener world, but the truth of the gospel (cf. Deuteronomy 6:5-9; 2 Timothy 3:14-15). Instead of being distracted by attempts to save our broken planet, we should focus on the primary mission God has given to the church. We can then look forward to the day when He will create a new earth that will last forever (Revelation 21–22).

5. We Must Rest in God's Sovereign Purposes

It is not a cop-out to entrust God with the global destiny of our planet. To be sure, God's sovereignty never excuses man to be lazy or irresponsible. But knowing that He is in control should guard Christians from the doomsday mentality that characterizes the global warming movement. After all, whether the ice caps are melting or not, God specifically promised that He would not flood the earth again (Genesis 9:11).

God has already revealed to us how this world is going to end—with Christ's return (1 Thessalonians 4:13–5:3) and reign (Revelation 20:1-6), followed by the creation of a new earth (2 Peter 3:10; Revelation 21:1-7). During the Great Tribulation, God Himself will do much worse to this planet than mankind ever could. There will be famine (Revelation 6:5-6), pestilence (6:7-8), cosmic disasters (6:12-17), vegetation that is burned up (8:7), sea life that is destroyed (8:8-9), waters that are contaminated (8:10-11), demonic "locusts" (9:1-12), deadly plagues (9:13-21), terrible sores (16:2), seas and rivers that are turned to blood (16:3), scorching heat (16:8-9), darkness and pain

(16:10-11), drought (16:12-16), and total devastation (16:17-21). After these divine judgments, Christ will come and establish His kingdom by force (19:11-21). A thousand years later (20:1-6), as the millennial kingdom transitions to the eternal state, God will ultimately destroy this world with fire (20:9; cf. 2 Peter 3:10-12) and create a new heaven and earth (21:1; cf. 2 Peter 3:13).

In spite of society's best attempts to cool down the planet, the Bible tells us how the world is going to end. It is going to get hot, but not because of carbon emissions. When God's divine fury is finally poured out on the world, no amount of environmental protection will be able to stop it.

Our Lord's words about anxiety, though specifically with regard to physical provision, serve as an appropriate reminder for those Christians who have allowed environmental fears to distract them from their God-given mission.

> Who of you by being worried can add a single hour to his life?...Do not worry then, saying, "What will we eat?" or "What will we drink?" or "What will we wear for clothing?" For the Gentiles eagerly seek all these things; for your heavenly Father knows that you need all these things. But seek first His kingdom and His righteousness, and all these things will be added to you. So do not worry about tomorrow; for tomorrow will care for itself. Each day has enough trouble of its own (Matthew 6:27,31-34).

In that same context, Jesus notes that the birds of the air and the lilies of the field need not worry, because God is taking care of them (verses 26-29). Just as the Creator oversees the animals and plants He has made (such that they need not worry about their future), He will also take care of those who give first priority to His kingdom purposes.

The Importance of an Eternal Perspective

The church must not get caught up in the doom-and-gloom

mentality fueling much of the contemporary hype about global warming and environmentalism. While we should be good citizens (as we submit to government restrictions), good neighbors (as we are sensitive to the needs of others), and good stewards (as we invest the resources God has individually bestowed to us into His kingdom work), we should not become preoccupied with agendas or concerns that distract us from our primary mission in this world. Though the message we preach is foolishness to the world (1 Corinthians 1:18), it is the wisdom and power of God (1 Corinthians 2:6-9; cf. Romans 1:16). The sinners we seek must understand that they are in rebellion against a holy God, and unless they repent and believe, they will spend eternity apart from Him in hell. Though having an eternal mind-set does not excuse us from temporal responsibilities, it should help keep them in right perspective. With that in mind, let us press forward with the truth and be faithful to the King.

14

FROM EVERY TRIBE AND TONGUE
Racism and Reconciliation in Church and Culture

MARK TATLOCK

Racism is the deeply held belief that one's ethnicity or cultural heritage justifies a sense of superiority over those of other ethnic backgrounds, resulting in discrimination, segregation, or unjust treatment toward them.

Creation and Race

God created one race, the human race. As a result, equality extends to all members of the human race.

In His design of man, God embedded His image (Genesis 1:26-27; James 3:9). As a result, man possesses an inherent dignity and value (Genesis 9:6; James 2:1-6). But racism violates this fundamental reality by elevating one ethnicity over another. Due to the Fall (Genesis 3:16-19), sinful man no longer submissively worships the Creator, but instead assumes a prideful position of superiority and, as a result, views others as inferior. At the heart of racism, then, is a consuming commitment to love self rather than others. Such pervasive pride is ultimately an affront to God and is consistently denounced in His Word (Proverbs 8:13; 16:19; James 1:9).

Having rejected the worship of the true God, unredeemed men

manifest behaviors and desires that are contrary to His nature (Romans 1:18-32). Only a total heart transformation through regeneration and sanctification can bring sinners back into a right relationship with God. At conversion, believers become reconciled image bearers, able to once again reflect the righteous character of God (cf. 1 Peter 1:14-16).

As redeemed image bearers, our capacity to reflect God's character is limited to His communicable attributes, such as His goodness, love, mercy, righteousness, justice, compassion, longsuffering, and forgiveness (cf. Galatians 5:13ff). Such attributes are seen most clearly in God's relationship to us. And we reflect them most clearly in our relationship to others. Because we are indwelt by the Holy Spirit, we can interact with and relate to others as God Himself does toward us. But when we demean other people or discriminate against them, we fail to reflect the nature of God. And when we claim to follow God but fail to reflect Him in our conduct, we justify the world's accusation of hypocrisy. Therefore, pursuing right relationships with those of other ethnic heritages is critical to the church's witness.

The Old Testament and Race

At creation, God gave a clear mandate for man to subdue and populate the earth (Genesis 1:28). This mandate was given so that man could rule, or manifest dominion, over the earth for the purposes of God's glory. The Fall, changing man's affections, produced in man the desire to exercise dominion for his own personal benefit. In Genesis 11, where mankind refused to fulfill this mandate, God Himself confused human language to assure His purposes would be achieved. Variations in language and geographical separation resulted in the development of very distinct ethnic traits, cultures, and identities.

Throughout the Old Testament we see illustrations of how man, now fallen in his thinking, perverted God's command to subdue and rule the earth, and in turn sought to have dominion over other peoples. We see this exemplified in Scripture by the Egyptians, the Philistines, the Babylonians, the Assyrians, and the Medes and Persians. War, slavery, and injustice stem from the violation of God's intended purpose for man to exercise dominion.

All through the Old Testament, the children of Israel often encountered people from other ethnic tribes and states. While many prohibitions were given to the Israelites to avoid making treaties or covenants, including marriage, with non-Jewish people, the intention of these restrictions was to limit the influence of idolatry. God had called out the nation of Israel to function as "a kingdom of priests and a holy nation" (Exodus 19:3-6). This mission required the Israelites to be lights to Gentile nations. They could not fulfill this call if they forsook the worship of the Lord and embraced the worship of the pagan gods of the nations (cf. 1 Kings 8:57-61; 11:1-4).

In the Old Testament, interracial marriage was not forbidden on the basis of ethnicity but rather idolatry. Since national membership and faith were linked in identity, ethnicity was linked to idol worship. The basis of God's prohibitions was to prevent false worship from being integrated into the Jewish culture; therefore, an Israelite could not marry a person who was not a true worshipper of God. This is still true for the believer today (2 Corinthians 6:14). For God's people, marriage has always been an issue of faith, not race.

At the same time, Israel was not to neglect the needs of foreigners. Repeatedly the law instructed the Israelites to practice hospitality to aliens and strangers by extending care, generosity, and protection (Exodus 22:21; 23:9; Leviticus 19:34; 25:35; Deuteronomy 27:19; 31:12). On many occasions the Israelites practiced hospitality to foreigners who, as a result, became followers of the Lord. Examples such as Rahab, Ruth, Namaan, the widow of Sidon, Nebuchadnezzar, the entire city of Nineveh, and others illustrate this point.

Christ and Race

With the inclusion of the Magi and the prophetic statement of Simeon in the nativity narrative of Luke 2, we see that from Christ's birth His love and ministry extended to men and women from every nation.

The issue of racism is seen as Christ began His earthly ministry. On several occasions, Christ identified Gentiles who demonstrated greater faith than the Jews of His day (Matthew 8:5-12; Luke 4:23-29). In so doing, Christ illustrated that in His kingdom there is no superiority of one race over another. There were valid reasons for the Jews to be angry and hostile toward Gentiles. Their long history had been benchmarked by periods when Gentiles abusively ruled over them. Whether the Egyptians, Assyrians, Babylonians, Medo-Persians, or the Romans, the Jews had suffered much under the tyrannical and inhumane rule of foreign rulers. Their longing for the Messiah and the coming of an earthly Jewish king was so intense that the very notion of a Gentile exercising true faith immediately stirred up anger from the Jewish mobs.

Christ understood racism, offering not just a temporal but an eternal solution. The gospel would not be limited by national or ethnic identity. All men were equally in need of God's undeserved grace. The gospel itself demands a rejection of pride and the acknowledgment of total humility (Luke 18:9-17). As the church again recovers the heart of the gospel, it discovers the ultimate solution for racism. It is not only human dignity (flowing out of creation), but primarily the gospel (flowing out of the cross) that is the ultimate equalizer. In the Beatitudes, the Lord delineates the distinct character of those who receive saving faith. The redeemed live according to kingdom values, which are inherently different than the values of the world.

This is no clearer than in Christ's call to be peacemakers (Matthew 5:9). To be a peacemaker is to be like God Himself (cf. Ephesians 5:1). Where conflict and divisions exist due to pride and envy (James 4:1), the Christian has the potential to display how God moved toward us in salvation. Peacemaking is a high standard, being met when we actively pursue reconciliation with our enemies and thereby make peace where it did not previously exist. Only a Spirit–filled, humble, compassionate believer can do such work. Because racial division is one of the most systemic evils in the world, there are few more dramatic contexts in which gospel love and peacemaking can be better illustrated.

On one specific occasion Christ confronted the sin of injustice. In so doing, He made it clear that any unjust abuse of power to prevail and take advantage of those who are helpless is contradictory to the values of the kingdom. The disciples John and Mark, looking for positions of prestige, boldly asked for seats of honor (Mark 10:35-45). As they did, Christ illustrated how Christian humility was to be understood in contrast to the world's lust for power and superiority. Christ responded to their request severely, telling them not to be like the Gentiles, who lord it over others (verse 42).

In rebuking His disciples, Christ identified the fact that unregenerate men seek power to mistreat, manipulate, or control others for personal benefit. He went on to explain that His followers must seek to serve their fellow men, not rule over them. "Lording over" is a biblical reference to injustice. This practice was repeatedly condemned in the Old Testament (Leviticus 19:15; Psalm 58:2; Proverbs 18:8; 22:8,22-23; Isaiah 61:8; Jeremiah 21:12; 22:13). Historically, injustice has been one of the most consistent characteristics of racism. As the disciples observed Christ model compassion for the Samaritan woman, or heard His account of the good Samaritan practicing Christian love, they began to see His equal love for all men and women regardless of ethnicity. His love confronted His disciples' established attitudes of superiority.

The New Testament and Race

The Great Commission (Matthew 28:19-20), given as Christ's final word to His disciples, clearly defines the scope of the kingdom as inclusive of men and women from every people group. To make disciples of all the nations fulfilled the historic and redemptive plan of God first expressed to Abraham in Genesis 12. The New Testament illustrates the outworking of this multi-ethnic mosaic of God's elect people.

Beginning on the Day of Pentecost in Acts 2, the global scope of the church would be displayed by the many languages represented when Peter first rose to preach. It was Peter, instructed through a vision that there was no longer any distinction between Jews and Gentiles, who would go and baptize the Roman Cornelius (Acts 10). It was Philip who would preach to the Samaritans and open the Scripture with a man from Ethiopia. It was Paul who, in meeting with the Jerusalem Council (Acts 15), would help his fellow apostles see that there must be no ethnic distinctions in the church. In 1 Corinthians 12, Paul definitively described the church as racially and economically diverse, with variations of gifts and abilities, yet unified as one body (verses 12-14). The gospel is the great equalizer. Understanding racism as a direct violation of the loving heart of God, and contradictory to the character of the gospel, requires believers to take racism seriously. Racism has led to great pain, separation, and division not only in society, but within the church.

The gospel enables the believer to see his identity in Christ as spiritual, not ethnic. Our ethnic and cultural identities are secondary as we assume the primary identity of citizens of God's kingdom. Here and only here can we find a common identity, which is an eternal one. This does not mean we are to ignore our cultural heritage, for God, in His providence, has ordained every aspect of our lives. Cultural differences provide us each with a framework to see the distinct and creative design of God, and with unique opportunities to minister the gospel within our own spheres of influence. But as those who are first and foremost citizens of God's kingdom, we must recognize that there may be parts of our own culture that run counter to a biblical worldview. In such cases, the Scriptures—not culture—must be upheld as the ultimate authority.

Racism in American History

The institution of slavery indelibly stamped the practice and effects of racism upon the American experience. The efforts of the church to either defend or renounce slavery led to significant denominational schism. Slavery also divided the nation as the issue of race, particularly attitudes of superiority toward blacks, left an indelible mark on early-American economics, education, and culture.

By the time of the Civil War, a number of major immigrant

populations were becoming established in the United States. Most came to the new country impoverished and took up residence in the industrially developing urban centers. Added to this was the northerly and westward expansion of blacks seeking employment in the cities. As these impoverished populations filled the city, North American churches, which had been primarily Protestant, began to witness a shift in urban demographics.

White Protestants, who were more established and therefore possessing greater economic resources, had the means to relocate beyond the cities. And churches often followed parishioners. While not all Protestant churches ignored or rejected these new urban populations, over time the dominant Protestant influence shifted from the cities to the suburbs. Between the Civil War and World War I, the urban population in the United States grew from 6.2 million to 42 million. Ethnic immigrants during this same period numbered over 26 million. Many of these immigrants were from less-developed, non-Protestant countries in Eastern and Southern Europe.

Following World War II, the development of affordable GI housing and the creation of manufactured housing developments established the suburbs as the home of the majority of whites. By the 1960s and 1970s, 85 percent of city growth was suburban. Money spent on constructing new churches in this period grew from $76 million to over $1 billion, almost all focused on suburban churches. Following the Civil Rights legislation of 1965, the United States expanded its quotas for immigrants to avoid ethnic discrimination. As a result, new immigrants to the United States over the last 40 years have come from Middle Eastern, Asian, and South American nations.

Understanding that city centers function as ports of entry for immigrants, the church should consider the city as strategic to the fulfillment of the Great Commission. The disengagement of Protestant churches from urban centers has led to a disengagement between ethnic churches and suburban communities. Pastors today must understand that ministry in the United States will be cross-cultural. Demographic trends show that minority populations will replace majority white populations in many states during the next quarter century. Today, the suburbs of the twenty-first century have become as multi-ethnic as the city centers. This is a strategic time to see the advancement of the gospel, a critical time for the church to think biblically about the issue of overcoming cultural barriers and ethnic distinctions.

In North America, where church and state are so clearly separated, we fail to appreciate that most of the world events we see unfolding today are an expression of deep-seated racial and religious conflict. It is critical to recognize that racial issues and discrimination are universal and affect every culture. They are not an American phenomenon. Whether it is caste clashes, genocide, ethnic cleansing, mass migration of refugees, or extreme nationalism, all are expressions of racism and religious conflict. Where race, state, and faith cannot be so easily separated, we can begin to understand why peace will never be ultimately achieved by human political instruments. Those involved in cross-cultural ministry, both in the States and overseas, must help their disciples understand the issue of racism and instruct the church to live biblically.

The future of the church provides the most comprehensive and beautiful picture of what God's intended plan has been for the ethnically diverse peoples of the earth. Gathered together as one community, one body, and one citizenship with one aim, we together will worship the Creator (Revelation 5:9-10; 7:9; 22:2). This has been God's agenda from creation, throughout history, for His church on earth and for eternity. Nowhere else in Scripture do you see the ultimate expression of God's redemptive love than in heaven. This picture, while perfect and eternal, serves as God's greatest illustration of what the church should look like today. It also reinforces that we as bearers of the gospel are stewards for every people group. God's church is global in nature, and we cannot afford to narrowly define the identity of our local church or the universal church along racial lines.

Considerations for Today's Church

1. The church must understand it was intended to encompass

men and women from every ethnicity. This should produce a humility in lifestyle that confronts sinful attitudes of racial superiority among the redeemed.

2. The church must recognize that, due to the Fall, every cultural context has at some point in its history experienced substantive racism. Christians should understand this history and honestly recognize the social, economic, and geographic effects on those who have been treated unjustly. Though individuals today may not be personally responsible for historical injustices, ignoring or denying these realities does not demonstrate God's loving concern and instead reinforces previous offenses.

3. The church must demonstrate a commitment to overcome racial strife, misunderstanding, or unintended offenses. Inviting the counsel of those in your congregation who are from different or minority populations (to help church leaders see their perspective on racial issues) will require trust, genuine interest, and an abiding commitment to growth and change.

4. The church must encourage those who have experienced the effects of injustice to be willing to practice forgiveness, faith, and hope, believing that God's people can work together to experience the unity that God promises is possible to enjoy within His church.

5. The church must discern the threats of a secular agenda of diversity, which, while attempting to address the right problem, relies solely on a rights-based and man-centered line of argumentation. A rights-based argumentation is inadequate. Christians can offer more than a rights-based solution; they can model a love-based and God-centered solution.

6. The church must anticipate that a secular agenda of multiculturalism also normalizes and equalizes every culture's

faith and religious worldview. While we must recognize the equality of every *race,* we cannot also affirm the equality of every *faith system.* Religious pluralism is a great threat to the church, often coming on the heels of the noble pursuit of cultural diversity.

7. The church must observe that dramatic shifts in global ethnic populations, patterns of legal and illegal immigration, and political conflicts require careful biblical and practical ministry responses. Simplistic attitudes or policies will not suffice to aid Christians to live out their faith in authentic ways.

8. The church must articulate a biblical perspective on the issues of interracial marriage, multiethnic families, and interracial adoption. Training its members to think biblically about these matters will also require that subtle racial attitudes or assumptions be confronted when demonstrated toward church members.

Racial reconciliation cannot genuinely happen unless people are born again. For only as redeemed individuals can we first be reconciled to God, and then possess the ability to be reconciled to one another. The goal of racial reconciliation, pursued apart from the gospel, will result in lesser accomplishments. Therefore, as believers who are indwelt by Christ, we have the greatest capacity to be peacemakers in our world today, both between men and God and between men and their fellow men.

15

When the Nations Come to Us

Illegal Immigration and Border Control

Pastoral Perspective

This chapter is adapted from pastoral staff discussions on this important issue. It is representative of the general position of Grace Community Church.

According to recent estimates, there are over 21 million people living in the United States illegally. On a political level, much controversy centers on how illegal immigration might be better regulated and how the government should respond to the immigrants who are already here. On an economic level, experts debate how the influx of immigrants has affected the American economy.

But our primary concern here is neither political nor economic. Rather, it is theological and pastoral. From a biblical and practical perspective, how should pastors, church leaders, and church members respond to this issue? As those who minister in Los Angeles, this question is not hypothetical for us. Nor is it hypothetical for a growing number of churches across our nation.

Though not an exhaustive response, below are ten considerations (organized under four headings) that outline Grace Community Church's pastoral perspective on this issue.

Illegal Immigration and U.S. Law

The Christian's Responsibility to Government

We affirm the fact that, in keeping with the Word of God, Christians are to submissively obey the laws of the government (Romans 13:1; 1 Peter 2:13-17; cf. Titus 3:1). The only exception to this general rule is when a government mandate requires believers to disobey God (Daniel 3:16-18; Acts 5:29). Nothing in current U.S. immigration law requires Christians to disobey God; thus, U.S. immigration laws are to be submissively obeyed by believers.

If a believer is illegally residing in the United States, he should take active steps to rectify that situation. This may involve seeking legal residency through whatever means are available to him (for which we would recommend consultation with an immigration lawyer), or it may necessitate leaving the United States until such a time as immigration can legally take place.

The Problems with Illegal Residency

In light of the biblical commands noted above, Christians who reside in the United States illegally should understand that doing so constitutes sin, and that such sin remains until their law-breaking status is resolved. Remaining an illegal resident also brings with it additional temptations—to lie and deceive (about one's status), to steal (by avoiding taxes and other fees), to worry (about getting caught), and so on. When known sin continues without repentance, the believer's relationship to God is seriously hindered (Psalm 66:18; Proverbs 28:9).

Like any sin, breaking the law in this regard can be forgiven through confession and repentance before God (cf. 1 Samuel 15:22; Psalm 32:5; Proverbs 28:13; 2 Corinthians 7:9-10). Repentance will manifest itself in a proactive attempt to make the situation right—either by attaining legal status through the appropriate means, or by leaving the country until such time as a legal immigration status can be obtained.

The Need to Understand Immigration Law

In all of this, we acknowledge that the U.S. government has been inconsistent in its enforcement of immigration law, resulting in widespread contradiction and corruption (cf. Prov. 29:12). Even from state to state and city to city, the enforcement of immigration policies differs widely. Nonetheless, the government still retains the right to enforce its policies, even if it does so inconsistently (Romans 13:1-7).

Although mixed signals on the part of government do not excuse illegal behavior on the part of individuals, they can create confusion. As a result, the issues involved in specific cases are sometimes complex, and must be handled with patience and compassion as biblical commands are applied to real-life circumstances.

Church leaders should become familiar with whatever state and regional laws apply to them and their congregation, perhaps even meeting with an immigration attorney to discuss such matters. Doing so will safeguard pastors from giving counsel that unknowingly violates current legislation.

Illegal Immigration and Pastoral Counseling

The Church's Responsibilities Regarding Citizenship Status

We do not believe it is the church's responsibility to police the immigration status of individual church attendees. Rather, the role of the church is to faithfully proclaim the truth of Scripture, trusting the Holy Spirit to prick the consciences of those believers who are in sin (cf. Psalm 19:7-14; John 16:8; Ephesians 6:17; Hebrews 4:12). The church may also provide private counsel to those who are struggling with how to submit to the government in their given circumstances (cf. 1 Peter 5:1-3; Hebrews 13:17). However, the pastor's role is not to give legal counsel, but rather biblical counsel, encouraging believers to honor the Lord by living according to what Scripture teaches. If legal counsel is requested, pastors should direct counselees to the appropriate channels (such as immigration attorneys).

At the same time, we do require all of our lay ministry leaders and church staff to be legal U.S. residents—actively inquiring as to their residency status if it is in doubt. The qualifications for spiritual leadership require individuals to be above reproach (1 Timothy 3:1-13; Titus 1:5-9). Someone willfully continuing in unrepentant law-breaking would be disqualified from any position or office of spiritual leadership. Moreover, in the spirit of Matthew 18:15-17, we would begin steps of private admonition and shepherding with that individual once his situation became known to us.

The Need to Shepherd New Believers

We recognize there are many believers who entered the United States illegally but did so before their conversion. Now, having come to faith in Christ, they have also come to realize that obedience to His Word means submission to the laws of the land (John 14:15,21; cf. Luke 20:25). Compassionate and confidential counsel can be given to such individuals; yet pastors must not compromise the biblical standard. Though it may be difficult, pastors should encourage counselees to do what is right and trust God for the results (cf. 1 Samuel 24 and 26, where David obeyed the law by sparing Saul's life and trusted God with the outcome).

Pastors should also explain to counselees that living in accordance with God's will starts by living in accordance with His Word (Psalm 119:105; Romans 12:2; Ephesians 5:17-18; Colossians 3:16). To persist in disobedience is to put oneself outside of God's will (cf. Colossians 1:9-10). Counselees can be confident that God, in His sovereign purposes, is fully aware of their struggles and concerns (Romans 8:28; cf. Matthew 6:25-34). Through prayer and supplication, they can rest in His parental care and trust Him as they seek to obey what the Bible teaches (Psalm 55:22; Philippians 4:6).

The Steps Toward Doing What Is Right

If a believer, being convicted of his sin in this area, determines the need to return to his home country, the church should do its best to make the transition as easy as possible. This may include financial help with travel and relocation costs, as well as an attempt to connect the individual with a church in that country. Because the individual was likely not a Christian when he left his native country, it is crucial that (with the church's help) he find a solid group of believers in his homeland with whom he can now fellowship and enjoy regular worship (cf. Hebrews 10:25). Though he came as a stranger, he leaves as a beloved brother in Christ, and the church must send him off accordingly (Ephesians 2:19; cf. Philemon 1:16).

Illegal Immigration and Evangelicalism

The Nations Have Come to Us

As evangelicals, we embrace the opportunity to preach the gospel to those who come to us, whether they come through legal channels or otherwise. Los Angeles, for instance, is home to people from over 140 countries speaking more than 220 languages and dialects. In a very literal sense, the nations have come to us, and this is true to varying extents throughout the United States. Thus, we have a unique opportunity to fulfill the Great Commission without going far from home (Matthew 28:18-20; Luke 24:47).

In evangelistic encounters with those who are illegal residents, if such is even possible to determine, the Christian's focus should be on reaching them with the gospel and not on confronting their immigration status. It may be that, in embracing Jesus Christ as their Lord and Savior, they will immediately recognize their need to make amends in this area. Or, more likely, conviction may come later through the hearing of God's Word, as the Spirit uses what is faithfully taught each week in the church to change the heart.

We Are Defined by the Gospel, Not Political Agendas

We do not agree with those who want the evangelical church to take a political stand on illegal immigration. While we affirm the right of each American citizen to vote according to his or her conscience, we believe it is an unnecessary distraction (away from the gospel) for churches to advocate political activism on issues such as this. Those who oppose illegal immigration run the risk of viewing illegal immigrants as enemies rather than a mission field (cf. Matthew 9:36). On the flip side, those who advocate increased immigrant rights must be careful not to promote attitudes of insubordination or contempt toward the government (1 Timothy 2:1-4; cf. Romans 13:1-7).

In both cases, the mission of the church becomes blurred when political issues overshadow biblical preaching and gospel-centered ministry. Evangelicals must take special care to remember that we are first citizens of heaven before we are citizens of earth (John 18:36; Philippians 3:20; cf. Hebrews 11:9-10). Biblical Christianity is not defined by political agendas, but rather by the truth of the gospel (1 Corinthians 2:2; cf. Galatians 2:20).

There Is No Room for Racism or Prejudice

We firmly denounce any perspective that would oppose immigration (either legal or illegal) on racist or prejudicial grounds. As Christians, we affirm that all people are created in the image of God (Genesis 1:27), and that there are no ethnic or economic barriers to full fellowship in the church, since all the redeemed are equal in Jesus Christ (Romans 3:22; Galatians 3:28; Ephesians 2:11-22). We recognize that we are all aliens and strangers in this world, and we look forward to the day when men and women from every tribe and tongue will join together in worship around the throne of Christ (Revelation 5:9-14).

Illegal Immigration and Employment

On a final note, we encourage Christian employers to carefully comply with all state and federal regulations regarding the employment of illegal immigrants. Employers sin if they knowingly violate the law, and may also be subject to legal penalties (Romans 13:1-7; 1 Peter 2:13-20). Though submitting to government requirements may cost more economically (due to higher wages and taxes), employers who do so should trust the Lord for the results. They can likewise rest in knowing that God is pleased when they do what is right.

If an employer needs to terminate an employee based on the employee's immigration status, the employer must treat the employee with dignity and fairness (Colossians 4:1). Moreover, Christian employers must never take advantage of any employee whom they learn is illegal—abusing or mistreating him because he is desperate to find work or afraid to report such abuses to the authorities. One day, employers will stand before Christ for how they have conducted themselves and their enterprise here on earth (Ephesians 6:9; cf. Leviticus 25:43). To that end, they must manage their business in a way that is neither contrary to Scripture or to their own consciences (cf. Romans 14:10-12).

Illegal Immigration and Honoring Christ

Illegal immigration is a real issue affecting millions of people currently living in the United States. Though it is a debated political topic, pastors and church leaders must not allow controversy or public opinion to determine their strategy for ministering to those affected. Rather, their approach must be governed by biblical principles as they seek to uphold the clear teaching of Scripture without compromise, while also extending pastoral kindness and compassion to those who need it. In the end, their primary concern should be the spiritual condition of every soul under their care—regardless of age, gender, race, or citizenship.

When the nations come to us, may we be faithful to greet them with the good news of salvation, and upon their conversion to graciously shepherd them in a way that honors Christ.

Part 4

TRAGEDY AND SUFFERING

SORROW, SUFFERING, AND THE SOVEREIGNTY OF GOD

Divine Providence, and the Problem of Evil

RICK HOLLAND

I f there were one word in the Bible I could change, I know what it would be. Two verses into his epistle, James wrote, "Consider it all joy, my brethren, *when* you encounter various trials" (emphasis added). How hopeful it would be had he used the word *if* instead of *when*. However, James's inspired quill is unmistakable; trials are inevitable. It is not *if* they will come, but *when*. No, I don't really wish it were a different word (then the blessings of the following verses would be forfeited), but I confess to a hard swallow when I think about this divine guarantee.

Sorrow, suffering, and difficulty are a part of life—everyone's life. Though there is a broad spectrum of the quantity and intensity of difficulty in people's lives, no exemptions are issued for facing the problems of pain, evil, and suffering. Our experience with evil is general and specific, communal and individual, global and personal. The question is not, Will I experience suffering? but rather, How will I respond when it comes?

There are two ways to approach "the problem of evil" as theologians and philosophers call it. We can wrestle with it *philosophically* or *emotionally*; however, both approaches inevitably end up addressing it *theologically*. The philosophical (or logical) approach involves *theodicy*. Theodicy is a defense of God's stated character in the Bible against the charge that He should not permit bad things to happen. The emotional (or individual) approach is *personal*. It is simply the effort to formulate a reasonable response to undesirable things when they do happen. Thousands of years of theologizing and study have not yielded an answer to the philosophical approach that is fully satisfying. And thousands of years of suffering have not diminished the pain we experience when suffering happens to us personally.

The Philosophical Problem of Evil

If millennia of history's foremost thinkers have not conclusively answered this problem, I am under no illusion that these few pages can. But understanding the formulation of the philosophical/logical problem of evil provides helpful perspective. Again, this is called *theodicy*. In this category the God of the Bible is on trial, and the charge against God is formulated like this: There are three theological propositions that the Bible puts forth, but logically, (it is argued) only two of them can be simultaneously true. Here are the propositions:

1. God is good (meaning He desires the good and happiness of His creatures).

2. God is sovereign (meaning He has power to do as He wills).

3. Evil exists (including natural disasters, personal tragedies, death, and sin).

So logically, if God is good and evil exists, then He must not be sovereign—that is, He is not powerful enough to prevent evil. Or, if God is sovereign and evil exists, then He must not be good—that is, He has no moral inclination to prevent evil. Or last, if God is good and He is sovereign, then evil does not exist—that is, evil is merely illusory. This last option is not a real one or we would not have the problem at all!

C.S. Lewis simplifies the problem: "If God were good, He would wish to make His creatures perfectly happy, and if He were almighty, He would be able to do what He wished. But His creatures are not happy. Therefore God lacks either goodness, or power, or both. This is the problem of pain in its simplest form."[1]

Admittedly, if this were the only way to formulate the problem, the only possible solutions would seem to invalidate the Bible's depiction of God and evil. However, this classic presentation of the problem of evil is incomplete. Yes, God is good. Yes, God is sovereign. Yes, evil exists. But there are other factors to consider.

When Abraham was pleading with God to spare Sodom and Gomorrah, he footnoted his arguments with this theological insight: "Shall not the Judge of all the earth deal justly?" (Genesis 18:25). In other words, Abraham asserted that God's actions are fundamentally righteous in all His dealings. Moses confessed the same when he sang, "The Rock! His work is perfect, for all His ways are just; a God of faithfulness and without injustice, righteous and upright is He" (Deuteronomy 32:4). Beyond God's goodness and sovereignty, His judgment to do what is right must be added to the equation. God Himself is the standard for all His actions. And the exercise of His sovereignty is always just (that is, right and righteous).

Another divine attribute should be considered as well—God's wisdom. God has morally sufficient reasons for the existence of evil that flow from His infinite wisdom. All things take place either by God's prescription or permission, and in perfect accordance with His sovereign purposes and unfathomable judgments (Romans 11:33-36). Divine reasons, then, exist for the evils of our world on both a massive scale (e.g., the events of 9/11, the Holocaust, and natural disasters) and on a personal level (e.g., sickness, pain, loss, and death). Sometimes the reasons for these evils are provided. For example, the greatest catastrophe in history, the worldwide flood, was preceded by a clear explanation of why it would happen (Genesis 6:5). But sometimes God's reasons are hidden, unavailable to the sufferers. Though the reader of the book of Job is privy to the goings on in heaven that precipitated Job's suffering (Job 1:6-12), Job was painfully uninformed (Job 31). Abraham was tested by the divine command to sacrifice his son Isaac. He too was unaware of God's purposes in this, his darkest hour (Genesis 22). Why does God inform some people of the reasons for their sufferings and not others? Because God's purposes concerning evil are always governed by His wisdom. And His wisdom sometimes works beyond the veil of our experience for reasons only He understands.

This raises an obvious question: Does God really send evil upon His creatures? To answer, we must first understand that this is actually two questions. The first question asks, Does God send evil things in our world and lives? The second question is, Does God commit evil in sending bad things into our world and lives? Both questions are answered by defining what *evil* is.

Lamentations 3:37-39 says, "Who is there who speaks and it comes to pass, unless the Lord has commanded it? Is it not from the mouth of the Most High that both good and ill go forth? Why should any living mortal, or any man, offer complaint in view of his sins?"

The word "ill" (*rāâ* in Hebrew) in verse 38 has an interesting range of meaning. It is translated with various terms that indicate its range: "calamity, evil, misery, trouble, disaster." The full force of this term is felt when we observe that it is used with God as its Sender (Job 2:10; Isaiah 45:7; Amos 3:6). Since God cannot sin (Psalm 5:4; 11:7; 145:17; Isaiah 5:16; Habakkuk 1:13; Hebrews 7:26; James 1:13; 1 Peter 1:14-16), these God-ordained "evils" cannot be understood as immoral or sinful when He sends them. Painful? Yes. Sinful? No.

The apostle Paul provides the most concise synthesis of this idea in Romans 8:28: "We know that God causes all things to work together for good to those who love God, to those who are called according to His purpose." Notice that "all things" are under the comprehensive direction of God's causation for His own purposes. This text does not say that He authors/causes sin, but that He causes all things—including sin—to work out for the good of those who love Him, and are called according to His purpose. The unveiled surprise of this verse is that perceived evils are a divine glove in which God's hand shapes good—but for Christians! Unbelievers have no reason to hope in the midst of difficulty except for the immediate suffering to end. Believers, however, have the assurance that God is causing their suffering to work for their good in time, His glory in eternity, and their increased enjoyment of heaven (Romans 8:18; 2 Corinthians 4:16-18).

Knowing these theological truths may provide understanding and comfort for some. But for most, the problem of pain is more difficult to handle emotionally, when we find ourselves in the middle of trouble and suffering.

The Emotional Problem of Pain

What about our personal pain and hardship? How can we respond?

What hope can be offered to my friends who walked into their baby's room to find him lying lifeless from SIDS? To a 28-year-old friend who was informed he has terminal brain cancer? To a young man in my ministry whose parents and two sisters were killed in a car crash? To loving parents who received a phone call letting them know their son had committed suicide? To my Mom, who called to tell me that she did not think I would make it to her bedside before she lost her final fight with cancer? What hope can be provided for these real people and their real heartaches?

Whether or not we have a philosophical answer to the problem of evil, we will all generate an emotional one when trouble finds us. When tragedy, suffering, and injustice are on God's agenda for His children, how can we respond?

A helpful protocol is to ask and answer three questions: What do I feel? What do I think? What do I believe?

When trials come our way, the first question to answer is, What do I feel? Shattered feelings are the soul's reflex to tragedy. And it is easier to tame wild animals than wounded feelings. When any kind of suffering visits us, we can expect our feelings to spike, sometimes in a predictable manner, other times in surprising ways. But identifying what we are feeling is the first step in generating a godly response. *Do I feel angry, fearful, threatened, sad, abandoned, alone, defensive, combative, embarrassed, jealous, or mistreated?* These are the initial questions to consider. It is remarkable how often we have these feelings without ever identifying and isolating them in our hearts.

The second question to answer is, What do I think? This is where our theology is tested in real life. Our thinking is like a boat with two possible rudders: feelings or beliefs. If left to feelings alone, thinking can become dangerous and erratic. Emotions that spring from difficult circumstances are almost always self-centered, self-protective, and self-interested. To be sure, God designed us with emotions that function protectively, but emotions rarely prompt God-focused thinking, at least at first. While feelings are hardwired to think of self, theology is inherently God-focused. For Christians, how we think must be governed first and foremost by what we know to be true, not by how we feel. Emotions should be the caboose on a train of thinking that is powered by true thoughts about God and His Word.

The third and most important question to answer when trouble comes is, What do I believe? Realities known to be true by faith can easily evaporate into doubt when the heat of emotion is applied. We don't always *feel* like our biblical convictions are true when sorrow and suffering come. Emotions such as fear, anxiety, and hurt can swallow perspective in one gulp. But confidence in theological realities is the only sure anchor in the tempests of trials. Truth can alter the course of our thinking and calm the storm of our emotions—but what truth?

Most of our emotional responses to evil, pain, and suffering fall into two general categories: fear and anger. These two responses are directly tied to theological doubts and their solutions are grounded in theological certainties. Fear has to do with loss, anger with trust.

Whenever there is the threat of loss, fearful anxiety can grip the heart. We fear the loss of anything that we believe will bring us happiness, comfort, joy, or pleasure. The prospect of losing our loved ones, our health, our money, our possessions, or anything we hold dear can stir up feelings of fear and anxiety. But all of these fears can be traced to a theological absence in our own hearts—the absence of confidence in God's sufficiency. In Romans 8:31-39, Paul described the kind of reasoning that should accompany trouble. His reference point is Christ. After writing a long list of the sources of sorrowful possibilities (especially verses 38-39), the persecuted apostle made an impressive theological assessment. These bad things—including tribulation, or distress, persecution, famine, supernatural powers, the past, the future, even death—have no power to "separate us from the love of God, which is in Christ Jesus our Lord" (verse 39; cf. Matthew 28:18; Acts 18:10). Paul pitted these evils against separation from God's love expressed in the gospel. All of these evils are fear-inducing threats, but none as threatening as being forsaken by God. Comforting perspective is gained by reminding ourselves of the gospel—that no threat can undo what God has done for us in Christ. After all, "if God is for us, who is against us?" (verse 31) Reorienting ourselves to the gospel forces us to make helpful comparisons as we realize that the trials of this life are outweighed by the glories promised in the next: "For I consider that the sufferings of this present time are not worthy to be compared with the glory that is to be revealed to us" (Romans 8:18). The apostle compared the worst possible threats to the horror of being separated from God. His argument is compelling. Since nothing can take away his greatest treasure—Christ—any other loss is manageable. This ability to compare the certainty of gospel security to the uncertainty of personal hardship was Paul's emotional and rational anchor.

Appropriate comparing should also bring solace to the angry heart. Difficulties can both whisper and scream the question, "Why?" Asking why something bad has happened is an admission that the event is contrary to our expectations. The default of our emotional expectations is that we don't deserve pain and suffering. Anger reveals a wrong worldview about what we deserve. "Man is born for trouble, as sparks fly upward" (Job 5:7; cf. 14:1). Why do bad things happen? The better question is, Why does so little happen to us? The expectations we have for our lives rarely match what we truly deserve. The greatest threat is eternity in hell. Since hell's threat has been eliminated for believers, any other painful event or circumstance can be relegated to the temporal. Again, Paul's example points toward the ability to compare: "For momentary, light affliction is producing for us an eternal weight of glory far beyond all comparison, while we look not at the things which are seen, but at the things which are not seen; for the things which are seen are temporal, but the things which are not seen are eternal" (2 Corinthians 4:17-18).

The great nineteenth-century Scottish preacher Horatius Bonar isolated the real issue when he wrote, "Man's dislike at God's sovereignty arises from his suspicion of God's heart." He added, "We are not always comfortable with the idea of being wholly at the disposal of God." To be angry at (or about) the events of life is to mistrust a loving God. How can we be suspicious of His heart when we remember His love for us in the gospel? But does God remember us? Is He beyond the reach of pain?

The Cross Is the Solution and Only Hope for Evil and Pain

God has not distanced Himself from the problem of evil. On the contrary, He met it straight on. During Jesus' trial before the Roman procurator of Judea, Pontius Pilate declared that he had the power and authority to determine Jesus' fate. The response of his Galilean prisoner must have been surprising. Jesus answered, "You would have no authority over Me, unless it had been given you from above" (John 19:11). Instead of pleading for His life, the Savior consented to His execution with a footnote. Jesus repudiated Pilate's misapprehension of his own authority and alerted him to the fact that God was the source of his governing power. God is the Conferrer of power and prerogative, not Rome or any other human authority.

The impending crucifixion of the Son of God constituted the greatest evil and injustice ever committed. But there was more going on than met the eye. What Jesus revealed to Pilate was that all perpetrators, conspirators, and evildoers ultimately act under the authority of God. So what was God doing in this horrific event? John Piper answers, "At the all-important pivot of human history, the worst sin ever committed served to show the greatest glory of Christ and obtain the sin-conquering gift of God's grace. God did not just overcome evil at the cross. He made evil commit suicide in doing its worst evil."[2] Any form of evil, every pain, all sorrow, every degree of suffering, each injustice, all sickness, every disease, and any "bad thing"—including death—lost its sting at the cross (cf. 1 Corinthians 15:54-57). God's sacrifice of His Son Jesus demonstrates His mysterious wisdom (Isaiah 53:10). The Father's unfathomable loss and the Son's incomprehensible suffering were the crux of God's predetermined plan for His own everlasting glory and our eternal good. "He who did not spare His own Son, but delivered Him over for us all, how will He not also with Him freely give us all things?" (Romans 8:32). The only appropriate response is to exclaim with Paul, "Oh, the depth of the riches both of the wisdom and knowledge of God! How unsearchable are His judgments and unfathomable His ways!" (Romans 11:33).

Heaven is the time and place where all believers will enjoy the absence of all evil and suffering and the presence of unmitigated joy. The problem of evil is the cry of the soul for that experience. It is placing upon this world expectations that can only be met in heaven. Considering our unworthiness in light of the infinite tributaries of God's goodness, sovereignty, wisdom, grace, and mercy can reset the troubled heart with the power of perspective.

The realities of heaven and hell bring evil and suffering into sharp focus. "For Christians, this present life is the closest they will come to Hell. For unbelievers, it is the closest they will come to Heaven."[3] God uses the troubles of our lives, culminating in the inevitability of our own deaths, to pry our grips off this world and refocus our hearts on what lies ahead with Him. As Maurice Roberts writes, "...the degree of a Christian's peace of mind depends upon his spiritual ability to interpose the thought of God between himself and his anxiety."[4] If a believer can keep his mind on God, no evil in this world can steal his peace. And that will be enough till heaven.

17

WHEN BAD THINGS HAPPEN TO GOD'S PEOPLE

Responding Rightly to Personal Hardship and Trials

IRV BUSENITZ

O n November 19, 1966, Rabbi Harold Kushner's home was rocked by the news that his only son, three-year-old Aaron, was afflicted with an extremely rare disease called *progeria*. Better known as the rapid aging disease, the progeria syndrome dramatically accelerates a person's physical aging. Eleven years later, Aaron passed away, driving Rabbi Kushner to search for answers to the question, How could God allow bad things to happen to good people? When he thought he had found the answer, he wrote the book *When Bad Things Happen to Good People*.

While Kushner's search for answers to his personal crisis is understandable, the title to the book is misleading. First, the reality is that there are no "good" people. Romans 3:23 confirms that "all have sinned and fall short of the glory of God." Isaiah 64:6 adds that "all our righteous deeds are like a filthy garment." Furthermore, Kushner's book is not about what to do *when* bad things happen; rather, it is about *why* bad things happen. The author's pursuit was about *why* or *how* a good God could allow bad things to happen to people whom he felt deserved better. That was really the question on the mind of Rabbi Kushner. He wanted to know *why*.

Habakkuk, in the first two chapters of his book in the Old Testament, asked himself the same question.

Habakkuk's First "Why?" Question (1:2-4)

Habakkuk was an Old Testament prophet who ministered during the final years of the southern kingdom of Judah, about a 100 years after Assyria had taken the northern ten tribes of Israel into captivity (722 B.C.). Following the moral path of her northern sister, Judah was engrossed in rampant sin. Habakkuk, outraged by the iniquity he saw around him, wanted to know why God didn't act. God appeared to be indifferent to Judah's sin, and the prophet asked God, in essence, "Why aren't You doing anything?"

God's Answer (1:5-11)

In reply, the Lord startled Habakkuk with a most unexpected answer: "I *am* doing something; punishment is on its way." God was sending the conquering Chaldeans (Babylonians) under the leadership of His servant, Nebuchadnezzar (Jeremiah 25:9). The picture was not a pretty one. The Chaldeans were a "fierce and impetuous people" who lived by their own rules (Habakkuk 1:6-7). With the swiftness of eagles, the tenacity of leopards, and the cunning of wolves (1:8-10), the Babylonian armies overwhelmed anyone or anything that stood in their path.

Habakkuk's Second "Why?" Question (1:12-17)

Habakkuk was bewildered by God's answer. In the prophet's thinking, God's reply was *unbelievable*. Though Habakkuk was pleased that God had heard his call for action, he was astonished by the drastic punishment God had chosen.

Habakkuk's perplexity is propelled by two concerns. First, Chaldea (Babylon) was *not* just another godless nation; it was the epitome of those who opposed God. The Chaldeans worshipped false gods and military might (1:15-16); yet, astonishingly, it seemed God was prospering their wickedness (1:16-17). Second, in Habakkuk's thinking, God's use of Chaldea as a means to punish Judea was an affront to His holiness! Israel was His "kingdom of priests" (Exodus 19:6). How could God now allow His prized possession (Exodus 19:5) to be overrun by a nation of unclean, uncircumcised, idolatrous "fishermen" (Habakkuk 1:14-17)? Wouldn't this, in essence, be looking with favor on wickedness?

The prophet, in his first query, questioned God's *in*action—evil was everywhere, and God was not doing anything about it. In the second question, he bemoaned God's *action*—something needed to be done, but to use the wicked Chaldeans was too extreme!

God's Answer (2:2-20)

God answered Habakkuk this second time by assuring him that He would judge the Chaldeans too. Emphatically so! They would be looted (2:6-8), shamed (2:9-11), and left to experience firsthand the temporal and vain nature of imperial ambitions (2:12-14). They would be disgraced, devastated (2:15-17), and left to suffer the full impact of the nothingness inherent in idolatry (2:18-19). In comparison to the God of Israel (2:20), the idols of Bel and Nebo could offer no protection from Babylon's certain destruction (cf. 1 Kings 18:27).

Within these judgments on Chaldea, the prophet was given two very important words of comfort. The first came in Habakkuk 2:4: "The righteous will live by his faith." God assured Habakkuk that His use of the Babylonians in no way justified them. Rather, right standing before God is by faith. The just will be both justified and preserved by faith. The second word of comfort came in Habakkuk 2:20: Contrary to the idols of Chaldea, which offered their worshippers no help, the God of Israel was still sovereign; the One who lives forever—the Lord—was still reigning "in His holy temple."

These verses (2:4,20) provided the theological foundation (that salvation is by faith and that God is on His throne) that Habakkuk needed to respond rightly in chapter three. They are the backbone of the book, the lifeline that rescued Habakkuk's thinking. They totally reshaped the prophet's outlook and sculpted his response. As a result, he no longer wanted to know *why*. Instead, he began to focus on how he would respond *when* the judgment and devastation came.

Chapter three provides a glimpse of Habakkuk's reoriented perspective. It offers a paradigm for how all believers should respond to difficult times—five godly responses that should characterize us *when* bad things happen.

Right Response #1: Relate the Matter to God (3:1)

Habakkuk begins by taking the matter to God in prayer. This is a remarkably different Habakkuk than in chapter one. There, he repeatedly demanded to know *why* (1:3, 13 [twice], 14). Not having the full picture, he was clearly struggling with God's plan.

But in 3:1 his response is different, especially noticeable in his attitude. God's words of comfort in 2:4,20 have totally changed his perspective. Yes, he is still very emotional about the whole matter (3:16). The heart is still beating fast! But, instead of telling God how He should respond, the prophet is now telling himself how to respond. He is dealing with his own response to God's perspective.

And remarkably, he begins with prayer. Prayer is the ultimate acknowledgment of God's sovereignty. Why else pray, right? Prayer recognizes that God is sovereign—He is totally in control of the circumstances and has the power to do something about the situation.

Prayer, in the midst of trial, brings strength. It did for Moses (Exodus 32:11; Numbers 14:13; 20:6; Deuteronomy 9:26), David (Psalm 55:16-17), and Daniel (Daniel 6:10; 9:20-23). Jesus, the Great High Priest, facing the ultimate cruelty of the crucifixion and weighed down with the sins of the world, spent His final night in prayer (Matthew 27:36-44; John 17).

We would do well to follow their example. Not only does prayer acknowledge God's sovereignty; it also takes the focus off our circumstances and puts our eyes on God. That is what prayer did for Habakkuk. In the first two chapters of the book, the prophet was focused on his situation. He was operating on the human level, trying to contrast the relative goodness of Israel with the relative wickedness of Babylon.

But once he took his eyes off himself, he caught a glimpse of God in His holiness (2:20), and suddenly those issues faded. Now all he saw was a holy and righteous God. In His instructions to the disciples, Jesus said, "Whatever you ask in My name, that will I do, *that the Father may be glorified*" (John 14:13, emphasis added). We focus so much on the first part of the verse (getting whatever we ask for) that we miss the second part (the goal, which is God's glory). Suddenly the focus is no longer on our need, but on giving glory to God!

Martyn Lloyd-Jones, commenting on this text, puts it this way:

> Our problems can nearly all be traced to our persistence in looking at the immediate problems themselves, instead of looking at them in the light of God. [Habakkuk] had to stop thinking in terms of the fact that the Chaldeans were worse sinners than the Jews and that God was going to use them…That attitude made him forget the sin of his own nation through concentrating on the sin of others, [making him] unhappy in mind and heart. But the prophet came… to see only the wonderful vision of the Lord in His holy temple. When things are seen from a spiritual viewpoint… the holiness of God and the sin of man are the only things that matter.[1]

Prayer may not change your circumstance, but it *will* change your perspective. It changed Habakkuk's perspective, and it will change yours too. That's what prayer does!

Right Response #2: Recognize Your Own Weaknesses (3:2,16)

In the first two chapters, Habakkuk was chaffing and battling (1:2-4; 2:1), challenging God on how to handle the situation regarding Judah's punishment by the Babylonians. He gave the impression that he knew what was best and expected God to respond in his way. But in Habakkuk 3:2,16 the prophet appeared to surrender and submit. And that was not an easy thing to do, because pride can get in the way (1 Peter 5:5-7).

Let's be honest: Habakkuk was still afraid (3:16). His stomach was churning and tied in knots. He knew the devastation would be lengthy; that it would last for *years* (3:2). But notice the contrast. The issue was no longer what Habakkuk wanted; it was now *"Your* work." Realizing that it was God's work and not his own, the prophet prayed that God would revive His work of grace toward Israel and reenact His deeds of power (3:3-15).

Recognizing his weakness, the prophet realized he needed divine strength. That was a crucial step for Habakkuk—and is key for us as well—for a number of reasons:

The first, quite obviously, is the *omniscience factor.* God is omniscient and can see the end from the beginning (Isaiah 46:9-10). We can't! We will never have the full picture (cf. Ephesians 6:12), but God does.

Second, there is the *instrumental factor.* Acknowledging our weakness allows God to work through us. Habakkuk, as a prophet, was to deliver God's message to God's people. Yet in the first two chapters of his book, he had it all wrong. He was telling God what to do! Until Habakkuk learned that he was only the instrument, God couldn't use him. The Lord told Zerubbabel that the building of the temple was "not by might, nor by power, but by My Spirit" (Zechariah 4:6). Gideon was told to first reduce his soldiers from 32,000 to 300; only then could God use him (Judges 7:2-7). We too are only clay pots—the instruments. Until we learn that, we are useless to God. The Lord does not give strength to the self-sufficient; He gives strength to the weak (2 Corinthians 12:9-10).

Third, there is the *maturation factor.* God often uses the valley of trials to expose our weaknesses and mature us. The apostle Paul exhorted us to exult in our trials and difficulties because the results are so grand: perseverance, proven character, and hope (Romans 5:3-4). James similarly commanded us to "consider it all joy" when we "encounter various trials, knowing that the testing of your faith produces endurance" (James 1:2-3). A.W. Tozer observed: "If the truth were known, the saints of God in every age were only effective after they had been wounded."[2]

Right Response #3: Review the Greatness of God (3:3-15)

Faced with the fear of the impending invasion, Habakkuk reminded himself of what he knew to be true. Emotion would not save him; reason would not save him. Only the knowledge of what he knew to be true about God would save him! And so he began reviewing God's great acts on behalf of His people, rehearsing the tremendous ways God had worked among them. Beginning with their deliverance from Egypt and entrance into Canaan, he highlighted God's works in Sinai (3:3), the Shekinah glory and the cloud between Israel and Pharaoh's army (3:4), the plagues in Egypt (3:5), crossing the Red Sea (3:8,15), the sun standing still at Gibeon (3:11), and seemingly even David killing Goliath (3:14).

Look at it this way: When you go to the bank for a loan, you are asked for your credit history. Why? Because the bank wants to know how you responded to loans in the past. Similarly, the record in Scripture is God's credit history. If He was faithful to His people in the past, He can be expected to be faithful in the future. Scripture gives us God's credit history, which we can review through reading (Psalm 119:105-107,109-112), meditation (Psalm 1) and memorization (Psalm 119:11), and even the singing of hymns (Colossians 3:16; cf. Acts 16:25).

Right Response #4: Reaffirm Your Faith in God (3:17-18)

Habakkuk knew the invasion of Nebuchadnezzar would bring massive famine—no food, no flocks or herds, no agricultural produce. Every source of food in ancient Israel is enumerated here, devoured by invading troops and snuffed out by the ravages of war. As a prophet in Israel, Habakkuk knew what Moses, some 800 years earlier, had predicted would happen if Israel failed to stay true to the Lord (Deuteronomy 11:16-17).

In spite of the inevitable gloom, the resolve of Habakkuk is absolutely remarkable. In contrast to his earlier response, the prophet reaffirmed his faith in God. No matter what happened, he would exult and rejoice in the Lord (3:18). Only when we keep our focus on God can we have that kind of perspective. As Joni Eareckson Tada, a quadriplegic for over 40 years, told Larry King, "A wheelchair is my passport to joy and peace in such a way I would never have dreamed possible."

And notice that Habakkuk's resolve came *before* the troubles arrived. Habakkuk knew it was coming, and he was prepared. His choice to exult was firmly established in his heart long before the heat of the trial (cf. Joshua 24:15). Like the prophet, we may not have time to decide the biblical course of action in the midst of a trial. Trials often come upon us unexpectedly and our resolve must be cultivated ahead of time, before the affliction itself clouds our judgment and perspective. That way, we will not be tempted to doubt in the dark the truth we embraced in the light.

Right Response #5: Rest in the Strength of the Lord (3:19)

The first four responses lead us to this amazing conclusion. If the first four take place, finding rest in God is the inevitable result. On the other hand, if the first four are absent, such rest is not possible.

Habakkuk's statement (3:19) is remarkable, especially in light of the earlier chapters. Instead of turmoil and fear (3:16), there is now strength and vitality. The message of 2:4 was being fulfilled in the life of the prophet: "The righteous will live by his faith." This was more than an intellectual assent for Habakkuk; it was a recognition that God was at work for his good and God's glory (2 Corinthians 4:16-18). It was an affirmation and commitment energized by the Spirit's application of the Word to his everyday life.

Every Christian's perspective on life must be invigorated by Habakkuk 2:4! It is not a promise to draw on from time to time as needed; rather, it is a truth designed to carry us continuously throughout our entire lives. Reiterated in the New Testament (Romans 1:17; Galatians

3:11; Hebrews 10:38), it represents the character of God's work in the life of every believer. Justification by faith not only inaugurates salvation, it is also the sum and substance of the believer's life. God's gift of faith initiates regeneration and then energizes and sustains that new life.

As Habakkuk so brilliantly portrays, there is no need to panic. There is no reason to fear or doubt God. Whether or not we see or feel it, God is orchestrating all things for His glory and our good. He is trustworthy. When it comes to trials, the prophet blazed a trail we would do well to follow.

Habakkuk's name means "one who embraces." By the end of the book, the prophet is found embracing God's sovereignty in the face of coming turmoil and suffering. He embraced God's plan because he knew God was faithful. God's credit history invites us to do the same!

18

WHY CHRISTIANS CAN TRUST GOD

Putting Your Hope in Your Heavenly Father

NATHAN BUSENITZ

O ur society is plagued with broken promises. They can be found in the family, at school, and in the workplace. They are present in the government—often in the campaign pledges of one or more aspiring candidates. Sometimes they even come to our very own mailboxes, with false assurances of instant winnings and millions of dollars.

Making a promise but never following through has become an American epidemic. In fact, according to the book *The Day America Told the Truth,* 91 percent of Americans admit to lying regularly. More specifically, 86 percent of Americans routinely lie to their parents, 75 percent to friends, 73 percent to siblings, and 69 percent to spouses.[1] As a result, our nation has developed a healthy sense of skepticism. We are all familiar with the saying that if something sounds too good to be true, it probably is. And when promises are made to us, we're told not to get our hopes up because we will likely be disappointed.

God Doesn't Make Empty Promises

The Bible, on the other hand, *invites* us to get our hopes up. Of course, Scripture is very specific as to what true hope includes. Hoping for instant riches to land in your mailbox is probably foolhardy. But hoping in the promises of God, both for this life and the next, is nothing less than the essence of faith (Hebrews 11:1). Unlike the broken and empty promises of so many people all around us, God's Word never fails (cf. 1 Kings 8:56-58).

But how do we know that we can trust God completely? What guarantees do we have that God will never disappoint?

The Bible gives us many reasons to take solace in God and His Word. Over and over again Scripture commands and compels us to trust God, both for the present and the future. The assurances that comprise our Christian hope are not too good to be true—and they are infinitely better than any earthly guarantee. They are certainties on which we can build both our lives and our eternities. They can be trusted because they come from a God who can be trusted.

In this chapter, we will consider five reasons Christians can confidently hope in God.

His Person: You Can Hope in God Because of Who He Is

First, believers can hope in God's promises because He is absolutely trustworthy—His Word can be trusted because He can be trusted. God's personality backs up the reliability of everything He says. Unlike the stereotypical used-car salesman, God's reputation does not contradict His promises. Thus, we can be confident that every assurance He makes will come to pass exactly as foretold, down to the smallest detail. But what is it about God's person that makes Him so trustworthy? To answer this question, at least three divine attributes must be considered:

1. *God is wise.* Believers can hope in God because He is perfectly wise. Psalm 147:5 notes that His understanding is infinite. And Paul, in Romans 11:33-34, exclaimed, "Oh, the depth of the riches both of the wisdom and knowledge of God! How unsearchable are His judgments and unfathomable His ways!" God needs no additional advice or help because He already possesses infinite understanding. He knows every situation, circumstance, and possibility in complete detail. He is never surprised or caught off guard.

As Christians, we can place our confidence fully in God's decisions because He knows exactly what He is doing. Our response to God's perfect wisdom, then, must be to trust in Him rather than in ourselves or anything else. Even Solomon, the wisest of men, advised, "Trust in the LORD with all your heart and do not lean on your own understanding" (Proverbs 3:5).

2. *God is righteous.* God's perfect righteousness also allows us to hope in Him completely. The Bible is clear: God is absolutely holy, without sin, and morally perfect in every way (Daniel 9:14; 1 John 1:5). In fact, God's holiness is a motivation for our own righteous living. Peter, quoting from Leviticus, urged his readers, "Like the Holy One who called you, be holy yourselves also in all your behavior; because it is written, 'You shall be holy, for I am holy'" (1 Peter 1:15-16).

So how does God's righteousness fit in with His trustworthiness? The answer is simple: Because lying is contrary to God's perfect character (Proverbs 6:16-17; 12:22; cf. John 8:44), His righteousness does not allow Him to have any part in it. Perhaps more to the point, God cannot lie because God cannot sin. His righteousness means that He will never act in any way that compromises or contradicts His perfect holiness. Unlike a crooked politician who says one thing but means another, our holy God always means exactly what He says. He can be trusted because He is pure and breaking His Word would violate His character (see John 17:17).

3. *God is unchanging.* Not only is God perfectly wise and perfectly righteous, but His character never changes. Psalm 102:26-27, contrasting God with His created works, says, "Even they will perish, but You endure; and all of them will wear out like a garment; like clothing. You will change them and they will be changed. But You are the same, and Your years will not come to an end." James 1:17 reiterates this point, noting that in God there is no shifting of shadows. Hebrews 13:8 says, "Jesus Christ is the same yesterday and today and forever." Whereas people are always changing, God remains constant. His character never changes.

God's immutable nature means that He will not suddenly change

His mind about promises He has made. He won't arbitrarily decide that salvation is no longer found in Christ or that eternal life is no longer available. We can trust Him because He is still the same as He has always been and will always be. We can cling tightly to His Word because an unchanging God can only make unchanging promises.

God's person—specifically, His wisdom, righteousness, and unchanging nature—allows us to trust Him because of who He is. His words are certain because His character is certain. On the other hand, for Him to violate His Word would be to contradict Himself. Yet that is not possible, for "it is impossible for God to lie" (Hebrews 6:18).

His Power: You Can Hope in God Because He Is in Control

A second reason to trust God, beyond His dependable character, is His perfect power. Again, the Bible is very clear: God is in control of everything at every moment of every day. His power is infinite, knowing no viable rivals or exclusions. God alone is King and He is King over all. Here are some passages that affirm the truth that God wields absolute authority:

- God is sovereign over Satan and demons (Job 1:12; 2:6; Luke 8:31; 22:31; 1 Corinthians 15:25; Revelation 20:10-15).

- God is sovereign over evil and sin (Proverbs 16:4; Lamentations 3:38; Luke 5:21).

- God is sovereign over the nations (2 Chronicles 20:6; Psalm 20:7; Proverbs 21:1; John 19:11; Acts 17:26; Romans 13:2).

- God is sovereign over nature, including natural disasters (Psalm 50:10; 107:29; Amos 4:7; Nahum 1:3-6; Matthew 5:45; Luke 8:24).

- God is sovereign over sickness, disease, and death (Exodus 15:26; Deuteronomy 32:39; 2 Kings 20:5; Matthew 4:23; Mark 6:56; John 9:3; 11:4; Acts 4:29-30; 1 Corinthians 15:26).

- God is sovereign over other people and their decisions

(Exodus 8:15; Ezra 6:22; Proverbs 21:1; Acts 13:48; Romans 9:17-18).

- God is sovereign over our personal plans (Proverbs 16:9; 19:21; James 4:13-15).

- God is sovereign over "chance" and "fate" (Job 20:29; Proverbs 16:33; Jonah 1:3-10; Acts 1:24-27).

- God is sovereign over everything in the universe (Psalm 115:3; 135:6; Romans 8:38-39; Ephesians 1:11).

Is there anything in the universe outside of God's control? No! Every potential danger we might face in life is under the supervision of an all-powerful God. Of course, this does not excuse us of our responsibilities—such as resisting temptation (James 4:7) or being properly prepared for the future (Nehemiah 4:9). But it does mean that we can put our hope fully in God and His guarantees. Because He is in control of all things, no circumstance, setting, or individual exists or acts without God's permission. So, when God promises to save us, we can be confident that nothing "will be able to separate us from the love of God, which is in Christ Jesus our Lord" (Romans 8:39). Nothing can thwart God's promises because, quite simply, His power won't allow it (John 10:28-29).

What comfort there is in knowing that nothing in this universe is greater than our God! Even the most powerful natural and man-made forces are subject to His reign. What comes to your mind when you think of great power? Maybe it is the military might of the United States military, which has well over a million soldiers in active duty, with personnel in more than 130 countries. Perhaps it is an earthquake or a volcano. Mount St. Helens, for example, was triggered by a 5.1-magnitude earthquake, shooting fire and lava 15 miles into the air. Or maybe it is the heavy winds of a hurricane or the brilliant flashes of a thunderstorm. Lightning bolts average 2 to 3 miles long with a current of 100 million volts, but some can stretch up to 75 miles in length.

You might think of the sea and the creatures that live there. The ocean covers 71 percent of the earth's surface, its deepest point being almost seven miles down. Or perhaps your thoughts turn to outer space, where the sun's volume alone could fit 1.3 million earths—and there are innumerable other stars that are larger than the sun. You may even contemplate spiritual forces, Satan and his minions, and the power they wield. Yet no matter what comes to your mind, God is more powerful still. He is the One who names and numbers the stars (Psalm 147:4), who regards the nations as a speck of dust (Isaiah 40:15), who quiets the seas with a word (Job 26:12; Matthew 8:26), and who will one day win the final victory (1 Corinthians 15:20-28). If God is our Refuge and Strength, we have nothing to fear (Psalm 62:6-8).

His Plan: You Can Hope in God Because He Knows Exactly What He's Doing

If God were merely all-powerful, haphazardly wielding brute force at random spurts throughout the universe, we might have reason to be anxious. But, as we have seen, God is not only all-powerful, He is also all-wise. This means He has a perfect plan that He is faithfully working out in history (Isaiah 25:1). In Isaiah 46:10 God describes Himself as "declaring the end from the beginning, and from ancient times things which have not been done, saying, 'My purpose will be established, and I will accomplish all My good pleasure.'" Psalm 33:11 echoes, "The counsel of the LORD stands forever, the plans of His heart from generation to generation." But what does God's plan include? The answer comes in at least two parts.

1. *God's plan mandates that He receive maximum glory.* Scripture says everyone and everything was created by God to bring Him glory and praise (1 Chronicles 16:2; 29:11; Psalm 8:1; 19:1; Isaiah 43:7; Ezekiel 43:2; 1 Corinthians 10:31). In fact, the primary reason God saved us was to further His reputation as a gracious God—that we would praise Him for His mercy (Romans 9:15-24). God's passion for His glory is not only right, but should be our greatest passion as well. He is the only One in the universe worthy of our honor and praise.

God's passion for His reputation guarantees that He will keep the promises He has made to His children. We can wholeheartedly trust God's Word because His name is at stake (cf. Exodus 32:9-14). For the sake of His glory, He will certainly follow through on what He has said He will do.

2. *God's plan mandates that believers receive maximum good.* In perfect conjunction with His glory, God's plan also includes the well-being of His people. The apostle Paul declares that "God causes all things to work together for good to those who love God, to those who are called according to His purpose" (Romans 8:28). God uses every circumstance and person in our lives for our spiritual betterment, to make us more like Christ. Granted, the good sometimes comes in the form of discipline (Hebrews 12:10) or trials (James 1:2-3). Yet even these are for our good, that through repentance or endurance we would grow stronger in the faith. God's definition of good does not necessarily include the temporal pleasures and wealth we so often desire. Rather, He defines it in terms of spiritual growth and eternal benefit.

In His perfect wisdom, God's plan merges both His passion for His glory and His concern for our good. Consequently, we find our greatest joy and satisfaction (or good) when we are pursuing Him—and His glory—most vigorously. And vice versa. As John Piper says, "God is most glorified in us when we are most satisfied in Him."[2]

Because God's plan includes our good, we can rest confidently in Him and His Word. Not only are His promises unbreakable because His reputation is at stake, but they are also spiritually beneficial. They can be trusted because they were made with our best interest in mind.

His Past Record: You Can Hope in God Because He's Been Faithful Before

Another reason we can embrace God and His Word is because He has never broken a promise. His track record is perfect. He has always kept His Word in the past and He will continue to do so in the future. The biblical record is clear: God is impeccably faithful.

In Psalm 100:5, we read, "The LORD is good; His lovingkindness is everlasting and His faithfulness to all generations." Earlier in the Psalms, Asaph overcame his despair by remembering "the deeds of the LORD; surely I will remember Your wonders of old" (Psalm 77:11). And 1 Chronicles 16:15 notes that God will "remember His covenant forever, the word which He commanded to a thousand generations." Ethan, in discussing God's promises to David, announced, "I will sing of the lovingkindness of the LORD forever; to all generations I will make known Your faithfulness with my mouth" (Psalm 89:1). And Psalm 119:90, speaking to God, echoes, "Your faithfulness continues throughout all generations."

God's faithfulness is not just an abstract part of who He is. Instead, it is an attribute that has been proven throughout history time and time again. As Christians, by remembering God's provision and protection in the past, we can hope expectantly in Him for the present and the future. Even in the midst of trials and suffering we can be confident that He who was faithful before is still faithful in all He does (Psalm 33:4).

His Parental Care: You Can Hope in God Because He Loves You

A final reason to trust God is found in the love He has for His children. In the Old Testament, God demonstrated His love to Israel again and again (Exodus 34:6-7; Deuteronomy 23:5). Over 25 times, in Psalms alone, is God's love called "unfailing" (see, for example, Psalm 6:4; 21:7; 90:14 NIV). We can trust in (Psalm 13:5) and "rejoice and be glad in" (Psalm 31:7) the love of God. Solomon, in 2 Chronicles 6:14, referred to God's promises as covenants of love (see also Nehemiah 1:5). Even Jeremiah, after Jerusalem's destruction, found comfort in His unfailing love (Lamentations 3:32).

God's great love for His children is found in the New Testament as well. It was on account of His great love that God sent His Son to this world (John 3:16; Ephesians 2:4; Titus 3:4; 1 John 4:19). Christ's death was the ultimate proof: "God demonstrates His own love toward us, in that while we were yet sinners, Christ died for us" (Romans 5:8). It was out of His love that He predestined us to salvation (Ephesians 1:4-5; 1 Thessalonians 4:9). Even in disciplining His children, it is God's love, not His wrath, that motivates His hand (Hebrews 12:6).

First Corinthians 13:8 clearly states that "love never fails." If God who is love (1 John 4:8) loves us (1 John 4:10), then we can be confident that He will never fail or forsake us (Romans 8:38-39; Hebrews 13:5). With Paul we can confidently assert that "hope does not disappoint, because the love of God has been poured out within our hearts through the Holy Spirit who was given to us" (Romans 5:5). We can cling to God's promises because He guarantees them as a loving Father.

Putting It All Together

We began this chapter by noting that this world is filled with false hopes and half-truths. From television ads to junk mail to electronic spam, our lives are inundated with empty promises. Even in places we might not expect, things are not always what they seem—a fact humorously illustrated by the statue of John Harvard that sits in Harvard Yard:

> For a university whose motto is "Veritas," you would expect the truth, the whole truth, and nothing but the truth. But check out the statue of the venerable school's namesake, John Harvard, standing right in front of University Hall. It's a pack of lies. In fact, it is informally called the Statue of Three Lies.
>
> The inscription beneath the statue reads JOHN HARVARD, FOUNDER, 1638. Not a word of it is true.
>
> John Harvard was not the founder of Harvard University. The college (it was a college back then) was founded in 1636 by the Massachusetts Bay Colony in what was then the village of Newtowne and later became Cambridge. John Harvard was an early benefactor of the college and it was named for him in 1639 after he donated his library to the school. Nor is the statue a likeness of John Harvard. There were no pictures or images of him, so the sculptor, Daniel Chester French,

randomly chose a student as his model and dressed him in seventeenth-century garb.[3]

In spite of what the inscription claims, John Harvard was not the founder of Harvard; the university wasn't founded in 1638, and the statue's likeness is not even of its namesake! All this in front of Harvard's University Hall, where the motto, ironically, is "Veritas" (which means "truth").

Like the Harvard motto, the Bible also claims the title "Truth." But unlike the statue of John Harvard, the Bible does not give us a false impression of who God is. It is His own self-revelation, and the claims that He makes are not stretched or misleading. Rather, they are absolutely certain. His attributes, as described in His Word, are not human inventions or mythical enhancements; they are the essence of who He really is. His Word is true because He is true, and we can wholeheartedly trust in Him.

The hope God offers His children is much more than just wishful thinking. The promises He has made to us are certain. They cannot be foiled because He is always in control. They cannot be broken because He always keeps His Word. Biblical hope is true hope. It can be embraced with confidence because of the God who guarantees it: "I am the LORD; those who hope in me will not be disappointed" (Isaiah 49:23 NIV). Our response, as Hebrews 10:23 urges, should be to "hold fast the confession of our hope without wavering, for He who promised is faithful."

Help for the Hurting and Hope for the Lost

Mercy Ministries and the Great Commission

Jesse Johnson

A few months ago, a Grace Community Church missionary was driving in Uganda when he saw a crowd gathered on the side of the road. He stopped his car, and discovered that a man had been hit by a car and left for dead. The man was still breathing, but he was quickly losing blood and the police were unable to locate an ambulance. The missionary scooped up the man, put him in his car, and took him to a hospital. He stayed while the doctors amputated the man's leg at the thigh. Days later, when the victim was released from the hospital, he had nowhere to go, so the missionary family opened their house to him, and he moved in. As the weeks went by, not only did the man learn to walk again, but he came to faith in Christ through the witness of this family.

What is one of the Bible's most frequent commands—to love and care for the poor and destitute—can sometimes seem abstract until the opportunity presents itself in an immediate way to care for the needy in our lives. When it does, the authenticity of our faith is put on display.

In the United States, legitimate opportunities to show mercy to the truly destitute can seem minimal. This is partly because many Americanized Christians have allowed their work ethic to eclipse the commands of Scripture to care for the poor. The average American has a view of poverty similar to the Jews' view of blindness in John 9—it has to be the result of someone's sin.

And there can be an element of truth to that. As a "Local Outreach Pastor," I have spent much time witnessing to the homeless. By far the most common reaction I receive to an offer of food or shelter is a critique of the quality of what is offered (e.g., "I don't like that shelter; they have a curfew"). It quickly becomes apparent that some needy people will accept help only on their terms—and thus cannot be helped. And sometimes giving out money isn't the right answer, either. So why, and how, should Christians respond to those in need?

The Foundation of Mercy Ministry: God's Compassion

Mercy ministry refers to meeting the needs of the poor and destitute, the widows and orphans, especially in the church but also in the world (Galatians 6:10). James describes this kind of ministry as religion that is "pure and undefiled" (James 1:27). It is a form of ministry that is woven into the fabric of Scripture because it has its foundation in the character of God Himself.

In the Mosaic law, if a person took a coat from someone as a pledge for future payment, he had to give the coat back by nightfall so the owner of the coat would not get cold. That was a fairly innocuous command, but notice the reason it was given: "for that is his only covering; it is his cloak for his body. What else shall he sleep in? And it shall come about that when he cries out to Me, I will hear him, for I am gracious" (Exodus 22:27). The Jews were to show compassion to the poor in their midst because they served a compassionate God. Moreover, the Jews were to never completely harvest their land so the poor could always find food (Leviticus 19:10; 23:22). While there were many specific commands throughout the law on how to care for the poor in Israel, here is a general one: "If there is a poor man with you, one of your brothers, in any of your towns in your land which the

L ORD your God is giving you, you shall not harden your heart, nor close your hand from your poor brother" (Deuteronomy 15:7).

Dozens of Old Testament verses stress the importance of showing compassion to those in need. Significantly, they are not followed by exceptions or disclaimers if the poverty was the result of rash decisions or sin. Often poverty *is* the result of foolish living. Nevertheless, to neglect the needy who cross our paths is to sin. It is worth noting that God destroyed Sodom not only for sexual perversion, but also because the people did not show respect to the poor (Ezekiel 16:49). Israel was exiled in large part because the people neglected to care for their poor (Jeremiah 5:28-29; Amos 5:12). The poor, who have no hope in this world, will always have hope in God because He is compassionate. He is the hope of the poor because He loves them and is gracious toward them (Psalm 12:5). Because God will defend those in poverty, Job could write, "so the poor have hope" (Job 5:16 NIV).

Throughout their history, the Jews did not keep the Sabbath year nor the year of Jubilee. They by and large ignored the commands of Deuteronomy 15, which is one of the reasons they were exiled. If they would not remember the poor, God would not remember them, and they would lose their land.

In the New Testament, God's compassion for the poor is restated and reaffirmed. When Zacchaeus repented, he gave half of his wealth to the poor (Luke 19:8). Jesus often used giving to the poor as a basic standard of righteousness (Matthew 19:21; Luke 14:13), and even specifically blessed them (Luke 6:20). When Paul received his ordination for ministry, he was charged with a different task than the other apostles. He was sent to the Gentiles, while they continued working among the Jews. When the apostles sent Paul out, they gave him only one specific charge: "They only asked us to remember the poor—the very thing I also was eager to do" (Galatians 2:10). How Paul fulfilled that command is noted in his epistles. He took collections from various churches to help meet the needs of destitute believers in Jerusalem (Romans 15:26). In fact, he told the church in Corinth to take this collection every week so that when he arrived, there would be no shortage for the poor in the Jerusalem church (1 Corinthians 16:1-4). It is evident that a care for the poor and needy, especially within the church, is a mark of New Testament ministry.

Is Compassion a Corporate or an Individual Command?

In the Old Testament, Israel was to show compassion to the poor in part because this was a way of displaying the wisdom of God through the Mosaic law (see Deuteronomy 4:5-7). When God was working through a nation, His nation had corporate commands that the people were held accountable to obey. Keeping those commands was a powerful evangelistic tool. Other nations would see how compassionate the people of Israel were and be drawn to the Lord because of the Jews' obedience (Deuteronomy 4:5-7; 1 Kings 8:41-43; 10:8-9).

But in the New Testament, God stopped working through the nation of Israel. At Pentecost, He began working through His church. In the Old Testament, Jews were not commanded to go into all the world and preach the gospel. They were commanded to stay in Israel and keep the Mosaic law so that the world would see the glory of God through their obedience. But in the New Testament, Christians are called to go into all the world and preach the gospel. When people receive the gospel and become believers, they are then added to the church, and they obey God out of their love for Him.

It should be noted at this point that there is a careful distinction in the New Testament between tasks given to the church corporately and tasks given to Christians individually. Individual Christians are to love their neighbors, their enemies, and those in need. They are to meet needs where they see them, as they are able. A Christian's first duty is to care for the needs of his family; his second duty is to meet the needs of those in the church; and his third duty is to those outside the church (Galatians 6:9-10; 1 Timothy 4:10; 5:4,8). Meanwhile, the church's main task is to spread the gospel throughout the world by equipping the saints for the work of the ministry. In addition, the church is called to care for the widows and the poor in her midst. In other words, the church is to care for Christians. The thrust of biblical commands concerning the poor, which were given to the church as a whole, relates to taking care of the needs of Christians, and not the poor in general.

When people look to the church to end poverty, halt human trafficking, bring drinking water to Africa, or cure AIDS, they are looking in the wrong place. The church was not commissioned to do any of these tasks. Elders are not appointed based on their ability to politic or irrigate. But as individual Christians live holy lives, they will inevitably find themselves in situations where they can make a difference.

Clarity is needed about what the Bible calls and does not call Christians to do. We are not called to end global hunger, fight homelessness, or feel guilty about having running water. We are called to show compassion to the poor, to open our hearts to them, to spread the gospel, and to hate materialism. We are to make sacrifices to advance the gospel around the world. And as the church is strengthened around the world, there will be more Christians loving the poor and caring for orphans in the neediest of places.

The Bible lays the obligation for mercy ministry at the feet (and in the hearts) of individuals. Individuals are called to love the poor and care for the needy as they have opportunity. Hiding behind a donation is not sufficient. As Paul explained in 1 Corinthians 13:3, it is possible to give all you have to the poor without loving them. But with such action, God is not pleased.

Mercy Ministry and Materialism

Why is it that Americans, who are some of the richest people in the world, are so quick to be calloused toward the poor? In some sense, it may be because we are immune to real poverty. Because of government intervention, social services, and the generosity of countless organizations, people generally do not starve to death in the United States. This does not minimize the suffering that many Americans do face—it can be difficult to provide for a family, to find work, or make rent. But for the most part, homelessness in America looks like a choice between shelters. And people understand that reality. They understand that the person on the side of the street with the "Will work for beer" sign is not the face of real poverty.

Thus there is a tension in many American churches between mercy ministry and "real" ministry, as though the two were mutually exclusive. To make matters worse, most ministries that do focus on mercy are so liberal or theologically unfocused that pastors steer their people *away* from them. It is possible, however, for churches to faithfully fulfill their primary duties (evangelizing the lost and edifying the saints) while also caring for the material needs of those in their midst. It is also possible for pastors to train their people to care for others as they spread the gospel through the context of their everyday lives.

So it must be unequivocally stated that Christians are to show mercy and kindness to all with whom they interact, both inside and outside the church. A shrewd business person may build bigger barns while closing his heart to his brother in need, but he cannot do so while having a true relationship with God (cf. Luke 12:16-21). The American Dream may prompt people to pursue health, wealth, and prosperity, but the gospel prompts Christians to a life of stewardship and sacrifice, all the while fleeing the love of money and cultivating a love for others.

Mercy Ministry and Missions

At the same time, it's important to note that the most needy people in the world are generally not in the United States, but overseas. Most of the poor in the world languish under the grip of corrupt governments and false religions. In many countries, disease is rampant, government is indifferent, and religion is oppressive. While poverty in the United States may look like food stamps, public transportation, and a lack of health insurance (and in extreme cases involves homelessness), in southern Africa, poverty looks like not having running water and dying of AIDS by age 30.

Because of this, many churches have rightly captured a passion for mercy ministry and focused their efforts overseas. In recent years there has been a push from evangelicals in the United States to take drinking water to Central America and mosquito nets to Africa. This resurgence of compassion is encouraging and is already making an impact in many countries that otherwise would be closed to missionaries.

However, mosquito nets are not the end for which God created the world. It is critical for churches to view missions for what they are: the expansion and strengthening of the church of Jesus Christ around the world. Consider this comment from the president of Detroit Baptist Seminary: "All missionary ministry should be intricately connected to the planting of local churches. Church planting is not *one* of the things that missionaries do—it is *the* thing!"[1] God's plan for social transformation is the gospel. Corruption will never be eliminated, and the poor we will always have with us. But the church in America can use her wealth to bring the gospel into the midst of poverty, and in doing so, lives will be changed. This is what it means to love the poor.

God's character is put on display in the ministry of His missionaries. A church can be established in the slums of México because the members of the church will love the poor there. A church can be established in Johannesburg because Christians will show South Africans the love that God has for them by the way the Christians love the orphans. As churches are established and pastors are trained, lasting social change comes. This change is never the primary goal, but is always a byproduct of authentic Christian living.

Compassion: Living with Love

To summarize, Christians are called to love the poor whom God brings their way, and this call cannot be fulfilled simply by writing a check or attending a church that has mercy ministries. It can only be fulfilled on an individual level—by fighting materialism, giving to missionaries, showing kindness to everyone we meet, and making sacrifices to promote the spread of the gospel. This kind of sacrificial living amplifies the gospel by demonstrating the love of Christ in addition to declaring it.

When that Grace Community Church missionary scooped up the bleeding body he found on the side of the road in Uganda, he did more than just minister to an anonymous man. He validated his ministry, and he validated the love of God as seen in the gospel. He showed the people there what kind of love God has for the world, and he encouraged others to show the same kind of love. It is surprisingly simple: When all is said and done, mercy ministry looks like nothing more than Christians being faithful to the Great Commission and being obedient to genuinely love people wherever they go. This is true mercy ministry, and this is true religion. We are to in turn be faithful to minister to those around us and to live sacrificially so that we can send people to places where needs are greater. This is the means God has established to bring hope to this hurting and broken world.

A Hope That's Fixed in a World That's Broken

The Gospel as God's Solution for Our Fallen World

Kevin Edwards

As the previous chapters have made clear, the world we live in is broken. Evil is abundant, righteousness is rare, crime is increasing, poverty is epidemic, natural disaster is imminent, and even the world as we know it is in jeopardy (though public opinion wavers as to whether global warming or global terror is the bigger threat to our planet). Why is the world falling apart? What can we do to make things right again? The Bible not only identifies the source of our world's problems, it also gives us the solution.

Our Fallen World

Our world is broken, but things were not always this way. When God first made the world, His evaluation of creation was that it was "very good" (Genesis 1:31). A holy God created a perfect world where He could lovingly care for man, and where man could perfectly respond with thankful devotion to his Creator. But when sin came on the scene, creation was contaminated and everything changed.

Broken Planet

The fall of man into sin resulted in man's ejection from God's perfect creation, placing the world on a path leading ultimately to destruction by its Creator (Genesis 3:24; 2 Peter 3:10; cf. Romans 8:20-22). Not long after the fall, the world plunged so deeply into sin that God judged the earth by destroying almost every human being and animal on the face of it (Genesis 6–7). This judgment was not an unrestrained reaction by God to man's evil heart. In fact, the potential for the destructive flood was something that God had designed and built into this world at creation. He made the earth with water hovering over its surface and with vast reservoirs of water under its surface (Genesis 1:7; 2 Peter 3:5-6). The world that God created was "formed out of water" (2 Peter 3:5), and it was this same water that God used to bring destruction by the Flood.

God did not completely destroy the earth with the Flood, but there will be an ultimate destruction in the Creator's plan in which everything sin has contaminated will be consumed. The apostle Peter described the coming destruction with these words: "By His word the present heavens and earth are being reserved for fire, kept for the day of judgment and destruction of ungodly men…But the day of the Lord will come like a thief, in which the heavens will pass away with a roar and the elements will be destroyed with intense heat, and the earth and its works will be burned up…the heavens will be destroyed by burning, and the elements will melt with intense heat!" (2 Peter 3:7,10,12).

The Creator has planned precisely how and when this world will end, and neither global warming nor global terrorism will be to blame. Just as with the Flood, the final destruction will be God's doing. This earth will not last forever. But a new earth will be created in its place, one which will last forever because it will never be touched by sin.

Broken Sinners

God could have destroyed the world at the moment of man's first sinful deviation from His will, but He instead responded with patience and kindness, offering mankind the opportunity to be made right with Him (Romans 2:4). Rather than readily embracing God's offer to be reconciled, man—in his rebellion—runs at full speed away from God. Instead of acknowledging the God of creation and finding meaning and purpose in Him, sinners deliberately suppress what they know about God, choosing to live without true purpose or sense (Romans 1:18-22).

Because sinners have rejected Him, God has abandoned them to their sin. The disastrous result of this is seen in human societies where sexual passion knows no restraint, where homosexual perversions are celebrated, and where each individual's conscience is terminally warped and full of corruption. Though man continually and blatantly rebels against Him, God patiently withholds the outpouring of His holy wrath against sin (Romans 1:18,24-32). Yet judgment is certainly coming.

Broken Souls

Is there anything that sinners can do to save themselves while there is still time, while God is still withholding final judgment on this broken world? God answers this question throughout the Bible, clearly showing how capable fallen man is to save himself:

> The LORD saw that the wickedness of man was great on the earth, and that every intent of the thoughts of his heart was only evil continually (Genesis 6:5).

> There is no one who does good. God has looked down from heaven upon the sons of men to see if there is anyone who understands, who seeks after God. Every one of them has turned aside; together they have become corrupt; there is no one who does good, not even one (Psalm 53:1-3).

> All of us have become like one who is unclean, and all our righteous deeds are like a filthy garment; all of us wither like a leaf, and our iniquities, like the wind, take us away (Isaiah 64:6).

> There is none righteous, not even one; there is none who understands, there is none who seeks for God (Romans 3:10-11).

All have sinned and fall short of the glory of God (Romans 3:23).

These and other passages make it clear that man's situation is hopeless, because there is nothing he can do in his own efforts to remedy his terminal condition. He is broken at the core with a corrupt heart that is capable only of sin. Thoroughly enslaved to sin, he is incapable of freeing himself from bondage. In fact, he is spiritually dead with no hope for eternal life or salvation without supernatural help from God.

Restoration Through Christ

Man's sin completely prevents him from being able, in his own wisdom or strength, to reestablish communion and peace with God. Many people try to seek after God through one of the myriad of religions in the world today, but no man-made religion can change the soul. The only reliable solution for man's problem of sin and separation from God is found in God's true Word, where the Lord Himself reveals the absolute truth about everything that man needs to know concerning his soul (Psalm 19; 119; 2 Timothy 3:16-17).

Souls Made Right in Christ

In the Bible, God declares that Jesus Christ is the only hope for guilty sinners before a holy God. Jesus Christ is eternally God and Lord of all (John 1:1-3,14; Philippians 2:9-11; Colossians 2:9). Being the second person of the Trinity, fully possessing all the excellencies of divinity, Christ became a sinless man, God incarnate—the only one who could pay the penalty for sin by dying on the cross and bringing salvation to all who would believe in Him (Isaiah 53:5-6; 2 Corinthians 5:21; Ephesians 1:7; Hebrews 4:15; 1 Peter 2:22-23). Christ's death paid the punishment that believing sinners deserved. Moreover, through the power of His Spirit, believers are freed from the power of sin and renewed from the inside out.

Christ's resurrection from the dead confirmed that God accepted

Christ's sacrifice. Those who embrace Jesus Christ and His sacrifice receive divine forgiveness for their sin and are made right before God (1 Corinthians 15:3-4; Colossians 1:20; 1 Peter 2:24; 3:18). Jesus' bodily resurrection also guaranteed a future resurrection for believers (John 5:26-29; 14:19; Romans 4:25; 6:5-10; 1 Corinthians 15:20,23). In resurrected bodies that are free from sin, believers will worship their Savior for all of eternity.

Sinners Made Holy in Christ

In order to be saved, sinners must truly believe in the Lord Jesus Christ (Acts 16:30-31), meaning, as Paul told the Romans, "If you confess with your mouth Jesus as Lord, and believe in your heart that God raised Him from the dead, you will be saved" (Romans 10:9). This is much more than a flippant or halfhearted decision for the sake of eternal fire insurance. The sinner must repent and turn from his sin to follow and trust Christ as Savior and as Lord (Ezekiel 18:30,32; Luke 9:23; 24:46-47; 1 Thessalonians 1:9).

The cost is high to follow Christ—it costs everything—and anyone desiring to be a disciple of Christ must consider this, as Jesus Himself pointed out:

> If anyone comes to Me, and does not hate his own father and mother and wife and children and brothers and sisters, yes, and even his own life, he cannot be My disciple. Whoever does not carry his own cross and come after Me cannot be My disciple. For which one of you, when he wants to build a tower, does not first sit down and calculate the cost to see if he has enough to complete it? Otherwise, when he has laid a foundation and is not able to finish, all who observe it begin to ridicule him, saying, 'This man began to build and was not able to finish.' Or what king, when he sets out to meet another king in battle, will not first sit down and consider whether he is strong enough with ten thousand men to encounter the one coming against him with twenty thousand? Or else, while the other is still far away, he sends a delegation and asks for terms

of peace. So then, none of you can be My disciple who does
not give up all his own possessions (Luke 14:26-33).

As new believers in Christ turn from their sin and pursue Christ,
God does not leave them alone in the journey. When sinners are saved,
they are instantaneously declared to be righteous before God, and
their hearts are made new to desire to seek after God (1 Corinthians
1:30; 2 Corinthians 5:17; Hebrews 10:14). The Holy Spirit indwells
them and works to bring them closer to Christ through obedience to
God's Word. This work is continued throughout the life of the believer,
bringing increasing holiness and a life that is more and more Christlike
(Romans 6:1-22; 2 Corinthians 3:18; 1 Thessalonians 5:23). The power
of the indwelling Holy Spirit enables victory over sin in the daily battle
against the flesh throughout the earthly life of the believer (Galatians
5:16-25; Philippians 3:12; Colossians 3:9-10; 1 Peter 1:14-16).

World Made New in Christ

In Christ the believer's hope goes beyond victory over sin in this life,
as believers and all of creation expectantly wait for the return and reign
of the glorified Christ on this earth. When He comes, the suffering,
opposition, and corruption of this world will give way to the glorious,
eternal, incorruptible splendor of our Lord (Romans 8:18-25).

While the saints eagerly wait for the Savior to make all things new,
unbelievers mistakenly assume that everything in our world will continue year after year just as it has in the past (2 Peter 3:3). The truth is
that creation is being sustained by God for ultimate judgment, when
everything will be destroyed by fire (2 Peter 3:7,10,12). Those who
are unsaved will spend eternity in conscious punishment in the lake
of fire (Matthew 25:41; Revelation 20:11-15). But those who are in
Christ will enjoy eternal life on a new earth where everything is right
and sin is no more. There, believers will worship their Savior and fellowship with Him face to face, and God will dwell among redeemed
men (Revelation 21–22).

God's Solution Is the Gospel

We began this chapter by noting that the world is broken. Even unbelievers recognize this fact. But the solution cannot be found in science, politics, philosophy, or any other human endeavor. Like those who put bandages on cancer, sinners err when they focus on temporal and material fixes for eternally significant spiritual problems. The reality is that our broken world cannot be fixed until God creates a new one; nor can the broken hearts of those who inhabit our world be fixed until God gives them a new heart. Thus, the gospel of Jesus Christ is the only lasting hope that our world has—not an uncertain hope, but one that is completely sure, secured by God Himself.

> If God is for us, who can be against us? He who did not spare his own Son, but gave him up for us all—how will he not also, along with him, graciously give us all things? Who will bring any charge against those whom God has chosen? It is God who justifies. Who is he that condemns? Christ Jesus, who died—more than that, who was raised to life—is at the right hand of God and is also interceding for us. Who shall separate us from the love of Christ? Shall trouble or hardship or persecution or famine or nakedness or danger or sword? As it is written: "For your sake we face death all day long; we are considered as sheep to be slaughtered."
>
> No, in all these things we are more than conquerors through him who loved us. For I am convinced that neither death nor life, nor angels nor demons, neither the present nor the future, nor any powers, neither height nor depth, nor anything else in all creation, will be able to separate us from the love of God that is in Christ Jesus our Lord (Romans 8:31-39 NIV).

TOPICAL
REFERENCE
GUIDE

Topical Reference Guide

Though this is not an exhaustive list of Scripture verses relevant to key issues, our hope is that this will help you begin to develop right thinking about these topics.

Addiction (including Substance Abuse)

Proverbs 20:1—Wine is a mocker, strong drink a brawler, and whoever is intoxicated by it is not wise.

Romans 6:12-18—Do not let sin reign in your mortal body so that you obey its lusts, and do not go on presenting the members of your body to sin as instruments of unrighteousness; but present yourselves to God as those alive from the dead, and your members as instruments of righteousness to God. For sin shall not be master over you, for you are not under law but under grace.

What then? Shall we sin because we are not under law but under grace? May it never be! Do you not know that when you present yourselves to someone as slaves for obedience, you are slaves of the one whom you obey, either of sin resulting in death, or of obedience resulting in righteousness? But thanks be to God that though you were slaves of sin, you became obedient from the heart to that form of teaching to which you were committed, and having been freed from sin, you became slaves of righteousness.

Romans 13:13-14—Let us behave properly as in the day, not in carousing and drunkenness, not in sexual promiscuity and sensuality, not in strife and jealousy. But put on the Lord Jesus Christ, and make no provision for the flesh in regard to its lusts.

1 Corinthians 6:12,19-20—All things are lawful for me, but not all things are profitable. All things are lawful for me, but I will not be mastered by anything...Or do you not know that your body is a temple of the Holy Spirit who is in you, whom you have from God, and that you are not your own? For you have been bought with a price: therefore glorify God in your body.

Ephesians 5:18—Do not get drunk with wine, for that is dissipation, but be filled with the Spirit.

Hebrews 12:1-2—Since we have so great a cloud of witnesses surrounding us, let us also lay aside every encumbrance and the sin which so easily entangles us, and let us run with endurance the race that is set before us, fixing our eyes on Jesus, the author and perfecter of faith.

2 Peter 2:19—By what a man is overcome, by this he is enslaved.

Anger and Violence

Proverbs 20:22—Do not say, "I will repay evil"; Wait for the LORD, and He will save you.

Matthew 5:21-22—You have heard that the ancients were told, "You shall not commit murder" and "Whoever commits murder shall be liable to the court." But I say to you that everyone who is angry with his brother shall be guilty before the court; and whoever says to his brother, "You good-for-nothing," shall be guilty before the supreme court; and whoever says, "You fool," shall be guilty enough to go into the fiery hell.

Romans 12:17-21—Never pay back evil for evil to anyone. Respect what is right in the sight of all men. If possible, so far as it depends on you, be at peace with all men. Never take your own revenge, beloved, but leave room for the wrath of God, for it is written, "Vengeance is Mine, I will repay," says the Lord. "But if your enemy is hungry, feed him, and if he is thirsty, give him a drink; for in so doing you will heap burning coals on his head." Do not be overcome by evil, but overcome evil with good.

Ephesians 4:26-27—Be angry, and yet do not sin; do not let the sun go down on your anger, and do not give the devil an opportunity.

Philippians 4:5—Let your gentle spirit be known to all men. The Lord is near.

James 1:19-20—This you know, my beloved brethren. But everyone must be quick to hear, slow to speak and slow to anger; for the anger of man does not achieve the righteousness of God.

1 Peter 3:8-9—To sum up, all of you be harmonious, sympathetic, brotherly, kindhearted, and humble in spirit; not returning evil for evil or insult for insult, but giving a blessing instead; for you were called for the very purpose that you might inherit a blessing.

Anxiety and Worry

Psalm 56:3-4—When I am afraid, I will put my trust in You. In God, whose word I praise, in God I have put my trust; I shall not be afraid. What can mere man do to me?

Matthew 6:25-34—For this reason I say to you, do not be worried about your life, as to what you will eat or what you will drink; nor for your body, as to what you will put on. Is not life more than food, and the body more than clothing? Look at the birds of the air, that they do not sow, nor reap nor gather into barns, and yet your heavenly Father feeds them. Are you not worth much more than they? And who of you by being worried can add a single hour to his life? And why are you worried about clothing? Observe how the lilies of the field grow; they do not toil nor do they spin, yet I say to you that not even Solomon in all his glory clothed himself like one of these. But if God so clothes the grass of the field, which is alive today and tomorrow is thrown into the furnace, will He not much more clothe you? You of little faith! Do not worry then, saying, "What will we eat?" or "What will we drink?" or "What will we wear for clothing?" For the Gentiles eagerly seek all these things; for your heavenly Father knows that you need all these things. But seek first His kingdom and His righteousness, and all these things will be added to you.

So do not worry about tomorrow; for tomorrow will care for itself. Each day has enough trouble of its own.

Romans 8:28—We know that God causes all things to work together for good to those who love God, to those who are called according to His purpose.

Philippians 4:6—Be anxious for nothing, but in everything by prayer and supplication with thanksgiving let your requests be made known to God.

1 Peter 5:6-7—Humble yourselves under the mighty hand of God, that He may exalt you at the proper time, casting all your anxiety on Him, because He cares for you.

Atheism and an Evolutionary Worldview

Genesis 1:1—In the beginning God created the heavens and the earth.

Psalm 53:1—The fool has said in his heart, "There is no God," they are corrupt, and have committed abominable injustice; there is no one who does good.

Proverbs 1:7—The fear of the LORD is the beginning of knowledge; fools despise wisdom and instruction.

Romans 1:20-22—Since the creation of the world His invisible attributes, His eternal power and divine nature, have been clearly seen, being understood through what has been made, so that they are without excuse. For even though they knew God, they did not honor Him as God or give thanks, but they became futile in their speculations, and their foolish heart was darkened. Professing to be wise, they became fools.

1 Corinthians 1:18; 2:14—The word of the cross is foolishness to those who are perishing, but to us who are being saved it is the power of God...a natural man does not accept the things of the Spirit of God, for they are foolishness to him; and he cannot understand them, because they are spiritually appraised.

2 Corinthians 10:5—We are destroying speculations and every lofty thing raised up against the knowledge of God, and we are taking every thought captive to the obedience of Christ.

1 Peter 3:15—Sanctify Christ as Lord in your hearts, always being ready to make a defense to everyone who asks you to give an account for the hope that is in you, yet with gentleness and reverence.

Covetousness and Discontentment

Ecclesiastes 5:10—He who loves money will not be satisfied with money, nor he who loves abundance with its income. This too is vanity.

Mark 7:21-23—From within, out of the heart of men, proceed the evil thoughts, fornications, thefts, murders, adulteries, deeds of coveting and wickedness, as well as deceit, sensuality, envy, slander, pride and foolishness. All these evil things proceed from within and defile the man.

Luke 12:15-21—Then He said to them, "Beware, and be on your guard against every form of greed; for not even when one has an abundance does his life consist of his possessions." And He told them a parable, saying, "The land of a rich man was very productive. And he began reasoning to himself, saying, 'What shall I do, since I have no place to store my crops?' Then he said, 'This is what I will do: I will tear down my barns and build larger ones, and there I will store all my grain and my goods. And I will say to my soul, "Soul, you have many goods laid up for many years to come; take your ease, eat, drink and be merry.'" But God said to him, 'You fool! This very night your soul is required of you; and now who will own what you have prepared?' So is the man who stores up treasure for himself, and is not rich toward God."

Philippians 4:11-13,19-20—Not that I speak from want, for I have learned to be content in whatever circumstances I am. I know how to get along with humble means, and I also know how to live in prosperity; in any and every circumstance I have learned the secret of being filled and going hungry, both of having abundance and suffering need. I can do all things through Him who strengthens me…And my God will supply all your needs according to His riches in glory in Christ Jesus. Now to our God and Father be the glory forever and ever. Amen.

Colossians 3:5—Consider the members of your earthly body as dead to immorality, impurity, passion, evil desire, and greed, which amounts to idolatry.

1 Timothy 6:6-8—Godliness actually is a means of great gain when accompanied by contentment. For we have brought nothing into the world, so we cannot take anything out of it either. If we have food and covering, with these we shall be content.

Hebrews 13:5—Make sure that your character is free from the love of money, being content with what you have; for He Himself has said, "I will never desert you, nor will I ever forsake you," so that we confidently say, "The Lord is my helper, I will not be afraid. What will man do to me?"

Death and Resurrection of Believers

John 6:39-40—This is the will of Him who sent Me, that of all that He has given Me I lose nothing, but raise it up on the last day. For this is the will of My Father, that everyone who beholds the Son and believes in Him will have eternal life, and I Myself will raise him up on the last day.

John 11:25-26—I am the resurrection and the life; he who believes in Me will live even if he dies, and everyone who lives and believes in Me will never die.

1 Corinthians 15:51-57—Behold, I tell you a mystery; we will not all sleep, but we will all be changed, in a moment, in the twinkling of an eye, at the last trumpet; for the trumpet will sound, and the dead will be raised imperishable, and we will be changed. For this perishable must put on the imperishable, and this mortal must put on immortality. But when this perishable will have put on the imperishable, and this mortal will have put on immortality, then will come about the saying that is written, "Death is swallowed up in victory. O death, where is your victory? O death, where is your sting?" The sting of death is sin, and the power of sin is the law; but thanks be to God, who gives us the victory through our Lord Jesus Christ.

2 Corinthians 5:6-9—Being always of good courage, and knowing that while we are at home in the body we are absent from the Lord—for we walk by faith, not by sight—we are of good courage, I say, and prefer rather to be absent from the body and to be at home with the Lord. Therefore we also have as our ambition, whether at home or absent, to be pleasing to Him.

Philippians 1:21-24—To me, to live is Christ and to die is gain. But if I am to live on in the flesh, this will mean fruitful labor for me; and I do not know which to choose. But I am hard-pressed from both directions, having the desire to depart and be with

Christ, for that is very much better; yet to remain on in the flesh is more necessary for your sake.

1 Thessalonians 4:13-14,18—We do not want you to be uninformed, brethren, about those who are asleep, so that you will not grieve as do the rest who have no hope. For if we believe that Jesus died and rose again, even so God will bring with Him those who have fallen asleep in Jesus…Therefore comfort one another with these words.

Fear of the Lord

Proverbs 1:7—The fear of the LORD is the beginning of knowledge; fools despise wisdom and instruction.

Proverbs 8:13—The fear of the LORD is to hate evil; pride and arrogance and the evil way and the perverted mouth, I hate.

Proverbs 9:10—The fear of the LORD is the beginning of wisdom, and the knowledge of the Holy One is understanding.

Proverbs 14:26-27—In the fear of the LORD there is strong confidence, and his children will have refuge. The fear of the LORD is a fountain of life, that one may avoid the snares of death.

Proverbs 15:3,16,33—The eyes of the LORD are in every place, watching the evil and the good…Better is a little with the fear of the LORD than great treasure and turmoil with it…The fear of the LORD is the instruction for wisdom, and before honor comes humility.

Proverbs 22:4—The reward of humility and the fear of the LORD are riches, honor and life.

Proverbs 23:17—Do not let your heart envy sinners, but live in the fear of the LORD always.

Ecclesiastes 11:9—Rejoice, young man, during your childhood, and let your heart be pleasant during the days of young manhood. And follow the impulses of your heart and the desires of your eyes. Yet know that God will bring you to judgment for all these things.

Romans 14:10-12—We will all stand before the judgment seat of God. For it is written, "As I live, says the Lord, every knee shall bow to Me, and every tongue shall give praise to God." So then each one of us will give an account of himself to God.

1 Corinthians 5:10—We must all appear before the judgment seat of Christ, so that each one may be recompensed for his deeds in the body, according to what he has done, whether good or bad.

Forgiveness

Matthew 5:43-45—You have heard that it was said, "You shall love your neighbor and hate your enemy." But I say to you, love your enemies and pray for those who persecute you, so that you may be sons of your Father who is in heaven; for He causes His sun to rise on the evil and the good, and sends rain on the righteous and the unrighteous.

Mark 11:25—Whenever you stand praying, forgive, if you have anything against anyone, so that your Father who is in heaven will also forgive you your transgressions.

Luke 6:35-36—Love your enemies, and do good, and lend, expecting nothing in return; and your reward will be great, and you will be sons of the Most High; for He Himself is kind to ungrateful and evil men. Be merciful, just as your Father is merciful.

Luke 17:3-4—Be on your guard! If your brother sins, rebuke him; and if he repents, forgive him. And if he sins against you seven times a day, and returns to you seven times, saying, "I repent," forgive him.

Ephesians 4:31-32—Let all bitterness and wrath and anger and clamor and slander be put away from you, along with all malice. Be kind to one another, tender-hearted, forgiving each other, just as God in Christ also has forgiven you.

Colossians 3:12-13—So, as those who have been chosen of God, holy and beloved, put on a heart of compassion, kindness, humility, gentleness and patience; bearing with one another, and forgiving each other, whoever has a complaint against anyone; just as the Lord forgave you, so also should you.

Gender Roles in Home and Church

Ephesians 5:22-27—Wives, be subject to your own husbands, as to the Lord. For the husband is the head of the wife, as Christ also is the head of the church, He Himself being the Savior of the body. But as the church is subject to Christ, so also the wives ought to be to their husbands in everything.

Husbands, love your wives, just as Christ also loved the church and gave Himself up for her, so that He might sanctify her, having cleansed her by the washing of water with the word, that He might present to Himself the church in all her glory, having no spot or wrinkle or any such thing; but that she would be holy and blameless.

Colossians 3:18-19—Wives, be subject to your husbands, as is fitting in the Lord. Husbands, love your wives and do not be embittered against them.

1 Timothy 2:9-15—I want women to adorn themselves with proper clothing, modestly and discreetly, not with braided hair and gold or pearls or costly garments, but rather by means of good works, as is proper for women making a claim to godliness. A woman must quietly receive instruction with entire submissiveness. But I do not allow a woman to teach or exercise authority over a man, but to remain quiet. For it was Adam who was first created, and then Eve. And it was not Adam who was deceived, but the woman being deceived, fell into transgression. But women will be preserved through the bearing of children if they continue in faith and love and sanctity with self-restraint.

Titus 2:3-5—Older women likewise are to be reverent in their behavior, not malicious gossips nor enslaved to much wine, teaching what is good, so that they may encourage the young women to love their husbands, to love their children, to be sensible, pure, workers at home, kind, being subject to their own husbands, so that the word of God will not be dishonored.

1 Peter 3:1-2,7—In the same way, you wives, be submissive to your own husbands so that even if any of them are disobedient to the word, they may be won without a word by the behavior of their wives, as they observe your chaste and respectful behavior...You husbands in the same way, live with your wives in an understanding way, as with someone weaker, since she is a woman; and show her honor as a fellow heir of the grace of life, so that your prayers will not be hindered.

Harsh Language

Proverbs 15:1—A gentle answer turns away wrath, but a harsh word stirs up anger.

Matthew 15:18-19—The things that proceed out of the mouth come from the heart, and those defile the man. For out of the heart come evil thoughts, murders, adulteries, fornications, thefts, false witness, slanders.

Ephesians 4:29—Let no unwholesome word proceed from your mouth, but only such a word as is good for edification according to the need of the moment, so that it will give grace to those who hear.

Ephesians 5:3—Immorality or any impurity or greed must not even be named among you, as is proper among saints; and there must be no filthiness and silly talk, or coarse jesting, which are not fitting, but rather giving of thanks. For this you know with certainty, that no immoral or impure person or covetous man, who is an idolater, has an inheritance in the kingdom of Christ and God.

Colossians 3:8—Now you also, put them all aside: anger, wrath, malice, slander, and abusive speech from your mouth.

Titus 2:6-8—Likewise urge the young men to be sensible; in all things show yourself to be an example of good deeds, with purity in doctrine, dignified, sound in speech which is beyond reproach, so that the opponent will be put to shame, having nothing bad to say about us.

Homosexuality

Genesis 19:4-7—Before they lay down, the men of the city, the men of Sodom, surrounded the house, both young and old, all the people from every quarter; and they called to Lot and said to him, "Where are the men who came to you tonight? Bring them out to us that we may have relations with them." But Lot went out to them at the doorway, and shut the door behind him, and said, "Please, my brothers, do not act wickedly."

Leviticus 18:22-23—You shall not lie with a male as one lies with a female; it is an abomination. Also you shall not have intercourse with any animal to be defiled with it, nor shall any woman stand before an animal to mate with it; it is a perversion.

Leviticus 20:13—If there is a man who lies with a male as those who lie with a woman, both of them have committed a detestable act; they shall surely be put to death. Their bloodguiltiness is upon them.

Matthew 19:4-6 (regarding the properness of heterosexual marriage)—[Jesus] answered and said, "Have you not read that He who created them from the beginning made them male and female, and said, 'For this reason a man shall leave his father and mother and be joined to his wife, and the two shall become one flesh'? So they are no longer two, but one flesh. What therefore God has joined together, let no man separate."

Romans 1:26-27—God gave them over to degrading passions; for their women exchanged the natural function for that which is unnatural, and in the same way also the men abandoned the natural function of the woman and burned in their desire toward one another, men with men committing indecent acts and receiving in their own persons the due penalty of their error.

1 Corinthians 6:9-11—Do you not know that the unrighteous will not inherit the kingdom of God? Do not be deceived; neither fornicators, nor idolaters, nor adulterers, nor effeminate, nor homosexuals, nor thieves, nor the covetous, nor drunkards, nor revilers, nor swindlers, will inherit the kingdom of God. Such were some of you; but you were washed, but you were sanctified, but you were justified in the name of the Lord Jesus Christ and in the Spirit of our God.

Hope and Confidence in God

Genesis 50:20—As for you, you meant evil against me, but God meant it for good.

Psalm 42:5—Why are you in despair, O my soul? And why have you become disturbed within me? Hope in God, for I shall again praise Him for the help of His presence.

Psalm 130:5-7—I wait for the Lord, my soul does wait, and in His word do I hope. My soul waits for the Lord more than the watchmen for the morning; indeed, more than the watchmen for the morning. O Israel, hope in the Lord; for with the Lord there is lovingkindness, and with Him is abundant redemption.

Lamentations 3:21-24—This I recall to my mind, therefore I have hope. The Lord's lovingkindnesses indeed never cease, for His compassions never fail. They are new every morning; great is Your faithfulness. "The Lord is my portion," says my soul, "Therefore I have hope in Him."

Micah 7:7—As for me, I will watch expectantly for the Lord; I will wait for the God of my salvation. My God will hear me.

Romans 8:31,38-39—What then shall we say to these things? If God is for us, who is against us?...For I am convinced that neither death, nor life, nor angels, nor principalities, nor things present, nor things to come, nor powers, nor height, nor depth, nor any other created thing, will be able to separate us from the love of God, which is in Christ Jesus our Lord.

1 Thessalonians 4:13-14,18—We do not want you to be uninformed, brethren, about those who are asleep, so that you will not grieve as do the rest who have no hope. For if we believe that Jesus died and rose again, even so God will bring with Him those who have fallen asleep in Jesus...Therefore comfort one another with these words.

1 Timothy 6:17—Instruct those who are rich in this present world not to be conceited or to fix their hope on the uncertainty of riches, but on God, who richly supplies us with all things to enjoy.

Love, Tolerance, and Truth

John 14:6,15—Jesus said to him, "I am the way, and the truth, and the life; no one comes to the Father but through Me...If you love Me, you will keep My commandments."

Romans 12:9—Let love be without hypocrisy. Abhor what is evil; cling to what is good.

1 Corinthians 13:6—[Love] does not rejoice in unrighteousness, but rejoices with the truth.

Ephesians 5:2-3—Walk in love, just as Christ also loved you and gave Himself up for us, an offering and a sacrifice to God as a fragrant aroma. But immorality or any impurity or greed must not even be named among you, as is proper among saints.

James 3:17—The wisdom from above is first pure, then peaceable, gentle, reasonable, full of mercy and good fruits, unwavering, without hypocrisy. And the seed whose fruit is righteousness is sown in peace by those who make peace.

1 Peter 1:22—Since you have in obedience to the truth purified your souls for a sincere love of the brethren, fervently love one another from the heart.

2 John 1:4,6—I was very glad to find some of your children walking in truth, just as we have received commandment to do from the Father...And this is love, that we walk according to His commandments. This is the commandment, just as you have heard from the beginning, that you should walk in it.

Lust and Sexual Sin

Job 31:1—I have made a covenant with my eyes; how then could I gaze at a virgin?

Proverbs 6:32—The one who commits adultery with a woman is lacking sense; he who would destroy himself does it.

Matthew 5:27-30—You have heard that it was said, "You shall not commit adultery"; but I say to you that everyone who looks at a woman with lust for her has already committed adultery with her in his heart. If your right eye makes you stumble, tear it out and throw it from you; for it is better for you to lose one of the parts of your body, than for your whole body to be thrown into hell. If your right hand makes you stumble, cut it off and throw it from you; for it is better for you to lose one of the parts of your body, than for your whole body to go into hell.

Romans 6:12-14—Do not let sin reign in your mortal body so that you obey its lusts, and do not go on presenting the members of your body to sin as instruments of unrighteousness; but present yourselves to God as those alive from the dead, and your members as instruments of righteousness to God. For sin shall not be master over you, for you are not under law but under grace

Romans 13:12-14—The night is almost gone, and the day is near. Therefore let us lay aside the deeds of darkness and put on the armor of light. Let us behave properly as in the day, not in carousing and drunkenness, not in sexual promiscuity and sensuality, not in strife and jealousy. But put on the Lord Jesus Christ, and make no provision for the flesh in regard to its lusts.

1 Corinthians 6:15-18—Do you not know that your bodies are members of Christ? Shall I then take away the members of Christ and make them members of a prostitute? May it never be! Or do you not know that the one who joins himself to a prostitute is one body with her? For He says, "The two shall become one flesh." But the one who joins himself to the Lord is one spirit with Him. Flee immorality. Every other sin that a man commits is outside the body, but the immoral man sins against his own body.

1 Thessalonians 4:3-6—This is the will of God, your sanctification; that is, that you abstain from sexual immorality; that each of you know how to possess his own vessel in sanctification and honor, not in lustful passion, like the Gentiles who do not know God; and that no man transgress and defraud his brother in the matter because the Lord is the avenger in all these things, just as we also told you before and solemnly warned you.

Hebrews 13:4—Marriage is to be held in honor among all, and the marriage bed is to be undefiled; for fornicators and adulterers God will judge.

1 Peter 2:11—Beloved, I urge you as aliens and strangers to abstain from fleshly lusts which wage war against the soul.

1 John 2:15-16—Do not love the world nor the things in the world. If anyone loves the world, the love of the Father is not in him. For all that is in the world, the lust of the flesh and the lust of the eyes and the boastful pride of life, is not from the Father, but is from the world.

Lying and Deceitfulness

Exodus 20:16—You shall not bear false witness against your neighbor.

Proverbs 6:16-19—There are six things which the LORD hates, yes, seven which are an abomination to Him: haughty eyes, a lying tongue, and hands that shed innocent blood, a heart that devises wicked plans, feet that run rapidly to evil, a false witness who utters lies, and one who spreads strife among brothers.

Proverbs 12:19,22—Truthful lips will be established forever, but a lying tongue is only for a moment…Lying lips are an abomination to the LORD, but those who deal faithfully are His delight.

John 8:44—You are of your father the devil, and you want to do the desires of your father. He was a murderer from the beginning, and does not stand in the truth because there is no truth in him.

Whenever he speaks a lie, he speaks from his own nature, for he is a liar and the father of lies.

Ephesians 4:25—Laying aside falsehood, speak truth each one of you with his neighbor, for we are members of one another.

Colossians 3:9-10—Do not lie to one another, since you laid aside the old self with its evil practices, and have put on the new self who is being renewed to a true knowledge according to the image of the One who created him.

Revelation 21:8—For the cowardly and unbelieving and abominable and murderers and immoral persons and sorcerers and idolaters and all liars, their part will be in the lake that burns with fire and brimstone, which is the second death.

Money and Generosity

Matthew 6:19-24—Do not store up for yourselves treasures on earth, where moth and rust destroy, and where thieves break in and steal. But store up for yourselves treasures in heaven, where neither moth nor rust destroys, and where thieves do not break in or steal; for where your treasure is, there your heart will be also.

The eye is the lamp of the body; so then if your eye is clear, your whole body will be full of light. But if your eye is bad, your whole body will be full of darkness. If then the light that is in you is darkness, how great is the darkness! No one can serve two masters; for either he will hate the one and love the other, or he will be devoted to one and despise the other. You cannot serve God and wealth.

Romans 12:10-13—Be devoted to one another in brotherly love; give preference to one another in honor; not lagging behind in diligence, fervent in spirit, serving the Lord; rejoicing in hope, persevering in tribulation, devoted to prayer, contributing to the needs of the saints, practicing hospitality.

2 Corinthians 9:6-8—Now this I say, he who sows sparingly will also reap sparingly, and he who sows bountifully will also reap bountifully. Each one must do just as he has purposed in his heart, not grudgingly or under compulsion, for God loves a cheerful giver. And God is able to make all grace abound to you, so that always having all sufficiency in everything, you may have an abundance for every good deed.

1 Timothy 6:9-10,17-18—Those who want to get rich fall into temptation and a snare and many foolish and harmful desires which plunge men into ruin and destruction. For the love of money is a root of all sorts of evil, and some by longing for it have wandered away from the faith and pierced themselves with many griefs… Instruct those who are rich in this present world not to be conceited or to fix their hope on the uncertainty of riches, but on God, who richly supplies us with all things to enjoy. Instruct them to do good, to be rich in good works, to be generous and ready to share, storing up for themselves the treasure of a good foundation for the future, so that they may take hold of that which is life indeed.

Parenting and Discipline

Deuteronomy 6:5-9—You shall love the LORD your God with all your heart and with all your soul and with all your might. These words, which I am commanding you today, shall be on your heart. You shall teach them diligently to your sons and shall talk of them when you sit in your house and when you walk by the way and when you lie down and when you rise up. You shall bind them as a sign on your hand and they shall be as frontals on your forehead. You shall write them on the doorposts of your house and on your gates.

Psalm 127:3-5—Behold, children are a gift of the LORD, the fruit of the womb is a reward. Like arrows in the hand of a warrior, so are the children of one's youth. How blessed is the man whose quiver is full of them; they will not be ashamed when they speak with their enemies in the gate.

Proverbs 13:24—He who withholds his rod hates his son, but he who loves him disciplines him diligently.

Proverbs 20:7—A righteous man who walks in his integrity—how blessed are his sons after him.

Proverbs 22:6,15—Train up a child in the way he should go, even when he is old he will not depart from it…Foolishness is bound up in the heart of a child; the rod of discipline will remove it far from him.

Proverbs 23:13-16—Do not hold back discipline from the child, although you strike him with the rod, he will not die. You shall strike him with the rod and rescue his soul from Sheol.

My son, if your heart is wise, my own heart also will be glad; and my inmost being will rejoice when your lips speak what is right.

Proverbs 29:15,17—The rod and reproof give wisdom, But a child who gets his own way brings shame to his mother…Correct your son, and he will give you comfort; he will also delight your soul.

Ephesians 6:1-4—Children, obey your parents in the Lord, for this is right. Honor your father and mother (which is the first commandment with a promise), so that it may be well with you, and that you may live long on the earth.

Fathers, do not provoke your children to anger, but bring them up in the discipline and instruction of the Lord.

Colossians 3:20-21—Children, be obedient to your parents in all things, for this is well-pleasing to the Lord. Fathers, do not exasperate your children, so that they will not lose heart.

Pride and Humility

Proverbs 11:2—When pride comes, then comes dishonor, but with the humble is wisdom.

Proverbs 16:5,18—Everyone who is proud in heart is an abomination to the LORD; assuredly, he will not be unpunished...Pride goes before destruction, and a haughty spirit before stumbling.

Proverbs 26:12—Do you see a man wise in his own eyes? There is more hope for a fool than for him.

Proverbs 29:23—A man's pride will bring him low, but a humble spirit will obtain honor.

Isaiah 66:1-2—Thus says the LORD, "Heaven is My throne and the earth is My footstool. Where then is a house you could build for Me? And where is a place that I may rest? For My hand made all these things, thus all these things came into being," declares the LORD. "But to this one I will look, to him who is humble and contrite of spirit, and who trembles at My word."

Matthew 23:11-12—The greatest among you shall be your servant. Whoever exalts himself shall be humbled; and whoever humbles himself shall be exalted.

Romans 12:3,16—Through the grace given to me I say to everyone among you not to think more highly of himself than he ought to think; but to think so as to have sound judgment, as God has allotted to each a measure of faith...Be of the same mind toward one another; do not be haughty in mind, but associate with the lowly. Do not be wise in your own estimation.

Philippians 2:1-5—If there is any encouragement in Christ, if there is any consolation of love, if there is any fellowship of the Spirit, if any affection and compassion, make my joy complete by being of the same mind, maintaining the same love, united in spirit, intent on one purpose. Do nothing from selfishness or empty conceit, but with humility of mind regard one another as more important than yourselves; do not merely look out for your own personal interests, but also for the interests of others. Have this attitude in yourselves which was also in Christ Jesus.

James 4:6—He gives a greater grace. Therefore it says, "God is opposed to the proud, but gives grace to the humble."

Stealing and Theft

Exodus 20:15—You shall not steal.

Proverbs 29:24—He who is a partner with a thief hates his own life.

Romans 13:1-2,6-9—Every person is to be in subjection to the governing authorities. For there is no authority except from God, and those which exist are established by God. Therefore whoever resists authority has opposed the ordinance of God; and they who have opposed will receive condemnation upon themselves…For because of this you also pay taxes, for rulers are servants of God, devoting themselves to this very thing. Render to all what is due them: tax to whom tax is due; custom to whom custom; fear to whom fear; honor to whom honor.

Owe nothing to anyone except to love one another; for he who loves his neighbor has fulfilled the law. For this, "You shall not commit adultery, you shall not murder, you shall not steal, you shall not covet," and if there is any other commandment, it is summed up in this saying, "You shall love your neighbor as yourself."

Ephesians 4:28—He who steals must steal no longer; but rather he must labor, performing with his own hands what is good, so that he will have something to share with one who has need.

Trials, Persecution, and Suffering

Matthew 5:10-12—Blessed are those who have been persecuted for the sake of righteousness, for theirs is the kingdom of heaven.

Blessed are you when people insult you and persecute you, and falsely say all kinds of evil against you because of Me. Rejoice and be glad, for your reward in heaven is great; for in the same way they persecuted the prophets who were before you.

Acts 5:40-42—After calling the apostles in, [the religious leaders] flogged them and ordered them not to speak in the name of Jesus, and then released them. So they went on their way from the presence of the Council, rejoicing that they had been considered worthy to suffer shame for His name. And every day, in the temple and from house to house, they kept right on teaching and preaching Jesus as the Christ.

Romans 5:2-5—We exult in hope of the glory of God. And not only this, but we also exult in our tribulations, knowing that tribulation brings about perseverance; and perseverance, proven character; and proven character, hope; and hope does not disappoint, because the love of God has been poured out within our hearts through the Holy Spirit who was given to us.

James 1:2-4—Consider it all joy, my brethren, when you encounter various trials, knowing that the testing of your faith produces endurance. And let endurance have its perfect result, so that you may be perfect and complete, lacking in nothing.

1 Peter 1:6-9—In this you greatly rejoice, even though now for a little while, if necessary, you have been distressed by various trials, so that the proof of your faith, being more precious than gold which is perishable, even though tested by fire, may be found to result in praise and glory and honor at the revelation of Jesus Christ; and though you have not seen Him, you love Him, and though you do not see Him now, but believe in Him, you greatly rejoice with joy inexpressible and full of glory, obtaining as the outcome of your faith the salvation of your souls.

1 Peter 2:20—What credit is there if, when you sin and are harshly treated, you endure it with patience? But if when you do what is right and suffer for it you patiently endure it, this finds favor with God.

Work and Laziness

Proverbs 6:6-11—Go to the ant, O sluggard, observe her ways and be wise, which having no chief, officer or ruler, prepares her food in the summer and gathers her provision in the harvest. How long will you lie down, O sluggard? When will you arise from your sleep? "A little sleep, a little slumber, a little folding of the hands to rest"—your poverty will come in like a vagabond and your need like an armed man.

Proverbs 13:4—The soul of the sluggard craves and gets nothing, but the soul of the diligent is made fat.

Ephesians 4:28—He who steals must steal no longer; but rather he must labor, performing with his own hands what is good, so that he will have something to share with one who has need.

Colossians 3:23-24—Whatever you do, do your work heartily, as for the Lord rather than for men knowing that from the Lord you will receive the reward of the inheritance. It is the Lord Christ whom you serve.

1 Thessalonians 4:11-12—Make it your ambition to lead a quiet life and attend to your own business and work with your hands, just as we commanded you, so that you will behave properly toward outsiders and not be in any need.

2 Thessalonians 3:10-12—Even when we were with you, we used to give you this order: if anyone is not willing to work, then he is not to eat, either. For we hear that some among you are leading an undisciplined life, doing no work at all, but acting like busybodies. Now such persons we command and exhort in the Lord Jesus Christ to work in quiet fashion and eat their own bread.

Worldliness

Matthew 5:13-16—You are the salt of the earth; but if the salt has become tasteless, how can it be made salty again? It is no longer good for anything, except to be thrown out and trampled under foot by men.

You are the light of the world. A city set on a hill cannot be hidden; nor does anyone light a lamp and put it under a basket, but on the lampstand, and it gives light to all who are in the house. Let your light shine before men in such a way that they may see your good works, and glorify your Father who is in heaven.

Matthew 13:22—The one on whom seed was sown among the thorns, this is the man who hears the word, and the worry of the world and the deceitfulness of wealth choke the word, and it becomes unfruitful.

John 17:14-17 (in Jesus' High Priestly prayer)—I have given them Your word; and the world has hated them, because they are not of the world, even as I am not of the world. I do not ask You to take them out of the world, but to keep them from the evil one. They are not of the world, even as I am not of the world. Sanctify them in the truth; Your word is truth.

Romans 12:2—Do not be conformed to this world, but be transformed by the renewing of your mind, so that you may prove what the will of God is, that which is good and acceptable and perfect.

Philippians 3:18-21—For many walk, of whom I often told you, and now tell you even weeping, that they are enemies of the cross of Christ, whose end is destruction, whose god is their appetite, and whose glory is in their shame, who set their minds on earthly things. For our citizenship is in heaven, from which also we eagerly wait for a Savior, the Lord Jesus Christ; who will transform the body of our humble state into conformity with the body of His glory, by the exertion of the power that He has even to subject all things to Himself.

2 Timothy 3:1-5,22—Realize this, that in the last days difficult times will come. For men will be lovers of self, lovers of money, boastful, arrogant, revilers, disobedient to parents, ungrateful, unholy, unloving, irreconcilable, malicious gossips, without self-control, brutal, haters of good, treacherous, reckless, conceited, lovers of pleasure rather than lovers of God, holding to a form of godliness, although they have denied its power; avoid such men as these.

James 4:4—You adulteresses, do you not know that friendship with the world is hostility toward God? Therefore whoever wishes to be a friend of the world makes himself an enemy of God.

1 John 2:15-17—Do not love the world nor the things in the world. If anyone loves the world, the love of the Father is not in him. For all that is in the world, the lust of the flesh and the lust of the eyes and the boastful pride of life, is not from the Father, but is from the world. The world is passing away, and also its lusts; but the one who does the will of God lives forever.

CONTRIBUTORS

(in order of appearance)

John MacArthur is the pastor-teacher of Grace Community Church. A nationally known author and preacher, he also serves as the president of The Master's College & Seminary and is heard daily on the *Grace to You* radio broadcast.

Rick Holland serves as the executive pastor at Grace Community Church, where he also pastors college students. He is the director of both the Resolved Conference and the Doctor of Ministry program in expository preaching at The Master's Seminary.

Austin Duncan has worked in student ministry for over a decade and currently serves as the high school pastor at Grace Community Church.

Kurt Gebhards gives oversight to the children's ministries department at Grace Community Church, while also pastoring career singles in a weekly fellowship group.

Tom Patton oversees membership and assimilation at Grace Community Church, while also pastoring young married couples and families in a weekly fellowship group.

Bill Shannon has served on pastoral staff at Grace Community Church for 20 years. He oversees discipleship counseling at the church and pastors a weekly fellowship group.

John D. Street is an elder at Grace Community Church and the chair of the graduate program in biblical counseling (MABC) at The Master's College.

Jonathan Rourke oversees conferences at Grace Community Church, including the Shepherds' Conference and Logos Equipping Ministry, while also pastoring a weekly fellowship group.

Mark Tatlock is an elder at Grace Community Church and the senior vice president and provost of The Master's College. He also participates in the theological training of pastors in cross-cultural ministry within urban and international contexts.

Irv Busenitz is an elder at Grace Community Church and the vice president for academic administration at The Master's Seminary. He is also a professor of Bible exposition and Old Testament at The Master's Seminary.

Nathan Busenitz serves as an associate pastor and assistant to John Mac-Arthur. He is the managing editor of *Pulpit* magazine and teaches historical theology at The Master's Seminary.

Jesse Johnson gives pastoral oversight to the local outreach ministry at Grace Community Church and teaches on evangelism at The Master's Seminary.

Kevin Edwards served as a missionary in Russia for ten years before becoming the pastor of outreach ministries at Grace Community Church, where he provides leadership for international missions.

NOTES

Introduction

1. For a more detailed exposition of Psalm 19, see my chapter "Embracing the Authority and Sufficiency of Scripture" in *Think Biblically!* (Wheaton, IL: Crossway, 2003), 21-35.

Chapter 1

1. Parts of this chapter were adapted from my article "Glorifying God in the Gray Areas," published online by *Grace to You* at http://www.gty.org/Resources/articles/44.

Chapter 2

1. "eHarmony Is Different," http://www.eharmony.com/why (accessed October 2008).
2. "We Find Truly Compatible Matches for You," http://www.eharmony.com/tour/finding (accessed October 2008).
3. Robert Epstein, "The Truth About Online Dating," *The Scientific American Mind*," January 30, 2007, http://www.sciam.com/article.cfm?id=the-truth-about-online-da& print=true.
4. Ibid.
5. For more on these principles see my chapter "The Guided Path" in *5 Paths to the Love of Your Life*, ed. Alex Chediak (Colorado Springs, CO: Th1nk, 2005), 89-121.
6. John Piper, "A Vision of Complementarity" in *Recovering Biblical Manhood and Womanhood*, eds. John Piper and Wayne Grudem (Wheaton, IL: Crossway, 1991), 33.

Chapter 3

1. Amanda Lenhart, Joseph Kahne, Ellen Middaugh, Alexandra Rankin Macgill, Chris Evans, and Jessica Vitak, "Teens, Video Games, and Civics," September 16, 2008, http://www.pewinternet.org/pdfs/PIP_Teens_Games_and_Civics_Report_FINAL.pdf.
2. Cf. Damon Brown, "Video Games for Grownups," July 24, 2008, http://www.aarp.org/leisure/games/articles/video_games_reviews.html.
3. HealthDay News published by Forbes.com, "Video Game Use May Be an Addiction," June 22, 2007, http://www.forbes.com/health/feeds/hscout/2007/06/22/hscout605801.html.
4. The Nielsen Company, "News Release," December 11, 2007, http://www.nielsen.com/media/2007/pr_071211a_download.pdf.
5. Leonard Sax, *Boys Adrift: The Five Factors Driving the Growing Epidemic of Unmotivated Boys and Underachieving Young Men* (New York: Basic Books, 2007), 131.
6. Mike Smith, "Wedding Woes: The Dark Side of Warcraft," February 13, 2008, http://videogames.yahoo.com/feature/wedding-woes-the-dark-side-of-warcraft/1186366.
7. Ibid.
8. Christine Rosen, "Playgrounds of the Self," *The New Atlantis*, Number 9, Summer 2005, pp. 3-27. Online at: http://www.thenewatlantis.com/publications/playgrounds-of-the-self.
9. John Piper, *Don't Waste Your Life* (Wheaton, IL: Crossway, 2007), 119-20.

10. Martha Irvine, "Games a Social Outlet" *Washington Times,* September 23, 2008, http://www.washingtontimes.com/news/2008/sep/23/games-a-social-outlet/?page=2.

11. Stephen Totilo, cited in "Grand Theft Auto IV," game review at http://www.pluggedinonline.com/games/games/a0004042.cfm. Plugged In Online is a ministry of Focus on the Family.

12. Cited from Albert Mohler, "Grand Theft Decency," May 1, 2008, http://www.albertmohler.com/blog_print.php?id=1141.

Chapter 6

1. The elders' perspective was originally published in 2000. For those interested in a more detailed discussion of this issue, we recommend John MacArthur's book *The Divorce Dilemma* (Leominster, UK: Day One Publishers, 2009).

2. On the other hand, God did not give a bill of divorce to the southern kingdom Judah, illustrating that an unfaithful partner can be forgiven.

3. This assumes that the second marriage was a biblically permissible marriage (following either the death of a spouse or a biblical divorce), or that it occurred before conversion.

Chapter 7

1. "Facts on Induced Abortion in the United States," July 2008, The Guttmacher Institute, online at http://www.guttmacher.org/pubs/fb_induced_abortion.html (accessed September 26, 2008).

2. Exodus 21:22-23, a passage that sometimes comes up in this discussion, refers to accidental and involuntary miscarriage. Thus, it cannot be used to support the intentional abortion of unborn babies. Moreover, it is likely from the context to imply that the death penalty would have been enacted if the premature baby died, and that a fine would have been imposed only if both the premature baby and the mother were without injury.

3. Gene Edward Veith, Jr., *Postmodern Times: A Christian Guide to Contemporary Thought and Culture* (Wheaton, IL: Crossway, 1994), 147.

4. Larry W. Epperson *Abortion the Lost Generation* (Geneva Industries booklet) June 11, 1998.

5. "Women's Suicide Rates Highest after Abortion, New Study," November 29, 2005, www.afterabortion.org/news/suicide205.html

6. Ibid.

7. Statistics from Alicia Geilfuss of the Pregnancy Resource Center of the San Fernando Valley (North Hills, CA). This center is only a few miles from Grace Community Church.

Chapter 8

1. As a side note, we would add that the story of Onan in Genesis 38:6-10 has no bearing on the current discussion of birth control. Onan's sin consisted of his direct disobedience in that instance; hence, his example does not serve as a categorical condemnation of birth control in general.

2. R. Albert Mohler, "Can Christians Use Birth Control?" March 30, 2004, http://www.albertmohler.com/commentary_read.php?cdate=2004-03-30.

3. A second type of OCP is the progesterone only pill, or POP. When taken by themselves, POPs have "a considerably higher breakthrough-ovulation rate than COCs" (William R. Cutrer and Sandra L. Glahn, *The Contraception Guidebook* [Grand Rapids: Zondervan, 2005], 108). On the other hand, there is no evidence to indicate that women using COCs

have a statistically higher rate of ectopic pregnancies (see Dennis M. Sullivan, "The Oral Contraceptive as Abortifacient: An Analysis of the Evidence," *Perspectives on Science and Christian Faith* 58/3, September 2006, 192).

4. Michael Frields, "Birth Control: A Biblical Perspective," *Faith and Reason Forum,* http://www.faithandreasonforum.com/index.asp?PageID=34&ArticleID=417.

5. Adding to the controversy is the fact that some manufacturers of the pill, in an effort to make their product sound more effective, do claim that their product will reduce the likelihood of implantation. Dennis M. Sullivan, a professor of biology from Cedarville University, explains why such claims should be taken with a grain of salt: "To be fair to [those] companies involved with the manufacture of these drugs, they are trying to reassure their potential customers that their products work well...The manufacturers of oral contraceptives are not necessarily concerned with 'fine points' of ethics, so they will understandably make somewhat biased claims to insure a strong market for their products" (Dennis M. Sullivan, "Oral Contraceptive as Abortifacient," 191).

6. William R. Cutrer and Sandra L. Glahn, *The Contraception Guidebook,* (Grand Rapids: Zondervan, 2005), 108.

7. Ibid., 104.

8. James P. Johnston, "Do Oral Contraceptives Cause Abortions?" January 7, 2005, http://www.prolifephysicians.org/abortifacient.htm. In the same article, Johnston explains that some prolife physicians are not convinced that OCPs cause abortions because "the third proposed method of action, the so-called 'hostile endometrium theory,' has little direct evidence to support it. Drug manufacturers have heralded it from the beginning without proof, and it has been echoed by two generations of investigators without verification. There is indirect evidence that the OC produces a thinner, less glandular, less vascular lining, and there is direct evidence from the field of in vitro fertilization that a thinner, less glandular, less vascular lining is less likely to allow the attachment of the new human being when it enters the uterus. However, when a woman taking OCs does ovulate, the corpus luteum (the ovarian follicle turns into the corpus luteum after ovulation) produces ten to twenty times the levels of both estrogen and progesterone seen in a non-ovulatory pill cycle. This results in the growth of stroma, blood vessels, glands, and glandular secretions to help prepare the lining for implantation. If there is no conception after ovulation, the corpus luteum ceases to function about two weeks after ovulation and menses follows. However, if conception occurs following ovulation, the embryo releases the human chorionic gonadotropin hormone (HCG), which stimulates the corpus luteum to continue its function until the placenta takes over hormone production two months later."

9. For more on the hormonal changes that take place see Rich Poupard, "Does Thin Uterine Lining Support the 'Pill as Baby Killer' Theory," *Life Training Institute Weblog,* June 16, 2008, http://lti-blog.blogspot.com/2008/06/does-thin-uterine-lining-support-pill.html.

10. Dennis M. Sullivan, "Oral Contraceptive as Abortifacient," 192.

11. Joel E. Goodnough, "Redux: Is the Oral Contraceptive Pill an Abortifacient?" *Ethics and Medicine,* Spring 2001, 37-51. Goodnough acknowledged that, at the time his article was written, more research was needed to determine whether implantation in OCP-users was as successful as in non-OCP users.

12. Michael Frields, "Birth Control: A Biblical Perspective." Dr. Frields is a graduate of the University of Arizona, where he received both Doctor of Pharmacy and a Doctor of Medicine degrees. He obtained his board certification in obstetrics and gynecology in 1982, and has practiced medicine at Glendale Adventist Medical Center in Glendale, California for several decades. Dr. Frields has served as both the Chief of Staff at Glendale Adventist and

as the Chairperson of Perinatal/Gynecology. He is also a member of Grace Community Church.

13. Joe DeCook, Susan A. Crockett, Donna Harrison, and Camilla Hersh, "Hormone Contraceptives: Controversies, and Clarifications" April 1999, American Association of Pro Life Obstetricians and Gynecologists Web site, http://www.aaplog.org/decook.htm. Dennis Sullivan, "The Oral Contraceptive as Abortifacient," 192, explains why the statistics about ectopic pregnancies are significant: "The key questions become: How often does the user of COCs ovulate and conceive, only to have such a conception fail to implant? How does this rate compare with non-Pill users? The baseline failure rate for implantation is an important statistic in this regard. A full 70% of fertilized ova fail to proceed to a full-term pregnancy, with three-fourths of these due to failure of implantation. Against this failure rate, the rarity of breakthrough ovulation makes statistical comparison of Pill users against non-Pill users difficult. Contraceptive opponents must make a difficult statistical case: (1) In instances of breakthrough ovulation (a rare event), a significant number of sperm must penetrate the thickened cervical mucous (presumably a rare event), thus evading both truly contraceptive effects of COCs; and (2) if fertilization does occur, an embryo must fail to implant in an endometrium at least somewhat prepared for it, or if it implants, fail to continue to term, and this failure rate must be greater than the 70% that occurs naturally...[A] higher ectopic rate means that more breakthrough ovulation pregnancies fail to implant, which bolsters the ethical case that these agents are abortifacients...[But] there would appear to be no specific evidence indicting COCs for [an] increase in ectopic pregnancies."

14. To read both the statement and a critical response, see Randy Alcorn, "Prolife Ob/Gyn's January 1998 Statement," Eternal Perspective Ministries, http://www.epm.org/artman2/publish/prolife_birth_control_pill/Prolife_Ob_Gyn_s_January_1998_Statement.shtml. Alcorn is a leading proponent for the view that OCPs can cause abortions.

15. "Position Statement: Birth Control Pills and Other Hormonal Contraception," *Focus on the Family,* December 30, 2005, http://www.family.org/sharedassets/correspondence/pdfs/miscellaneous/Position_Statement-Birth_Control_Pills_and_Other_Hormonal_Contraception.pdf. On balance, "A minority of the experts feel that when conception occurs on the pill, there is enough of a possibility for an abortifacient effect, however remote, to warrant informing women about it."

16. Cf. Dennis Sullivan, "The Oral Contraceptive as Abortifacient," 193.

Chapter 9

1. Romans 1:26, παρα φυσιν, "contrary to nature"; in contrast see Romans 11:21, κατα φυσιν, "according to nature."

2. First Corinthians 6:9, μαλακοι, often used as a technical term in the first century. It refers to male prostitutes who assume the role of the female, hence effeminate. Such people in verse 9 are labeled "the unrighteous" and have not been "justified in the name of the Lord Jesus Christ."

3. A real letter from a former pastor with references to personal identification removed. He had seen more than one psychologist claiming to give him "Christian" counsel.

4. Study Jesus Christ and His masculinity. Carefully counsel the role of man's leadership in the home and church as a provider and protector (Matthew 20:25-28; 1 Timothy 3:1-7; 5:8; Titus 1:5-9; 2:2,6-8; 1 Peter 5:1-5). This is not the search for self-focused significance and identity that is popularized by Alfred Adler and many "Christian" psychologists. It is the theological identity, a true identity, that is so important in the New Testament.

5. See "Homosexuality in the Ministry," *Journal of Modern Ministry,* Fall 2004.

6. In Romans 7, the apostle Paul is speaking of his struggle with sin as a Christian. See of verse 24 the emphatic personal pronoun (εγω) points to a present tense as the apostle is writing this epistle.

7. Jay E. Adams, *The Christian Counselor's Manual* (Phillipsburg, NJ: Presbyterian and Reformed, 1973), 206-07.

8. In answering such claims, it is helpful to demonstrate that biblical love abhors evil and speaks the truth (cf. Romans 12:9; 1 Corinthians 13:6). Therefore, to confront homosexuality as sin and call for repentance is not "unloving." The truly unloving response would be to say nothing, in spite of the fact God's Word is clear on the subject.

Chapter 10

1. Statistics from the World Health Organization, "Suicide Prevention," February 16, 2006, http://www.who.int/mental_health/prevention/suicide/suicideprevent/en/. Also referenced is John L. McIntosh, "U.S.A. Suicide: 2005 Official Final Data," January 24, 2008, http://www.suicidology.org/associations/1045/files/2005datapgs.pdf.

2. Statistics obtained from Amnesty International, "Death Sentences and Executions in 2007," April 15, 2008, http://www.amnesty.org/en/library/asset/ACT50/001/2008/en/b43a1e5a-ffea-11dc-b092-bdb020617d3d/act500012008eng.html.

3. These definitions adapted from Keith H. Essex, "Euthanasia," *The Master's Seminary Journal*, Fall 2000, 200-04. Our staff is indebted to Dr. Essex's helpful work on this topic.

4. Ibid., 211-12.

5. Ibid., 212.

6. Neither Jesus' words in John 10:18 nor Paul's words in Philippians 1:21-26 can be misconstrued to support suicide (despite the attempts of some). Jesus was put to death by violent men (Acts 2:23; 3:14-15); and Paul's point was not that he desired death *per se*, but that he eagerly looked forward to the "gain" of one day being with Christ (cf. 2 Corinthians 5:8).

7. Those who truly commit the unpardonable sin inevitably continue in unrepentant unbelief for their entire lives. By contrast, those who fear that they may have committed the unpardonable sin but who have confessed their sins to Christ and long for His forgiveness demonstrate that they have not, in fact, committed the unpardonable sin.

8. Robert Culver, *Toward a Biblical View of Civil Government* (Chicago: Moody Press, 1974), 256.

9. Paul S. Feinberg and John D. Feinberg, *Ethics for a Brave New World* (Wheaton, IL: Good News Publishers, 1993), 147.

Chapter 13

1. Brett McCracken, "The Greening of Evangelicals," *Biola* magazine, Fall 2008, 18-25.

2. There is good reason to believe that today's consensus science has misidentified the cause of global warming. Trends in temperature show that "the recent warming trend since about 1850 appears to be the continuation of the warming following the Little Ice Age, rather than a sudden upsurge after a long period of relatively uniform temperatures" (Larry Vardiman, "Does Carbon Dioxide Drive Global Warming?" Institute for Creation Research, October 1, 2008, http://www.icr.org/article/4128/). Moreover, evidence from oceans and ice cores indicates that the increase in "carbon dioxide is the result, not the cause, of global warming."

3. "God's Earth Is Sacred: An Open Letter to Church and Society in the United States,"

National Council of Churches USA, February 14, 2005, http://www.ncccusa.org/news/
godsearthissacred.html.

4. Ibid. Emphasis in original.

Chapter 11

1. For additional perspective on the topic of Christians and government, see my books *Why Government Can't Save You* (Nashville: Thomas Nelson, 2000) and *Can God Bless America?* (Nashville, TN: W Publishing Group, 2002).

Chapter 16

1. C.S. Lewis, *The Problem of Pain* (New York: Macmillan, 1962), 26.
2. John Piper, *Spectacular Sins* (Wheaton, IL: Crossway, 2008), 12.
3. Randy Alcorn, *Heaven* (Carol Stream, IL: Tyndale, 2004), 28.
4. Maurice Roberts, *The Thought of God* (Carlisle, PA: Banner of Truth, 1994), 7.

Chapter 17

1. D. Martyn Lloyd-Jones, *From Fear to Faith* (Grand Rapids: Baker, 1985), 59-60.
2. A.W. Tozer, *Men Who Met God* (Harrisburg, PA: Christian Publications, 1986), 59.

Chapter 18

1. James Patterson and Peter Kim, *The Day America Told the Truth* (New York: Prentice Hall, 1991), 45, 48.
2. John Piper, *Desiring God* (Sisters, OR: Multnomah, 1996), 238.
3. Bruce Gellerman and Erik Sherman, *Massachusetts Curiosities* (Guilford, CT: Globe Pequot, 2004), 66-67.

Chapter 19

1. David M. Doran, *For the Sake of His Name* (Allen Park, MI: Student Global Impact), 128. Emphasis added.